Muslim–Christian Polemics in Safavid Iran

Edinburgh Historical Studies of Iran and the Persian World

Published in association with Elahé Omidyar Mir-Djalali, Founder and Chair, Roshan Cultural Heritage Institute

ROSHAN
CULTURAL HERITAGE
INSTITUTE

Series General Editor: Stephanie Cronin, Elahé Omidyar Mir-Djalali Research Fellow, University of Oxford

Series Advisory Board: Professor Janet Afary (UC Santa Barbara), Professor Abbas Amanat (Yale University), Professor Touraj Atabaki (International Institute of Social History), Dr Joanna de Groot (University of York), Professor Vanessa Martin (Royal Holloway, University of London), Professor Rudi Matthee (University of Delaware), Professor Cyrus Schayegh (The Graduate Institute, Geneva)

Covering the history of Iran and the Persian world from the medieval period to the present, this series aims to become the pre-eminent place for publication in this field. As well as its core concern with Iran, it extends its concerns to encompass a much wider and more loosely defined cultural and linguistic world, to include Afghanistan, the Caucasus, Central Asia, Xinjiang and northern India. Books in the series present a range of conceptual and methodological approaches, looking not only at states, dynasties and elites, but at subalterns, minorities and everyday life.

Published and forthcoming titles

Religion, Orientalism and Modernity: The Case of the Babis and Baha'is in Iran
Geoffrey Nash

Remapping Persian Literary History, 1700–1900
Kevin L. Schwartz

Muslim–Christian Polemics in Safavid Iran
Alberto Tiburcio

edinburghuniversitypress.com/series/ehsipw

Muslim–Christian Polemics in Safavid Iran

Alberto Tiburcio

EDINBURGH
University Press

Edinburgh University Press is one of the leading university presses in the UK. We publish academic books and journals in our selected subject areas across the humanities and social sciences, combining cutting-edge scholarship with high editorial and production values to produce academic works of lasting importance. For more information visit our website: edinburghuniversitypress.com

Edinburgh University Press Ltd
The Tun – Holyrood Road
12 (2f) Jackson's Entry
Edinburgh EH8 8PJ

First published in hardback by Edinburgh University Press 2020

Typeset in 11/15 Adobe Garamond by
Servis Filmsetting Ltd, Stockport, Cheshire

A CIP record for this book is available from the British Library

ISBN 978 1 4744 4046 2 (hardback)
ISBN 978 1 4744 4047 9 (paperback)
ISBN 978 1 4744 4048 6 (webready PDF)
ISBN 978 1 4744 4049 3 (epub)

Contents

Acknowledgements vi

Introduction 1

1 The Profile of a Convert in Safavid Iran 9

2 A Cycle of Polemics and Translation Projects 38

3 Jadid al-Islam and the Signs of the Prophecy 66

4 Appropriating Shiʿi Tradition and Engaging Christian Sources 94

5 Defending the Prophet and Condemning Christian Morality 123

6 Sufis as the Christians of the Umma 154

Conclusions 179

Bibliography 185

Index 215

Acknowledgements

This book grew out my dissertation at McGill University, where I worked under the supervision of Rula Abisaab. Throughout my studies, I benefitted from the support of McGill's Faculty of Arts. Their funding was essential for my fieldwork at the Archivio Storico di Propaganda Fide in Rome and at the Majlis Library in Tehran. I am grateful to Reza Pourjavady for introducing me to the work of ʿAli Quli Jadid al-Islam, to Aun Hasan Ali for encouraging me to pursue this project and to Pouneh Shabani-Jadidi for her support and patience throughout my training in Persian. I thank the Seifzadeh family, as well as my friends Sajjad Nikfahm and Fateme Savadi for hosting me in Iran, as well as Mansur Sefatgol for a very productive conversation at the University of Tehran. I dedicate this book to my friends at McGill and elsewhere in Montreal: Pascal Abidor, Vinay Khetia, Christopher Anzalone, Eliza Tasbihi, Shirin Radjavi, Bariza Umar, Kathy Kalemkerian, Farah Kawtharani, Sean Swanick, Michael Nafi, Usman Hamid, Heather Empey and Rashed Chowdhury. Here it is as a testament to all the great moments and conversations.

Revisions from the dissertation phase into the book version were undertaken during my postdoctoral contract at the Philipps-University of Marburg, where I worked for the *Dynamics of Transmission* project, funded jointly by the *Deutsche Forschungsgemeinschaft* and the *Association Nationale de la Recherche*. I am grateful to Christoph Werner for this opportunity, and to the whole team, especially to Maria Szuppe, Francis Richard, Michele Bernardini, Albrecht Fuess, Sandra Aube and Anthony Quickel. I would also like to thank the staff of the division of Iranistics at Marburg's Center for Near and Middle Eastern Studies, particularly Brunhilde Schäfer, as well as my friends Christine Kämpfer, Anna Heller, Goulia Ghardashkhani, Felix Otter, Bianca Devos and Anna Martin for many wonderful occasions.

Throughout the period of revisions, I benefitted from feedback from different sources. The comments and suggestions from Rudi Matthee and Sajjad Rizvi were of utmost importance in the preparation of the final version of this book. I would also like to acknowledge Dennis Halft, Catherina Wenzel, Kim Siebenhüner and Lejla Demiri for their feedback at various forums, to Christian Windler and Willem Floor for sharing with me their findings on Jadid al-Islam, and to Norbert Hintersteiner and Haila Manteghi for sharing with me their research on Jerome Xavier. Stefan Winter and Giancarlo Casale also deserve special mention for their advice on professional matters of different kind.

Finally, I would like to thank Nicola Ramsey and Kirsty Woods from Edinburgh University Press for their seemingly infinite patience throughout the process of elaboration of this book, and George MacBeth and Eddie Clark for their work during the copy-editing process. And last, but indeed most importantly, I thank my parents Alberto and Alicia, and my sister Natalia for their unconditional love and support.

Introduction

The study of Muslim–Christian relations in the Middle East during the age of the 'Gunpowder Empires' has, until relatively recently, remained a rather marginal topic. Archival limitations can partially explain this neglect. The amount and the nature of the sources at our disposal varies considerably from one empire to the other.[1] It would hardly come as a surprise to the initiated that the Ottoman archive is much richer than the Iranian and Mughal ones, which explains why Ottomanist scholarship on the matter has developed faster. In addition, the status of the Ottomans as the quintessential antagonist of Christendom in the Western imagination, the large number of Christian subjects in the Ottoman realm and the frontier wars fought between the Ottomans and the Habsburgs make the study of Muslim–Christian interactions in this empire an attractive scholarly endeavour.[2]

In the Persianate world, the subject's appeal has lagged behind, not without justification. To begin with, the sources are more constrained in terms of both number and scope. Court chronicles, which comprise the most important indigenous body of documentation, are notably lacking in their portrayal of the non-elites, including of course, religious minorities. Other indigenous archives, which are often richer for social history, such as the Armenian and Georgian ones, pose an unsurmountable linguistic obstacle for many Iranologists (including myself). Nonetheless, scholars with the adequate linguistic expertise, such as Vazken S. Ghougassian, Edmund Herzig, Gorgio Rota, Hirotake Maeda, Helen Giunashvili and Tamar Abuladze have provided us with important studies on the histories on these communities.[3] For the broader picture however, European travelogues, together with missionary and diplomatic correspondence, remain indispensable despite the obvious limitations of their European gaze. Scholars of both the Iranian and

Indian worlds at large, such as Rudi Matthee and Jorge Flores, to name only two major examples; as well as specialists on Catholic missions in Asia, such as John M. Flannery and Christian Windler, have produced important works of scholarship drawing partly from these sources.[4]

Yet, the greatest obstacle to the development of scholarship on Muslim–Christian relations in the Persianate world is perhaps more thematic than archival: while the presence of indigenous and European Christians played an important role in both Iran and India, in neither place did Christians constitute the most important religious minority nor the major antagonists to the politically-dominant group. In Mughal India, the Muslim political elite ruled over a diverse population composed primarily of Hindus and other Indian religious groups. In Safavid Iran, the main religious 'others' in the eyes of the Shiʿi dynasty were the Sunni Afghans and Baluchis of the frontier regions – which eventually brought the Empire to its demise – together with other Muslim (even nominally Shiʿi) groups whose practices did not adhere to the legalistic Shiʿi views espoused by the ulama at any given time.

This brings us to an important theoretical consideration concerning the study of interreligious interactions in this period. A debate has ensued in recent years regarding the pertinence of the paradigm of confessionalisation when examining the relationship between religion and power in the Muslim world in this period. The term *confessionalisation* is associated with the work of Wolfgang Reinhard and Heinz Schilling on early modern Europe; and refers to the process through which the Lutheran and Catholic political spheres were shaped, partly through state coercion, following the principle of *cujus regio ejus religio* (whose reign, his religion).[5] The adaptation of this term into discussions of the Muslim world has had both enthusiastic supporters and fierce critics. Tijana Krstić has been at the forefront of its use, arguing that the Ottoman Empire underwent a similar process, legitimising its power as the guardian of Sunni Islam vis-à-vis the Christian Habsburgs and vis-à-vis Shiʿi Iran.[6] She links the project of Sunnitisation to the development of an institutional apparatus comprised of mosques and *medreses*, which according to this narrative would have promoted an 'official' version of the state religion.[7] She sees evidence of confessional demarcation reflected in the composition of conversion narratives, stories of martyrs and other similar documents from the different confessional communities within the Empire.[8]

Marc D. Baer, however, has criticised this thesis, considering it to be Eurocentric and as failing to account for the complex reality of the Ottoman Empire, in which multiple and competing religious groups were constantly negotiating their status. He has pointed out, for example, that while Catholicism could be forcibly banished from the Protestant realms to which it had belonged before the Reformation; Safavid Shiʿism was never part of the Ottoman Empire and could not have been banished through a process of confessionalisation. He has also noted that the Ottoman State did not pursue a forcible Sunnitisation of its population through any form of centralised state-led initiative comparable to that of the German Church.[9] Other critiques of the confessionalisation paradigm question its lack of nuance. For example, in his study on the portrayals of ʿAli and the family of the Prophet (*ahl al-bayt*) in Ottoman historiography and *belle-lettres*, Vefa Erginbaş has observed that these portrayals are anything but monolithic: some show traces of what Robert McChesney called 'ahl al-baytism'; that is, a degree of devotion for the *ahl-bayt* among Sunnis which is nonetheless void of the theological implications of Shiʿism.[10] This was even more true in the case of those who could claim descent from the Prophet (*sayyids*/*sharīfs*), for whom sectarian lines were less defined, as Kazuo Morimoto has shown.[11] Others, however, were indeed adamant in their condemnation of the Shiʿa, who were unsurprisingly dismissed as extremists (*ghulāt*) and unequivocally associated with the Qizilbash, the Turkoman tribes that gave rise to the Safavid Empire.[12] This condemnation was nonetheless circumscribed to the context of Safavid emergence, and did not translate into a generalised anti-Shiʿi attitude within the Ottoman realm.[13]

While this debate has also been dominated by Ottoman specialists, Iran's potential pertinence to it is undeniable, given the sectarian project behind the foundation of the Safavid State. In her brief reference to Iran, Krstić speaks of Safavid Shiʿitisation as a parallel development to Ottoman Sunnitisation, with the Ottoman case starting to develop perhaps even slightly later.[14] Erginbaş's findings also seem to suggest that the most staunchly Sunni discourses in Ottoman historiography appear after the emergence of the Safavid state's Shiʿism, somehow as a reaction to it.[15] Whatever the case, the nature of Safavid state-sanctioned sectarianism would be the obvious point of departure for any incorporation of Iran into the broader discussion of interreligious and inter-sectarian relations in the Muslim Gunpowder Empires. This, despite the relatively marginal role of non-Muslims in Iranian society. The idea of a process of confessionalisation does not preclude the possibility of there being various religious antagonists or even a hierarchy of primary and secondary 'others' Therefore, Iranian confessionalisation – should we choose to accept this paradigm – could be said to have had non-Shiʿi Muslims as its main target, while retaining some loose shots to scapegoat non-Muslim subjects whenever politically convenient, especially during the decline of the Safavid dynasty.

There is, however, enough room for objection against applying this paradigm to the history of Safavid Iran: as is well known and as we will partially see in this book, the height of repression against non-Shiʿi and non-Muslim minorities in the Safavid period coincided with the last decades of the Empire, at the moment when the state was at its weakest. This implies that there would have been an inversely proportional relation between the coercive capacity of the state and the phenomenon of sectarian repression. This would at least demand some nuance regarding the principle of enforced religiosity at the heart of the paradigm in question. Further, this model ascribes disproportionate agency to the state at a time in which the technology of governance was rather limited. But there is yet another – perhaps even more fundamental – shortcoming to this approach to the study of religious minorities and sectarian politics. This model tends to favour an almost exclusively sociological and political reading of the sources, often to the neglect of intellectual and cultural developments that result from interreligious encounters.

As it happens, even with the confessionalisation paradigm remaining a marginal debate within Middle Eastern studies, scholarship on this period of Middle Eastern history in general, and Iranian in particular, has been mostly dominated by political and social historians. This is not in itself a negative thing. Essentially all of the abovementioned scholars have pursued this approach, contributing greatly to our understanding of questions related to identity-formation, political and religious self-fashioning, communal practice and even issues of realpolitik. However, this approach has not done enough justice to another, non-negligible, body of sources which is best engaged through a closer textual analysis, namely that of interreligious theological polemics. To be sure, questions regarding the motivations behind the writing of polemics or whether or not the authors of these texts enjoyed any kind of state patronage are not only legitimate, but indeed necessary for understanding the circumstances in which this kind of literature was conceived. Nonetheless, the richness of these works can only be fully accounted for through a close examination of their structure, their use of tropes and their intertextual engagement with other sources, whether as direct intellectual interlocutors in a debate, or as auxiliary aids of argumentation.

In this latter sense, many studies have of course paved the way for our assessment of the evolution of interreligious polemics as a genre. Some have done so in broad terms, accounting for the genre as a whole, as in the case of the classic studies by Hava Lazarus-Yafeh or more recently by David Thomas.[16] Others have chosen to focus on the work of a single author. Among the latter, it is hardly surprising that the most detailed and rigorous studies have been devoted to authors from the classical or, at most, from the early post-Mongol periods: from Gabriel Said Reynolds's study on the Muʿtazili scholar ʿAbd al-Jabbar (d. 1025) or Diego Sarrió Cucarella's work on the Maliki jurist Shihab al-Din al-Qarafi (d. 1285), to Dominique Urvoy and Samuel Martin-Behloul's studies on Ibn Hazm of Cordoba (d. 1064), attention has been given primarily to the study of the early classics of the genre.[17] Others have concentrated, understandably, on Muslim Spain and the Maghreb, where the process of *Reconquista* makes the history of Muslim–Christian relations a central topic. Among these, Míkel de Epalza's classic book on the convert and polemicist Anselm Turmeda (d. 1423) remains one of the most complete monographs ever written on an author of theological polemics.[18]

However, despite the undeniable progress made in the study of Muslim–Christian polemics, the early modern corpus has received relatively little attention. A plausible explanation could be the general biases that intellectual history of the post-Mongol Muslim world tends to face. Luckily, in many subfields, particularly in philosophy, the dismissal of postclassical intellectual production as derivative has been long questioned and superseded. However, at a superficial level, polemics seem easier to characterise as formulaic, given that they do tend to follow a set of standard rhetorical conventions. This could explain, at least partially, why early polemics have been the subject of close textual analyses, while later developments tend to be read mostly for their social and contextual value. As notable exemptions to this trend, we could cite two studies on the Persian-language polemics of the Jesuit missionary Jerome Xavier (d. 1617): one would be Arnulf Camps's classic book on this missionary and the other a more recent study by Jorge Flores.[19] In addition, Dennis Halft's work on the circulation of Biblical translations in Safavid Iran and their use by Muslim polemicists represents the most important contribution to the subject in a specifically Safavid Iranian context in Western academia.[20] In Iran, in addition to the rich production of critical editions of primary sources, polemics have been used in broader studies on social and political history, with studies by Rasul Jaʿfariyan, Maryam Sadiqi, ʿAbdul-Hadi Haʾiri and Sayyid Hashim Aghajari as representative examples.[21]

Scope and Structure of this Book

The present book focuses on the work of the convert and polemicist ʿAli Quli Jadid al-Islam (d. 1734). This character was by no means the only major polemicist of the period, and in fact his work is linked to a cycle of refutations that connected India, Rome and Iran. However, I have chosen to focus on his case given the particularity of his condition as a convert. As we will see, throughout different periods and places, converts have always played a major role in the development of the genre, as they could use their knowledge of their previous religion to their advantage. They could use it to present themselves as credible 'native informants' who could enrich their theological disputations with insider expertise. As noted above, however, this study does not seek to provide a purely sociological reading of the case in question, nor to simply provide an overview of the circumstances behind the composition of Jadid al-Islam's work. Instead, it uses his case to connect the thematic axes listed above: the history of Muslim–Christian engagement in Iran, the history of interreligious polemics in the early modern period and the history of the transmission of knowledge across Iran, Europe and the broader Persianate world. The first two chapters of the book are largely contextual, while the remaining four focus more closely on the author's work. In Chapter one, I briefly introduce the scarce biographical data on this character, followed by an overview of the status of Christians in the Safavid Empire. In Chapter two, I trace the genealogy of the polemical cycle to which Jadid al-Islam responded. The cycle in question extended throughout Iran, Mughal India and Rome, and developed throughout the entire seventeenth century and beyond. Chapter three situates Jadid al-Islam's work within the centuries-old tradition of *dalāʾil al-nubuwwa* (signs of the prophecy) literature, which among other rhetorical devices uses the Bible as a proof of the coming of Islam. In this chapter I also begin to examine the specifically Shiʿi character of the author's take on the genre. Chapter four explores the author's appropriation of sources from both the Shiʿi and the Christian intellectual archives, looking at how he makes use of them to legitimise his position as an intellectual authority on both traditions. The fifth chapter is devoted to debates on ritual practice and moral conduct among Christians, both in broad terms as well as in the context of Jadid al-Islam's response to his main intellectual adversary, Filippo Guadagnoli (d. 1656). Finally, the sixth chapter explores the connections between the author's anti-Sufi and anti-Christian works. To conclude, I revisit the question of what would be implied by speaking of *confessionalisation* in the late Safavid period, given the context of a weak state and of competing understandings of proper Shiʿi orthodoxy.

Notes

1. I am using, of course, the term coined by Marshall Hodgson. See Hodgson, *The Venture of Islam*, vol. 3.
2. For representative studies on the matter, see Krstić, *Contested Conversions to Islam*; Baer, *Honored by the Glory of Islam*; Graf, *The Sultan's Renegades*; Frazee, *Catholics and Sultans*; Malcolm, *Useful Enemies*.
3. Ghougassian, *The Emergence of the Armenian Diocese of New Julfa*; Herzig, 'The Deportation of the Armenians'; Rota, 'The Death of Tahmāspqoli Xān Qājār'; Hirotake Maeda, 'Slave Elites Who Returned Home'; Giunashvili and Abuladze, 'Researches on Persian and Georgian-Persian'.
4. Matthee, 'Christians in Safavid Iran'; Matthee, 'The Politics of Protection'; Matthee, 'Poverty and Perseverance'; Flores, *Unwanted Neighbours*; Flannery, *The Mission of the Portuguese Augustinians*; Windler, 'Katholische Mission und Diasporareligiosität'; Windler, 'La curie romaine et la cour safavide'; Windler, *Missionare in Persien*.
5. Reinhard, 'Gegenreformation als Modernisierung?'; Reinhard, 'Zwang zur Konfessionalisierung?'; Schilling, 'Die Konfessionalisierung im Reich'.
6. Krstić, *Contested Conversions to Islam*, pp. 12–16, 23–5.
7. Ibid. p. 14.

8. Ibid. pp. 121–64.
9. Baer, 'Review of: *Contested Conversions to Islam*'. In a conversation between Baer, Ussama Makdisi and Andrew Shryock, Makdisi emphasises the importance of not confisung the coexistence of different religious groups in the Ottoman Empire with modern notions of 'tolerance'. See Baer, Makdisi and Shryock, 'Tolerance and Conversion in the Ottoman Empire', pp. 928–9
10. Erginbaş, 'Problematizing Ottoman Sunnism', pp. 621–6, 630–5. For the term *ahl al-baytism*, see McChesney, *Waqf in Central Asia*, pp. 33–4, 268–9.
11. Morimoto, 'How to behave towards *sayyids* and *sharīfs*', p. 17.
12. Erginbaş, 'Problematizing Ottoman Sunnism', pp. 626–8.
13. Ibid. pp. 641–2.
14. Krstić, *Contested Conversions to Islam*, pp. 12–16.
15. Erginbaş, 'Problematizing Ottoman Sunnism', pp. 626–30, 635–41.
16. Lazarus-Yafeh, *Intertwined Worlds*; Thomas, *Christian Doctrines in Islamic Theology*; Thomas, *Routledge Handbook of Christian-Muslim Relations.*
17. Said Reynolds, *A Muslim Theologian in a Sectarian Milieu*; Sarrió Cucarella, *Muslim-Christian Polemics across the Mediterranean*; Urvoy, 'Le sense de la polémique anti-biblique chez Ibn Ḥazm'; Behloul, 'The Testimony of Reason'.
18. Epalza, *La Tuḥfah, autobiografía y polémica islámica.* (Reprinted as Epalza, *Fray Anselmo Turmeda (Abdallāh al-Taryumān) y su polémica islamo-cristiana*).
19. Camps, *Jerome Xavier S.J. and the Muslims*; Flores, *The Mughal Padshah.*
20. Halft, 'The Arabic Vulgate in Safavid Persia'. See also Halft, 'Schiitische Polemik gegen das Chrsitentum'; Halft, 'Hebrew Bible Quotations'.
21. Jaʿfariyan and Sadiqi, *Az Darband ta Qaitf*; Jaʿfariyan, *Din va siyasat*; Haʾiri, *Nakhustin ruyaruyiha-yi andishihgaran*; Aghajari, *Muqaddimih-i bar munasibat.*

I

The Profile of a Convert in Safavid Iran

In the last decade of the seventeenth century, the Catholic missions in Isfahan were struck by the news of the apostasy of two Portuguese clerics from the Augustinian Order. The first case was that of Padre Manuel de Santa Maria, who embraced Islam in 1691 and adopted the name of Hasan Quli Beg.[1] It was, however, the second case that proved more scandalous. As the Bishop of Isfahan Louis Marie Pidou de Saint Olon (d. 1717) explained in a letter dated on 25 October 1697, the most troubling aspect of the case of this latter convert was that: 'having made himself a doctor of the Qur'an, it [was] said that he [was] writing a book against the Christian Religion (*ayant se fait docteur de l'Alcoran, on dit qu'il compose un livre contre la religion chrétienne*)'.[2] This second apostate was Padre António de Jesus, who the scholarly consensus has identified with the late ʿAli Quli Jadid al-Islam (d. 1734). The identification, although not completely uncontestable, rests on a reasonable deduction: Padre António is the only one of the two who is said to have written polemics after his conversion and ʿAli Quli Jadid al-Islam is the only polemicist from the period who presents himself as a former priest, as we will later see in more detail.[3] Past scholarship worked under the assumption that he could have died during the 1722 Afghan invasion.[4] However, Willem Floor has recently discovered a document from the Dutch East India Company, which says that the renegade 'Alie Coelie Beek' died on 10 March 1734.[5] As we will see shortly, the circumstances surrounding his conversion are not entirely clear. In the absence of clarity about the conditions in which he converted and his motives for doing so, the next relevant task is to ask what his case reveals about larger societal and epochal trends.

As we will also see, the confessionalisation paradigm applied to the Muslim world appears to be inadequate or insufficient for this late period of Safavid history. If we were to accept the idea of there having been a process of confessionalisation in Safavid Iran, the obvious thing would be to look at the early years of the empire and its 'conversion' to Twelver Shiʿism. In this case, the target of conversion would have been Sunni Muslims, who until then comprised the majority of the Iranian population.[6] However, by the time in which the apostasies of these missionaries took place, there was no longer a need to convert Iran to Shiʿism, as by then Iran was a majority Shiʿi society with established Shiʿi institutions. Furthermore, neither Christians nor other non-Muslims could be said to have ever been systematically targeted for conversion in their entirety. This, it must be said, is also true of the Ottoman Empire, as critics of importing the confessionalisation paradigm to the Muslim world have noted.[7] There were many instances of religious repression against these communities in Iran indeed, but they occurred under specific and often short-lived circumstances. Therefore, a close examination of Jadid al-Islam's character and work should take into account some key considerations: first, we must distinguish between cases like his and that of the mass – and perhaps often insincere – conversions that occurred among indigenous Christian communities. Second, we must account for the geopolitical role of the missionary orders as diplomatic entities, the weakening of which seem to have resulted in defections from their ranks. And third and more importantly, while understanding the immediate circumstances behind both Jadid al-Islam's conversion and the composition of his polemics is important, a serious historical genealogy of his work must also situate it within the larger context of the history of the genre. For this reason, a purely sociological reading of his work would be insufficient, and hence the need to delve deeper into his use of literary devices and discursive strategies. A short overview of the context of Jadid al-Islam's milieu is nonetheless pertinent as a point of departure.

Christians and the Safavid State in the Seventeenth Century

Throughout most of the Safavid period, the state's attitude toward Christian and other non-Muslim groups was fraught with contradiction. Christian groups such as European missionaries and Armenian merchants were favoured at moments when they were deemed politically useful and repressed when they became convenient scapegoats. When assessing their status and their overall experience throughout the more than two centuries of Safavid rule, we must bear in mind Rudi Matthee's note of caution regarding their over-representation in European sources. These often give the false impression that Christian minorities were more central to Safavid society than they probably were, especially considering the relative failure of Catholic missions in Iran.[8] As for their appearance in Persian chronicles, they are rather scattered and schematic, since these sources are overwhelmingly centred on the court and on the battlefield, leaving little space for details on social history. Overall, even at times when Christian groups were repressed, they tended to fare better than other non-Muslim groups. Also, as Roger Savory has correctly pointed out, Christians of European origin could always count on a certain level of political leverage through their diplomatic connections with European powers, while indigenous religious minorities did not enjoy these sorts of connections.[9]

During the first half of the seventeenth century, Armenian Christians played a central role in the Safavid economy. In 1604–5, in the midst of the Safavid–Ottoman wars, Armenian merchant communities were massively relocated from the town of Julfa in the Caucasus to what became the district of New Julfa in Isfahan. Much debate has surrounded the question of whether this was indeed a forced migration deliberately planned by Shah ʿAbbas I (r. 1587–1629). Edmund Herzig, relying on Armenian sources, has argued that this was rather unplanned, as the Iranian army had to resort to scorched-earth policy in the Armenian homeland in order to cut provisions for the advancing Ottoman forces.[10] This view of the events coincides with the report of the Augustinian missionary Belchior dos Anjos, who speaks of an orderly yet expeditious retreat followed by the burning of all crops. According to another Augustinian, António de Gouvea (d. 1628), they were given a two-day notice to leave their lands and were given camels and pack animals to ease their journey.[11] Whatever the case, once settled in New Julfa, Armenians enjoyed royal protection and became the cornerstone of the Iranian silk trade with both Europe and the Ottoman Empire. As Christians, they had access to trading routes which remained inaccessible to Shiʿi Iranians due to the sectarianism of the time.[12] This of course did not mean that the Shah trusted them unconditionally. At times, he became wary that their contact with European missionaries could bring them too close to the Church of Rome, which could lead them to compromise their loyalty. To prevent this, he often barred them from visiting the missionaries' houses.[13]

However, this status of apparent protection did not prevent conversions from occurring, often under circumstances of repression. For instance, around the year 1621 a group of Armenians in the region of Faridun in Gilan embraced Islam. According to the chronicler Iskandar Beg Munshi (d. 1632), they were encouraged to do so to gain the Shah's protection against Luri and Bakhtiari raids at the frontier, since the Shah could not otherwise guarantee their safety as *dhimmīs* (protected minorities, belonging to the People of the Book).[14] Roger Savory has noted that many Armenians remained sceptical about the Shah's motivations, saying that he harboured a deep hatred against them, instigated by the Shaykh al-Islam of Isfahan, the famous Baha' al-Din al-ʿAmili (hereon Shaykh-i Bahaʾi) (d. 1621). However, Savory has rejected this thesis based on the overall contextual evidence and on other policies championed by Shaykh Bahaʾi.[15] In any case, what is clear is that the Shah soon realised that these forced conversions of Armenians could have a detrimental effect on the Iranian economy and decided not to pursue them any further.[16]

Another group of indigenous Christians that played an important role in Safavid society were the Georgians. Since the early sixteenth century, the Safavid shahs had raided and plundered the Georgian kingdoms of Kartli and Kakhet'i. In 1554, under Shah Tahmasp (r. 1524–76), as many as 30,000 people (chief among them Georgians) were captured from the Caucasus and sent to Iran. This number would only continue to increase during Shah ʿAbbas I's tenure, who in 1616 captured close to 200,000 Georgians.[17] As a result, by the mid-seventeenth century, King Teimuraz I of Kakhet'i (d. 1663) made many attempts to keep Iranian invaders away. The Safavid–Ottoman war brought a truce between Iran and the Caucasian Kingdom. Hoping to alleviate hostilities, Teimuraz went as far as to send his sons and his mother, Queen Ketevan (d. 1624), to the court of Shah ʿAbbas, where they were held captive. Following the reestablishment of peace with the Ottomans, the Queen was martyred, and the Shah reinitiated his campaigns against Georgia. The hitherto independent Bagrationi Dynasty (r. 575–1810) was then forced to accept puppet-governments appointed by the Shah, effectively making Georgia an Iranian suzerainty.[18]

Through these raids and political interventions, many Georgians were brought into Iran to serve as mercenaries and royal slaves, forming – together with a minority of Armenians and Circassians – the *ghulām* corps (royal military slaves). This became the Safavid equivalent of the *mamlūk* soldiery of early Turkic dynasties and of the Ottoman *devşirme* system.[19] Up until the enthronement of Shah ʿAbbas I, Safavid politics had been dominated by strife between the Turcoman Qizilbash tribes, which had helped the Safavid order come to power at the beginning of the sixteenth century. However, Shah ʿAbbas I then appointed *ghulāms* to positions of power to create a force that would be loyal to him alone, thus neutralising the political influence of the Qizilbash.[20] Many Georgians converted to Islam and became powerful *ghulāms*, going on to hold influential positions in the administration.[21] Scholars have of course questioned the sincerity of their conversions, with some, like Giorgio Rota, finding evidence that many of them remained secretly attached to their original faith.[22] Moreover, as Babak Rezvani has correctly noted, while Georgians who became part of the Iranian elite (be it as *ghulāms* or as concubines of the Shah) were Islamised, the popular classes had less incentive to convert to Islam, and many simply assimilated into the Armenian Christian community.[23] This of course did not imply that there were never efforts to preach among the community, as suggested by the existence of an anonymous text from Shah ʿAbbas's time, known in Persian as the *Risalih-i shinakht* (*Treatise on Knowledge*), which defends the tenets of Twelver Shiʿism in the Georgian language.[24]

Later, under Shah ʿAbbas II (r. 1642–66), Jews, Hindu Banyans, Zoroastrians and Christians came under increased religious restriction and suppression. At the beginning of his reign, ʿAbbas II showed signs of tolerance towards other religions, leading the chronicler Jean-Baptiste Tavernier (d. 1689) to describe him as a 'courageous and generous (*vaillant et généreux*) prince' who 'loved foreigners' and who 'took pleasure and was at ease seeing the works that [people] brought to him from Europe, especially the French'.[25] However, the sources continued to register more cases of repression and conversion from the time between the mid-1640s and the 1650s. Rudi Matthee has suggested that the instigator of these campaigns was the grand vizier Khalifih Sultan (r. 1645–54), who perhaps in order to prove himself as a God-fearing functionary targeted practices proscribed by the shariʿa, such as wine-drinking, and directed campaigns against coffeehouses, brothels and taverns.[26] Khalifih Sultan's predecessor, Muhammad Saru Taqi (r. 1634–45) had already demonstrated his hostility towards Jews and Armenians by asking the Shah to enforce *dhimmī* dress codes more strictly. However, it was the former who pursued the harshest policies, forcing Armenian and Jewish merchants to close their shops so that they could not compete with their Muslim counterparts.[27] Pressure continued under Muhammad Beg's tenure as grand vizier (r. 1654–61), who in 1654 ordered the closure of churches and prohibited the building of new ones. By 1657, European missionaries and workers of the East India Companies were the only Christians allowed to stay within the city limits of Isfahan.[28] Even though it was the ulama's role to ensure the preservation of Shiʿi doctrinal and ritual customs, the sovereigns came under sharp criticism whenever members of the royal household indulged in acts that contravened the shariʿa. Therefore, repression of non-Muslims was often part of a more comprehensive demand for a strict application of religious and moral rules, which served to legitimise both the monarchs and the high administrators. Yet, in moments when such legitimacy could be taken for granted, these rules became apparently laxer and they were only enforced from time to time. Also, by its very nature as a pre-modern entity, the Safavid State's ability to fully implement and police such laws was limited. Let it suffice as a proof that throughout this period prostitution needed to be banned repeatedly, which indicates that it was never truly eradicated and oftentimes seemingly tolerated.[29]

Towards the last decades of the seventeenth century – that is, during the reigns of Shah Sulayman (r. 1666–94) and Shah Sultan Husayn (r. 1694–1722) – what many scholars have seen as the period of Safavid decline began. Earlier scholars blamed this on the fact that, having spent most of their formative years secluded in the harem, the latter shahs failed to develop strong statecraft skills and lost control of their political affairs.[30] This undoubtedly played a role, but as Rudi Matthee has argued, other factors were more important: Iran's coinage underwent a process of debasement, its military resources were drained, frontier wars became widespread and harsh natural disasters became more frequent.[31] For our purposes however, what matters is that this period is often seen as one of increased hardship for non-Shiʿi (let alone non-Muslim) groups. Many scholars have attributed this trend to the growing influence at the court of ulama such as Muhammad Baqir Majlisi (d. 1699). Some sources associate the latter with the forced conversion of Armenians, the destruction of Hindu temples and the deportation of Banyan merchants to India.[32] He is also said to have advocated oppressive measures against Jews, and even against Sufis and Sunni Muslims.[33] However, Matthee has persuasively argued that it was Shah Sulayman's chief musketeer Budaq Sultan and his grand vizier Shaykh ʿAli Khan Zanganih (d. 1689), himself a Sunni, who should bear most of the responsibility for these policies.[34] Scholars who single out Majlisi for these measures tend to rely on European sources or on some of Majlisi's own polemical writings.[35] Whether it is possible to establish a causative link between polemical writings and actual hostilities on the ground is something that could and should be problematised in studies of intellectual history. For now, however, suffice it to note that this has been one of the dominant narratives in Western scholarship dealing with Safavid historiography.

In the early 1670s, after having been banned from the Muslim quarters of Isfahan, many prominent Armenians converted to Islam, among them the famous *kalāntar* (communal head) Aqa Piri.[36] In 1671, an Armenian archimandrite (*vardapet*) by the name of Yovhan embraced Islam and sought the protection of the Shaykh al-Islam, leading to a dispute with another *vardapet* and with the Bishop of New Julfa.[37] The latter accused Yovhan of translating the Qurʾan into Armenian and of writing a refutation against it. The renegade was then brought before an 'inquisitorial tribunal of that faith [Islam]', where thirty Muslim witnesses testified to the charges. During the trial, the convert pretended to be illiterate, claiming that his role within the Church consisted only of preaching through the performance of good deeds and the transmission of good teachings. After unsuccessfully trying to bribe the judge, he was sentenced to be burnt at the stake, only to be liberated later through the intercession of the Queen Mother.[38] His accusers were then imprisoned for conspiracy.[39]

Finally, in 1678 a group of ulama blamed Armenians and Jews for causing a drought. This led to the execution of rabbis and to the levying of fines against both groups. However, the Queen Mother interceded on behalf of the Armenians to ease their financial burden.[40] In addition, Armenians were less affected by a series of fiscal measures imposed on the *dhimmīs* during the

1690s.[41] In this decade there was a failed attempt to enforce strict purity laws, such as prohibiting non-Muslims from leaving their homes during times of rain and snow.[42] At the turn of the eighteenth century, Shah Sultan Husayn withdrew from Armenians the royal patronage they had enjoyed until then.[43] They were then banned from selling food to Muslims, from importing corn and wheat to New Julfa, and from building their houses along the banks of the Zayandih Rud River.[44] More importantly, inheritance laws whereby converts could inherit the property of their non-Muslim families were enforced more widely.[45] These kinds of measures led the Polish Jesuit missionary Jan Tadeusz Krusinski (d. 1751) to say that although, since the reign of Shah ʿAbbas, 'great infringements had been made on their [Armenians] Privileges by his Successors, yet none of them did it so enormously as Schah [Sultan] Hussein has done'.[46]

The aforementioned forms of pressure notwithstanding, mass conversions of Armenian Christians remained a statistical anomaly. Many of them had more to lose than to gain from changing their faith. This was partly because merchants from the Julfan network were more likely to collaborate with each other than with Armenians from other regions. More importantly, belonging to the Armenian Orthodox Church strengthened the network's sense of trust and community.[47] In his autobiography, known to us under the title of *Iʿtirafnamih* (*Confession Book*), the Armenian convert to Islam Abgar ʿAli Akbar Armani gives some examples of how much was at stake for renegades who lost their connection to the trading network. In his case, his family denied him lodging during a trip to Venice, where he was imprisoned in retaliation for rumours concerning the abuse of Christians in Iran.[48] However, this same source also suggests that through their integration into Muslim social circles, renegades could acquire material benefits and social status, and also become socialised into circles of relative influence through marriage bonds.[49] This is of course clearer among the Georgian *ghulāms*, even if their conversions were not exempt from ambiguity. Thus for example, Levan Khan (d. 1709)[50] – known for his participation in campaigns against the Afghans and the Baluchis – is said to have requested the Pope to secretly recognise him as a Catholic after having been forced to convert to Islam.[51] In many other instances, *ghulāms* were reprimanded for behaviour that contravened the shariʿa, such as drinking wine, eating pork, or indulging in 'depravities proper of drunkards' (*fisq va fujūr kih lāzimih-i mastān ast*) inside the mosque, which of course puts in doubt the deepness of their commitment to their new religion.[52]

Comparatively speaking, however, Christians tended to fare better than other non-Muslim groups. For example, the sources mention many instances of forced conversions of Jews during the 1650s, under the auspices of Muhammad Beg, who offered them the options of conversion, exile to troubled regions of the country, or martyrdom.[53] At some point, a community was relocated almost in its entirety to the Zoroastrian quarter of Gabrabad in order to incite the Zoroastrians against them.[54] Further, a Judeo–Persian epic that narrates the fate of the Jews of Kashan during the last decades of the dynasty, recounts how a group of Jews were punished for feasting on the night of the commemoration of the killing of Husayn. According to this source, the royal musketeers (*qurchīs*) incited both Christians and Zoroastrians to break into the Synagogue and to partake in the public shaming of the Jews.[55]

However, the fact that such instances of repression occurred did not mean that religious minorities did not have ways of negotiating their status. For instance, the local chronicle *Tazkirih-i Safavi-yi Kirman* tells a story from 1673 in which the son of Khvajih Sharif, an influential functionary of the Divan, lures a young Zoroastrian woman into conversion in order to consummate a temporary marriage (*mutʿa*).[56] After the woman's parents complain to the *kalāntar* of Kerman, the latter reprimands Khvajih Sharif, who in turn plots with the vizier – a sworn enemy of the *kalāntar* – to orchestrate a self-robbery of the Divan and to blame it on the Zoroastrian community. The vizier, who owed favours to Rustam-i Majus, a former Zoroastrian who served as a collector of the *jizya* (poll tax paid by non-Muslims), entrusts the latter with the operation, allowing him to keep the booty as payment.[57] However, since Rustam-i Majus already had a history of trying to extort the Zoroastrian community, a group of them anticipates the plot and has him lynched beforehand. The *kalāntar* then tries to intervene on Rustam's behalf, but the community warns him that this was an internal issue, which had to be solved by them alone. Upon hearing the news, the vizier wants a restitution to be given to Rustam's heirs. The *kalāntar* then takes sides with the Zoroastrian commoners, a mistake which eventually led to his own political assassination at the hands of the vizier's allies.[58] What the account seems to indicate is that relations between non-Muslim (or non- Shiʿi) communities and the Shiʿi majority were complex, shifting and multifaceted. On the one hand, there seems to have been a certain degree of adherence to social and legal rules, such as the payment of *jizya* or the necessity to convert before consummating the *mutʿa*. However, there also seems to have been a certain degree of fluidity in such relations: communal boundaries and legal norms were transgressed from time to time by political manoeuvres and by alliances with 'the others', as is shown by the vizier's alliance with Rustam-i Majus and by the *kalāntar's* backing of the Zoroastrians.

Missionaries in Safavid Iran

By the time that Padre António was sent to Iran to proselytise, corresponding to the reign of Shah Sultan Husayn, most Catholic missionaries had already abandoned any hopes of converting the Shah or any substantial portion of the Muslim population. At the very beginning of the Safavid period, Europeans misread the advent of Shah Ismaʿil (r. 1501–24) as that of a redeeming figure who would convert Iran to Christianity.[59] The Habsburgs in particular saw in Iran a potential ally in their quest to establish an anti-Ottoman axis. By contrast, for most of the duration of Safavid rule, the French aligned themselves with the Ottomans given their common rivalry with the Habsburgs.[60] These kinds of alliances were not a development new to the sixteenth century. A century earlier, the Venetians had cooperated with the Aq Quyunlu (White Sheep Turk) Confederation (1378–1501) against the Ottoman Sultan Mehmed II (r. 1444–6 and 1451–81).[61] Later, throughout the seventeenth century, missionaries would serve as diplomatic attachés of the states to which each of them were most closely associated, in conjunction with trading emporia like the Dutch, English, or French East India Companies.[62]

Padre António's people, the Portuguese, were among the first Europeans to venture into Iran and the Persian Gulf during the Safavid period. Afonso de Albuquerque (d. 1515) invaded the island of Hormuz in 1507 and consolidated his rule in it in 1515.[63] The capture of Bahrain followed suit in 1521. From the beginning of the Portuguese seaborne enterprise in Asia, Vasco da Gama (d. 1524) had made it his mission to explore the edges of the world in search of 'Christians and spices'.[64] However, having realised that indigenous Asian Christians were negligible in India, the Portuguese rapidly started to prioritise spices and trade. Consequently, their empire remained largely confined to coastal regions, where it could dominate trading routes without needing to penetrate the continent.[65] Yet the Portuguese still sent diplomatic and religious missions to various strategic locations in Asia, including mainland Iran.

Before the advent of the Safavids, the Dominican order had already sought to establish a mission in Iran in the fourteenth century,[66] but the height of Catholic missionary activity came in the mid-Safavid period. The first Portuguese missionaries to venture into the Safavid realm were Jesuits, although with little success. Their presence was restricted to Hormuz and lasted only two decades before all their missionaries were sent to Goa in 1568.[67] Later in 1581, an Armenian who served as the Neapolitan and Indian ambassador to the Shah claimed that the Persian crown prince had converted to Christianity. This had allegedly happened after the prince had been miraculously cured of an illness by the mere sight of a crucifix. According to the story, the princess, a daughter of the Alexander II of Kakhet'i (r. 1574–1605), had guided him to his conversion, and as a result the Shah had requested the King of Spain to send Catholic priests to Iran. While almost no European dignitary seemed to believe this story, Philip II (r. in Portugal 1581–98) – who reigned over both Spain and Portugal at that time – sent a diplomatic mission in response. At the head of it was the Augustinian Simão de Moraes, who worked for the viceroyalty of Goa. His mission was brief, but he did manage to convert a number of Iranians – including supposedly an unnamed major philosopher – before returning to Goa in 1584. [68] After Moraes, the Augustinian Order sent Nicolau de Melo (d. 1615), who was in charge of negotiating an anti-Ottoman alliance between Iran, Spain, England, Poland, Scotland and France. De Melo's mission in Persia was brief, but he did have the opportunity to meet with Shah ʿAbbas, who allegedly said to him: 'what is the reason that the Moghul and the Turk have priests in their lands while they are the enemies of the Christians, whereas I, who am so fond of them, have none?'[69] De Melo was sent to Russia in the mid-1590s to explore alternative routes for the silk trade, since both Iran and the European powers wanted to avoid Ottoman territory. There, he would meet a tragic fate due to intra-Christian conflicts. He was imprisoned for allegedly baptising an

Orthodox girl in accordance with the Catholic rite, and after experiencing many other hardships he was killed in Astrakhan in 1615.[70]

At the turn of the seventeenth century, having had the precedent of the abovementioned embassies, the Augustinian Order persuaded the king and the viceroy of Goa to entrust them with the founding of a permanent mission in Iran, citing concerns that the Jesuits had already pretensions to this regard.[71] Thus, with royal support, the Augustinians established their convent in Isfahan around the year 1602. That year, however, the Portuguese sought to reclaim their presence in Bahrain, where they encountered resistance from the Shah. The latter established a temporary strategic alliance with the English in order to expel the Portuguese from the island. Knowing that in this context it would have been inconvenient to have the Portuguese Augustinians at the forefront of the Catholic mission, Pope Clement VIII (p. 1592–1605) dispatched instead a Carmelite mission in 1604.[72] The Pope preferred to entrust the mission to the Carmelites, probably because – as Pedro Ortega García has suggested – he saw the Augustinians functioning more as diplomats than as a proper religious order.[73] He was wary that their politically charged closeness to the Spanish-Portuguese crown could affect Iranians' perception of Christianity. The Carmelites represented an ideal candidate because they were accountable only to Rome and not to any other crown. As a result, the Carmelites arrived in Iran in 1607 with a contingent of mostly Spanish missionaries, although responding to the authority of the Italian branch of their order.[74] With the establishment of these two orders, Rome and Madrid intensified their diplomatic relations with Iran. Through Augustinian intercession, the Carmelites were given a house to stay in. As a sign of their largesse, the Carmelites presented the Shah with portraits of the Madonna and Saint Michael, a crucifix and an illuminated Arabic Bible from the thirteenth century.[75]

Hostilities between Iran and the Portugese culminated in the expulsion of the latter from Hormuz in 1622. This did not entail the end of Portuguese Augustinian presence in Iran and Georgia, where another convent had been established a year before.[76] However, the missionaries and their followers did experience some hardship that year, when five Muslim apostates were executed for converting to Christianity.[77] Tensions eased over time, which again led Europeans to entertain false hopes of converting Shah ʿAbbas I, citing his favourable disposition to them and the fact that he had a Georgian wife or that he offered pork during a banquet for Christmas.[78] The monarch certainly made some gestures that could have been interpreted as an overture to Christians, such as visiting the Augustinian convent in Isfahan on one occasion.[79] More importantly, there were many instances at which the Shah intervened in favour of the missionaries, as they struggled against local Muslim governors and met with opposition from members of the Orthodox Armenian clergy who strongly resisted the missionaries' efforts to bring their community under papal control.[80] In reality, however, it seems that the Shah's only motivation in doing so was to secure European cooperation against the eternal Ottoman threat and possibly even – as Matthee has suggested – to use the Europeans as a counterweight to the political influence of his own clerics.[81]

In the second half of the seventeenth century, with the Portuguese presence waning in Iran, France saw an opportunity to curtail the Iberian influence in the country and establish a new diplomatic sphere of influence. Given their healthy relations with the Ottomans, the French, under Louis XIII (r. 1610–43) offered to mediate between Shah ʿAbbas I and Sultan Murad IV (r. 1623–40).[82] As a result, in 1628, the French Capuchins were allowed to establish their convent in Isfahan.[83] French–Iranian relations continued to evolve until in 1665 Louis XIV (r. 1643–1715) struck a deal with Shah ʿAbbas II to get the same concessions for silk purchases that the Dutch and the English had enjoyed in the early decades of the seventeenth century.[84] Although there were Capuchins and Theatines among the French missionaries, the Jesuits constituted France's main clerical branch.[85] Their mission was first entrusted to François Rigordi (d. 1679), who in 1647 managed to obtain a decree from Shah ʿAbbas II allowing them to purchase land. He would then leave Iran for a short period, during which time the mission was entrusted to Alexandre de Rhodes (d. 1660), who had earned a reputation for his proselytising work in Japan and Vietnam. Rigordi was to return to Iran in 1652, accompanied by Aimé Chézaud (d. 1664), who would become a prominent figure of missionary intellectual life in this period, going as far as to debate Shiʿi religious scholars and to write polemical treatises against Islam, as we will see later.[86]

However, from the beginning, missionaries realised that winning the hearts and minds of Muslims would have been a nearly impossible task.

They knew that pursuing this goal might lead to political problems with Iran and that the European powers at the time had more important priorities than providing supplies and protection for the missions. Seeing this, they concentrated their efforts on the local Armenian and – to a lesser extent – Georgian Orthodox populations, which they sought to bring under the tutelage of Rome. This does not mean that there were no Armenian Catholics in the region before. Indeed, one of the things that struck the Augustinians was the story, related by a group of Armenians Catholics, of Bartholomew, a legendary figure who had allegedly converted many villages to Catholicism four centuries earlier.[87] However – as would remain the case even after these missionary activities – the Gregorian Church managed to retain its independence, and with it, the religious adherence of most Armenians. In addition, the Gregorian leadership of New Julfa enjoyed the protection of the Safavid authorities, including the Queen Mother, the patron of the suburb.

Nonetheless, European missionaries did have some success stories. For instance, in 1607, the patriarch David IV (d. 1629) promised to recognise the authority of Rome after visiting the Augustinian monastery of Isfahan. He sought Rome's support to remain at the head of his community, at a time when he was facing the opposition of another bishop by the name of Melchizedek.[88] The plan for unification with Rome failed for many reasons: the missionaries had been unable to persuade the Orthodox population on theological questions regarding the divine nature of Christ, and they had also been inflexible regarding the possibility of allowing Armenians to retain certain customs. But more importantly, David IV's project not only faced the opposition of many bishops, but also that of many powerful merchants. This began to affect the missionaries even at a diplomatic level, as Shah ʿAbbas I was concerned that by converting, Armenians would potentially revolt against Iranian authority with European support. As a result, the patriarch was forced to retreat from his initial intentions.[89]

One exception to this general failure was the successful conversion to Catholicism of the Shahrimanians, a wealthy and influential merchant family, who on various occasions granted the missionaries asylum while subsidising their building activities.[90] One of the members of this family, Basil, became a priest and studied at the *Colegio Urbano* in Rome.[91] However, many members of this family were pressured into becoming Muslim at the turn of the eighteenth century.[92] Missionary documentation from this period speaks of constant pressure against the orders. According to the missionaries' own accounts, most hostilities against them came, not from Muslims, but from what they called the *schismatici* (that is, the Gregorian Armenians). In a letter from 1694, Bishop Elia di San Alberto (d. 1708) claimed that the Armenian bishop of Julfa sent people to plunder the Carmelite church. During this operation, the Armenians levied fines of 850 *scudi*[93] against the members of the Shahrimanian family for collaborating with the Catholics and threatened them with bastinado. In despair, the Catholics sent a delegation to Shah Sulayman's court, hoping that the ruler would intervene on their behalf. Yet, since the latter had died before they could reach the court, they had to wait until the coronation of his successor.[94] In the same year, a missionary by the name of Father Beauvoilier suggested that seeking Shah Sulayman's intervention would have been useless anyway, since 'the defunct king no longer occupied himself with anything (*il Re defonto non s'intrigava più in niente*)' – referring to Shah's disappearance into his harem during the last years of his life.[95] Beauvoilier recounted a story that seems to refer to the case of the abovementioned renegade *vardapet*, adding the detail that the Armenians had brought donkeys and horses to desecrate the church, but that the Portuguese Augustinians intervened. They threatened to denounce the Armenian bishop for writing a book against the Qur'an and for sending the king over 50,000 gifts in bribes. They managed to have him sent to prison where he had his toenails pulled off through cane-strokes. Armenian churches were then closed, no masses were held in them and the population demanded the appointment of a new bishop.[96]

As for the damaged Carmelite convent, in 1708 Shah Sultan Husayn allowed the order to rebuild it and issued a royal edict (*raqam*) as a guarantee of protection.[97] Some years before, in an undated letter to Pope Innocent XII (papacy 1691–1700), the Shah had also authorised the establishment of a Polish Jesuit mission in Kerman.[98] After the reparation of the Carmelite church, the Shah sent the Georgian prince Vakhtan Mirza (d. 1737) to punish a group of Armenians for troubling the Capuchin Fathers in Tiflis.[99] However, the Armenians did retain some bargaining power, and in 1710 they were able to convince the Shah to seize property previously given to the Catholics.[100]

Finally, we should emphasise that – as we have hinted at before – the Catholic orders continued to engage in internal rivalries, in great part reflective of the longstanding French–Iberian rivalry mentioned above. For example, in 1706 a priest from the order of Santa Sabina by the name of Antonio di Poschiavo complained that the Jesuits wanted their church to be instituted as the official parish of New Julfa, to the exclusion of all others.[101] Further, upon the apostasy of the two Portuguese Augustinians, Pidou de Saint Olon proposed a measure, which, by hurting the Augustinians, could indirectly benefit the Jesuits. He stated as the most urgent priority:

> « [. . .] obtenir du Roy de Portugal quelque résolution par le Convent des Augustins d'Ispahan et d'y employer que d'agents séculiers comme les anglois et hollandois et jamais d'ecclésiastiques.»[102]
>
> [. . .] to obtain from the King of Portugal some resolution for the Augustinian Convent of Isfahan and to employ there only secular agents such as the English and the Dutch, and never clerical ones]

As these anecdotes suggest, the status of the orders as political liaisons of competing European powers meant that their institutional structures and agendas often reproduced the same quarrels. We should of course be careful not to draw general conclusions from these isolated cases nor to explain the phenomenon of apostasy solely in terms of social and political convenience. However, we should also be mindful that as certain states saw their influence in the region waning, it is hardly surprising that the orders and other institutions attached to them would face defections from their ranks.

ʿAli Quli Jadid al-Islam: The Profile of a Convert

Virtually all we know about Jadid al-Islam's life comes from missionary and diplomatic correspondence. A short note from the Augustinian archives says that he was born in Lisbon and entered the order in 1681 and took the vows a year later.[103] He was deployed to Bengal in 1687 and to Isfahan in 1691, having arrived in the retinue of Gaspar dos Reis, who he eventually succeeded as the prelate of the Augustinians in Isfahan in October of 1696.[104] He appears as a co-signatory of the abovementioned 1694 letter in which Bishop Elia di San Alberto recounted the story of the apostasy of Vardapet Yovhan.[105] In addition, in the chronicle of his ambassadorial mission to Iran and the Persian Gulf, Gregório Pereira Fidalgo recounts many instances of interactions with Padre António, who played a pivotal role as an intermediary between the Portuguese diplomats and the Safavid court. Pereira was the diplomatic envoy from the Portuguese *Estado da Índia* in charge of ratifying a joint Persian-Portuguese alliance against the sultans of Oman.[106] Portugal had been interested in establishing an anti-Omani alliance after losing Muscat to the Yarubid Sultans in 1650. Since Shah Sultan Husayn also perceived Omani hegemony in the Persian Gulf as a threat, the two parts reached an agreement whereby the Portuguese committed to mobilise their sea vessels while Iran cooperated with land forces.[107] Pereira was on his way to discuss the terms of this alliance when he first arrived at the island of Kong on 1 June 1696. There, Padre António received him in his capacity as an envoy from the Shah in order to settle some customs-related arrangements to which the Portuguese were obliged.[108] Their second meeting occurred on 4 November, when Padre António informed him that the Shah could not deploy military personnel to Kong.[109] Already in Shiraz, on 26 December, Pereira received news that the Augustinian father had gone to Bandar ʿAbbas to negotiate a peace settlement with the Omanis.[110] However, perhaps Pereira's most revealing anecdote involving Padre António is one from 30 January 1697: according to this story, an Armenian apostate from New Julfa who had lived in Goa and had travelled extensively in Europe was spreading the rumour that the Portuguese no longer held any significant power in Goa and only pretended to do so to manipulate the Shah. In revenge, Pereira and some people from his retinue ambushed and lynched the man. Upon hearing this, Padre António became very upset, fearing reprisals from the Shah.[111] After this episode, relations between Pereira and Padre António gradually deteriorated. In September, the latter was among the signatories of a letter in which members of the Armenian Orthodox community requested the expulsion of Elia di San Alberto as the bishop of Isfahan. However, Jean Aubin found evidence that he also signed a letter denouncing the persecution of the bishop.[112] Finally, Pereira recounts that the missionary had apostatised and remained stubborn in his decision, rejecting a merciful offer from the Pope to forgive apostates and to retain them in their missionary posts.[113] This stubbornness is confirmed by another document from the superior of the Augustinians in Isfahan, António de Desterro.[114]

According to letters collected in the *Chronicle of Carmelites*, after his conversion Jadid al-Islam played a role in a case involving various members of the Shahrimanian family. The account tells the story of Gaspar Shahrimanian, who – like all the members of his family – was baptised and had enjoyed privileged access to European courts. He had even married into the family of the famous merchant-traveller Jean-Baptiste Tavernier. To the outrage of the missionaries, Gaspar apostatised and gained access to the Shah's court, where, as the alleged heir of Tavernier, he went on to claim the right to inherit the 28,000 tomans that the latter had lent to other members of the Shahrimanian family. At the trial, in which only apostates were called as witnesses, he brought another Armenian apostate – the nephew of an Orthodox priest – to advocate on his behalf. However, other Shahrimanians were secretly cited to testify, which led Gaspar to confess that the whole story had only been a plot to extract money from the Catholics so that they could not rebuild their churches and could not continue to attract Armenians to the Church of Rome.[115] In a follow up to this case, two other Shahrimanians, Michael and Markar, said they had been forced into conversion to avoid paying Gaspar a heavy sum. When reporting this case to Rome in 1697, the Carmelite Vicar Provincial Substitute accused Jadid al-Islam of plotting against the Shahrimanians and against the missionaries, saying:

> The miserable Antonio the Portuguese, formerly Prior of the Augustinians in Isfahan, who became a renegade three years ago, is plotting to ruin us, and it was he who advised the enemies of the Sharimans and he will do us enormous damage. He is a rascal to a superlative degree.[116]

This letter suggests that Jadid al-Islam's conversion would have occurred in 1694 and not in 1697, thus contradicting the evidence from the rest of the relevant documentation and the chronology of events. To add to the confusion, Jean Aubin has identified a letter from a Portuguese agent by the name of Cunha Rivara, in which he speaks of Jadid al-Islam's 'fidelity to the Portuguese nation' even after his conversion.[117] Could he have hidden his conversion from the Europeans in order to work more effectively as a diplomat and perhaps even as a spy? As to what triggered his conversion, one can only speculate. Flannery has noted that the first Augustinian apostate, Manuel de Santa Maria/ Hasan Quli Beg had taken advantage of church property and engaged in a lifestyle that was not compatible with his religious investiture, and thus feared repercussions from the Portuguese authorities.[118] However, as he also correctly notes, Jadid al-Islam's case was more ambiguous. We know that he also married and that at some point he wrote a treatise against the Catholic precept of priestly celibacy entitled *Fava'id-i izdivaj* (*The Benefits of Marriage*).[119] As we have seen, the petty fights between Pereira's retinue and the Armenian renegade had put the Portuguese in a vulnerable position. Moreover, Francis Richard has also identified a citation in which Padre António complained about the Capuchin Raphaël du Mans (d. 1696) and his retinue for bribing Muslims into conversion.[120] In a letter, Du Mans says that Padre António had informed him of his intention to convert. Du Mans tried to dissuade him by telling him that he was once approached by the grand vizier (*I'timād al-dawla*), who asked him why he refused to become Muslim. Showing his priestly grey garments and his bare feet, Du Mans responded that even with that modest attire he had more access to the court that many rich Muslim men. This did not impress Padre António, who rejected Du Mans's 'deceitful arguments (*arguments mensongers*)'.[121]

Apart from this, we know that after his conversion Jadid al-Islam replaced Du Mans as interpreter of European languages at the court of Shah Sultan Husayn. In contrast with Du Mans, he actually received a salary for performing these functions.[122] Three documents from the Dutch East India Company – dated between 1713 and 1715 – mention him, either as Alie Koelibeg or as Alie Koelichan, as an interpreter for the King of Persia.[123] As evidence of the degree of power he achieved in this position, in 1719 the Portuguese representative at Kong, Lino de Faria Rodrigues, was advised to maintain good relations with 'Aly Culy Beque' at all times, given how prone the latter was to deception.[124]

In the preface to one of his treatises, Jadid al-Islam describes his conversion as the result of a purely spiritual and intellectual process:

> In the years when I belonged to the Christian faith, I enjoyed a privileged position among priestly circles, to the point to which they [Christians] knew me as a leader and a high priest (*muqtadā va pīshvā*). Their men and women, who believed that I had been infused with the Holy Spirit, would come to me to ask for forgiveness for their sins. But suddenly, the Grace of

> God and the Light of Faith illuminated the hovel of the heart of this poor man. In a matter of a few years, through the affection of the Leader of the Imams (may salutations and praise be upon him), [I] walked freely into the path of the lamp of Islam, releasing my mind from the alley of doubt and from the darkness of the Christian path. I then spent much time diligently collecting Christian books and putting all my endeavours into refuting their false arguments. By scrutinizing the terminology of their books, through blessings and pride I have borne witness to the Truth of the Islamic Faith, to the prophetic mission of the Messenger of the Final Days and to the guidance of the Leader of the Imams (pbuh) until the Day of Judgement.[125]

As most scholarship on conversion narratives has shown, this 'narrative non-event' – to use Krstić's words – was characteristic of the medieval Muslim archive, which contrasts with the narrations of climatic epiphanies from their Christian counterparts, modelled after Saints Paul and Augustine.[126] While Jadid al-Islam's treatise is of course not the equivalent of a conversion narrative, his brief prologue certainly follows this thematic trend. His case could thus evoke comparisons with other convert-polemicists from the Ottoman period, such as the Athenian Muhammad b. ʿAbd Allah or the Jewish renegade Yusuf b. ʿAbdüdeyyan, who was also said to have followed a purely intellectual path towards conversion.[127]

Further, as David Snow and Richard Machalek have warned us in their studies on the sociology of conversion, it is important to distinguish between superficial shifts in someone's religious loyalties and deep changes in doctrinal conviction. This is because the degree of individual commitment to a given faith or the level of participation within a religious organisation can vary from case to case, and throughout different periods of the life of each convert.[128] Snow and Machalek have also warned us against giving too much credence to the importance of a particular event to explain a case of conversion. Doing so would be myopic given that such events usually correspond only to the moments in which the convert publicises his or her change of allegiance and often take place in situations where converts feel considerable pressure to prove themselves before their new coreligionists.[129] It is of course clear that Jadid al-Islam's case was in this sense different from that of the many cases of Georgian *ghulāms* and probably from that most of the Armenian renegades so far described. In Jadid al-Islam's case, there is evidence of a radical change in what Snow and Machalek have called the *universe of discourse*, defined as the 'system of common social meanings' which provides a 'broad interpretative framework in terms of which people live and organize experience'.[130]

However, to better account for the complexity of Jadid al-Islam's case, we need to transcend the purely biographical approach. For instance, at a first glance, his case may invite comparisons with that of the famous Uruch Beg Bayat (d. *c.* 1650), an Iranian who embraced Catholicism during the reign of Shah ʿAbbas and adopted the name of 'Don Juan de Persia'. The similarities transcend the mere fact that both were converts, although heading in the opposite direction, so to speak. First, in neither case were their conversions completely isolated: in the same way that Manuel Santa Maria/ Hasan Quli Beg's apostasy occurred around the same time as Padre António's, so too Don Juan's conversion coincided with those of ʿAli Quli Beg and Bunyad Beg, who became known respectively as Don Felipe de Persia and Don Diego de Persia. Second, like Jadid al-Islam, Don Juan de Persia too was a diplomatic envoy – in his case on behalf of Shah ʿAbbas to Spain – who ended up 'switching sides' politically, as much as he did religiously. And third and most importantly, Don Juan de Persia too went on to produce his own writings, while enjoying courtly patronage. In his case, he dedicated his famous *Relaciones de Persia* to Philip III of Spain (r. 1598–1621).[131] However, as João Teles e Cunha has correctly noted, Don Juan de Persia's *Relaciones* offered a rich amount of information on Iranian history and society, and was therefore of great use for the Spanish authorities in their diplomatic dealings with Shah ʿAbbas.[132] The same cannot be said of Jadid al-Islam's work, which was by its very nature seemingly concerned only with perennial theological truths. This might make it seem as disconnected from its own time and space. However, as I hope to demonstrate throughout this study, theological polemics, when analysed closely, do indeed offer subtle glimpses into the particularities of the intellectual – and to a certain extent political and social – developments of the historical milieus from which they emerge.

Jadid al-Islam's Intellectual Production

Unfortunately, not all of Jadid al-Islam's writings are extant, nor are all of the surviving ones integrally preserved. Reza Pourjavady and Sabine Schmidtke believe that his *Ithbat al-nubuwwa* (*The Proof of the Prophecy*) might be identical with his *Radd bar yahud*, a polemic against Judaism, of which only one manuscript has survived.[133] He wrote a couple of short treatises (*risālas*), both of which have been edited by Rasul Jaʿfariyan. These are the *Radd-i jamaʿat-i sufiyan* or *Radd-i ʿaqaʾid-i sufiyan* (*Refutation of the community – or of the beliefs – of the Sufis*) and the abovementioned *Favaʿid-i izdivaj*.[134] These are now kept respectively at the Sipahsalar Library and at Iran's National Library in Tehran.[135]

However, his major works are two full-length treatises called respectively *Hidayat al-zallin (or al-muzillin) va taqviyyat al-muʾminin* (*A Guidance for Those Who are Led (or who Lead) Astray and a Strengthening for the Believers*) and *Sayf al-muʾminin fi qital al-mushrikin* (*The Sword of the Faithful to Fight the Idolaters*). The first one was originally written in 'the language of the Franks' (*bi-zabān-i farangī*) and then translated into Persian, and it aims to provide proof of the truthfulness of Islam using Christian scriptures.[136] Two manuscripts of this work are held in Qom at the Malek and the Marashi Libraries, and two others at the Old Majlis Library in Tehran and at the Astan-i Quds-i Razavi Library in Mashhad.[137] His second major work, the *Sayf al-muʾminin* – written under the encouragement of the famous jurist Bahaʾ al-Din Muhammad b. al-Hasan al-Isfahani, known as Fazil-i Hindi (d. 1724/5) and dedicated to Shah Sultan Husayn – was conceived as a refutation of an important Christian polemic, the *Apologia pro Christiana Religione* (*Apology of the Christian Religion*) by Filippo Guadagnoli (d. 1656), as we will see in more detail throughout the next chapter.[138] Three manuscripts of this work survive and can be found respectively at the Astan-i Quds-i Razavi Library in Mashhad, in the private collection of Sayyid Muhammad ʿAli Rowzati in Isfahan, and at the Library of the Congregational Mosque in Qom. As for the date of completion of this work, one of the manuscripts gives the date 15 of the month Rabiʿ al-Akhar of the year 1123 Hijri, which corresponds to 2 June 1711 in the Gregorian calendar.[139] Rasul Jaʿfariyan has published a critical edition of this source. My study will focus primarily on this latter work, the genealogy and the aims of which will be explored throughout the next chapter.

Notes

1. *Propaganda Fide*: *Fondo di Persia, Messopotamia e i Caldei*, vol. 2, ff. 16, 19–20. See also Richard, 'Un augustin portugais renégat', p. 73; Alonso, 'El convento agustiniano de Ispahán', p. 145; Flannery, *The Mission of the Portuguese Augustinians*, pp. 96–7; Windler, *Missionare in Persien*, p. 272; Aubin, 'Introduction', pp. 21–2; Jaʿfariyan, 'Muqaddimih', p. 14.
2. *Propaganda Fide*: *Fondo di Persia, Messopotamia e i Caldei*, vol. 2, f. 219; Alonso, 'El convent agustiniano de Ispahan', p. 17; Richard, 'Un augustin portugais renégat', p. 74; Jaʿfariyan, 'Muqaddimih', pp. 13–15; Windler, *Missionare in Persien*, pp. 272–3; Flannery, *The Mission of the Portuguese Augustinians*, pp. 96–7; Tiburcio, 'Muslim-Christian Polemics and Scriptural translations', p. 247; Tiburcio,'ʿAlī Qulī Jadīd al-Islām, António de Jesus', p. 266.
3. Reza Pourjavady and Sabine Schmitdke have cautiously noted that the identification is based on indirect evidence. See Pourjavady and Schmidtke,'ʿAlī Qulī Jadīd al-Islām'. For Jadid al-Islam's own account, see Jadid al-Islam, *Sayf al-muʾminin*, p. 56. [From here on, references to this source will appear as SM].
4. Richard, 'Un augustin portugais renégat', p. 74; Tiburcio, 'Muslim-Christian Polemics and Scriptural Translations', p. 247; Tiburcio, 'ʿAlī Qulī Jadīd al-Islām, António de Jesus', p. 266; Tiburcio, 'Convert Literature', p. 46.
5. *Vereenigde Oostindische Compagnie* (*United East India Company*), 2323, Extract uyt 'tSpahan dagregister (extract from the Isfahan factory diary), 11 September 1733 to 15 July 1734, f. 973. (I am indebted to Willem Floor for sharing this information with me).
6. For a study on how this process of conversion took place, see Abisaab, *Converting Persia*.
7. Baer, 'Review of: Contested Conversions to Islam'. See also Baer, Makdisi and Shryock, 'Tolerance and Conversion in the Ottoman Empire'.
8. Matthee, 'Christians in Safavid Iran', pp. 3–4.
9. Roger Savory, 'Relations between the Safavid State and its Non-Muslim Minorities 1', p. 444.
10. Herzig, 'The Deportation of the Armenians', p. 64.
11. Flannery, *The Mission of the Portuguese Augustinians*, pp. 123–5.
12. For instance, in 1514, following the Battle of Chaldiran when the troops of Selim I (r. 1512–20) put an end to Shah Ismaʿil's (r. 1501–1524) westward

expansion, the Ottomans boycotted Iranian trade. See Matthee, *The Politics of Trade*, p. 22. For comprehensive studies on the Julfan trading networks, see Aslanian, *From the Indian Ocean to the Mediterranean*; Aslanian, 'Social Capital, Trust, and the Role of Networks', pp. 383–402; Faroqhi, *The Ottoman Empire*, p. 139. See also Herzig, 'The Family Firm'.

13. Matthee, 'Christians in Safavid Iran', p. 22.
14. Savory, 'Relations between the Safavid State and its Non-Muslim Minorities 1', p. 447; Munshi, *History of Shah ʿAbbās the Great*, vol. 2, pp. 1181–2.
15. Savory, 'Relations between the Safavid State and its Non-Muslim Minorities 1', p. 447.
16. Amanat, *Jewish Identities in Iran*, pp. 41–2; Matthee, *The Politics of Trade,* p. 83.
17. Matthee, 'Georgia vii. Georgians in the Safavid Administration'.
18. For good summary of Safavid-Georgian military and political relations, see Alonso, *Misioneros Agustinos en Georgia*, pp. 13–26.
19. For a comprehensive history of the various social roles of the *ghulām*, see Babaie, Babayan, McCabe and Farhad (eds), *Slaves of the Shah.*
20. Babayan, *Mystics, Monarchs, and Messiahs*, pp. 10–12.
21. For example, by the time of ʿAbbas II (r. 1642–66), twenty-one out of the ninety-two most powerful positions at the administration, including twenty three out of thirty seven appointed *amīrs*, were held by *ghulāms.* See Matthee, 'Georgia vii. Georgians in the Safavid Administration'.
22. Rota, 'The Death of Tahmāspqoli Xān Qājār', pp. 54–63.
23. Rezvani, 'The Islamization and Ethnogenesis of the Fereydani Georgians', pp. 600–2.
24. Anonymous, 'Risalih-i shinakht'.
25. Tavernier, *Les six voyages*, p. 522. See also Amanat, *Jewish Identities*, p. 42; Spicehandler, 'The Persecution of the Jews of Isfahan', p. 337.
26. Matthee, 'The Career of Mohammad Beg', p. 27.
27. Matthee, 'Christians in Safavid Iran', p. 26. For more on Saru Taqi, see Floor, 'The Rise and Fall of Mirza Taqi'.
28. Matthee, 'Christians in Safavid Iran', p. 27.
29. Matthee, *The Pursuit of Pleasure*, pp. 26, 74, 92.
30. Roemer, 'The Safavid Period', pp. 311–13; Savory, *Iran under the Safavids*, pp. 239–41; Lockhart, *The Fall of the Safavid Dynasty.*
31. Matthee, *Persia in Crisis*, pp. 244–50.

32. Matthee has identified a document from the Dutch East India Company that reproduces these claims. See Matthee, *Persia in Crisis*, p. 192. See also Sifatgul, *Sakhtar-i nihad*, p. 221.
33. See for instance Savory, *Iran under the Safavids*, pp. 237–8.
34. Matthe, *Persia in Crisis*, pp. 192–3. For Majlisi's anti-Sufi writings, see Rizvi, 'The takfīr of the Philosophers', p. 252. For an example of his anti-Jewish polemics, see Moreen (ed. and tr.), 'Risāla-yi Ṣawāiq al-Yahūd'.
35. For some examples of this trend, see Turner, *Islam without Allah?*, p. 149; Browne, *A Literary History of Persia*, vol. 4, pp. 120, 366, 403–4; Lockhart, *The Fall of the Safavid Dynasty*, pp. 70–2.
36. Matthee, *Persia in Crisis*, p. 193; Matthee, 'Christians in Safavid Iran', p. 30
37. Ghougassian, *The Emergence of the Armenian Diocese of New Julfa*, pp. 158–9; Chick (ed.), *A Chronicle of Carmelites*, vol. 1, pp. 467–8
38. Chick (ed.), *A Chronicle of Carmelites*, vol. 1, pp. 467–8.
39. Ghougassian, *The Emergence of the Armenian Diocese of New Julfa*, p. 159.
40. Matthee, 'Christians in Safavid Iran', p. 31.
41. Matthee, *The Politics of Trade*, p. 205
42. Matthee, 'Christians in Safavid Iran', p. 32.
43. Matthee, *The Politics of Trade*, p. 206.
44. Matthee, 'Christians in Safavid Iran', p. 32.
45. Ghougassian, *The Emergence of the Armenian Diocese of New Julfa*, p. 161.
46. Krusinski, *The History of the Late Revolutions*, vol. 2, p. 44.
47. Aslanian, 'Social Capital, Trust, and the Role of Networks', p. 392.
48. Armani, 'Iʿtirafnamih', pp. 66–8. See also Sifatgul, 'Muqaddimih', pp. 51–38; Tiburcio, 'Some Aspects of Conversion Narratives', p. 354; Tiburcio, 'Abgar ʿAli Akbar Armani'. A partial translation of this work has recently been made available, see Matthee, 'Confessions of an Armenian Convert'.
49. Armani, 'Iʿtirafnamih', p. 72; Tiburcio, 'Some Aspects of Conversion Narratives', p. 355.
50. The date of 1709 is given by Matthee in his entry on Gorgin Khan for the *Encyclopaedia Iranica* (see next footnote), yet the *Chronicle of Carmelites* mentions him being alive as late as 1711
51. *A Chronicle of Carmelites*, vol. 2, pp. 812–13.
52. Tihrani, *Mirʾat -i varidat*, p. 109.
53. Moreen, 'The Problems of Conversion among Iranian Jews', p. 217. Amanat, *Jewish Identities in Iran*, p. 42.
54. Spicehandler, 'The Persecution of the Jews in Isfahan', p. 334.

55. Moreen, *Iranian Jewry during the Afghan Invasion*, p. 28.
56. Mashizi, *Tazkirih-i Safavi-yi Kirman*, pp. 575–6.
57. Ibid. p. 577.
58. Ibid. pp. 578–80.
59. Matthee, 'The Politics of Protection', p. 249.
60. Matthee, 'Poverty and Perseverance', p. 467. For a good overview of Iran-Spain relations, see Cutillas, 'Spain: Relations with Persia'.
61. Teles e Cunha, 'The Eye of the Beholder', pp. 13–15.
62. For useful overviews of the activities of the trading companies, see Floor, 'Dutch-Persian Relations'; Kroell, 'East India Company (French)'; Ferrier and Perry, 'East India Company (The British)'.
63. Teles e Cunha, 'The Eye of the Beholder', pp. 16–18. See also Matthee, 'Introduction', pp. 1–7.
64. Subrahmanyam, *The Career and Legend of Vasco da Gama*, p. 129.
65. For a study on the dynamics of this process, see Chaudhuri, *Trade and Civilisation in the Indian Ocean*, pp. 98–118.
66. Matthee, 'The Politics of Protection', p. 245.
67. Matthee, 'Poverty and Perseverance', p. 466.
68. Flannery, *The Mission of the Portuguese Augustinians*, pp. 47–9. For a general overview of Portuguese–Iranian diplomacy during this period, see Matthee, 'Diplomatic Contacts between Portugal and Iran'.
69. Gulbenkian, *Translation of the Four Gospels into Persian*, p. 18.
70. Flannery, *The Mission of the Portuguese Augustinians*, pp. 49–51.
71. Ibid. p. 54.
72. Matthee, 'The Politics of Protection', p. 246. See also Loureiro, 'The Persian Ventures of Fr. António de Gouveia', pp. 251–4.
73. Ortega García, 'Juan Tadeo de San Eliseo', p. 168.
74. Windler, 'La curie romaine et la cour safavide', p. 507; Windler, 'Katholische Mission und Diasporareligiosität', p. 187. For a general overview of the order's activities, see Richard, 'Carmelites in Persia'.
75. Windler, 'La curie romaine', pp. 511–12.
76. For a chronicle of the mission, see Alonso (ed.), 'El convento agustiniano de Ispahán', pp. 247–308. See also Alonso, *Misioneros Agustinos en Georgia.*
77. Flannery, *The Mission of the Portuguese Augustinians*, 71; Windler, 'La curie romaine', p. 514.
78. Matthee, 'Christians in Safavid Iran', p. 20.
79. Matthee, *The Politics of Protection*, pp. 251–2, 259.

80. Matthee, 'Christians in Safavid Iran', pp. 18–20.
81. Matthee, *Persia in Crisis,* p. 179.
82. Calmard, 'Fance ii. Relations with Persia'.
83. Matthee, 'Poverty and Perseverance', pp. 466–7; Richard, 'Capuchins in Persia'.
84. Kroell, *Louis XIV, la Perse et Mascate*, p. 5.
85. Matthee, 'Jesuists in Safavid Persia'.
86. Richard, 'Le Père Aimé Chézaud', pp. 7–9; Jaʿfariyan and Sadiqi, *Az Darband ta Qatif*, pp. 48–51; Matthee, 'Poverty and Perseverance', pp. 468–70; Ha'iri, 'Reflections on the Shiʿi Responses', pp. 153–5. For a general overview of Chézaud's career, see Tiburcio, 'Aimé Chézaud'; Matthee, 'Jesuits in Safavid Persia'.
87. Flannery, *The Mission of the Portuguese Augustinians*, p. 119.
88. Ibid. pp. 132–3.
89. Ibid. pp. 136–8.
90. *Propaganda Fide: Fondo di Persia, Messopotamia e i Caldei*, vol. 2, f. 44.
91. Ibid. vol. 2, f. 42.
92. Chick (ed.), *A Chronicle of Carmelites*, vol. 2, 812.
93. Coinage unit of the Papal States until 1866
94. *Propaganda Fide*: *Fondo di Persia, Messopotamia e i Caldei*, vol. 2, ff. 110–11.
95. Ibid. vol. 2, f. 119.
96. Ibid. vol. 2, f. 119.
97. Ibid. vol. 3, f. 327.
98. Ibid. vol. 3, f. 301.
99. Ibid. vol. 3, f. 328
100. Kroell, *Louis XIV, la Perse et Mascate*, p. 42.
101. *Propaganda Fide*: *Fondo di Persia, Messopotamia e i Caldei*, vol. 2, f. 490.
102. Ibid. vol.2, f. 219.
103. Alonso, 'El convento agustiniano de Ispahán', pp. 171, 163 ; Richard, 'Un augustin portugais renégat', p. 82, fn. 7.
104. Richard, 'Un augustin portugais renégat', p. 74. For the mention of his career in Bengal, see Alonso, 'El convento agustiniano de Ispahán', p. 163.
105. Chick (ed.), *A Chronicle of Carmelites*, vol. 1, p. 469.
106. Aubin, 'Introduction', p. 16.
107. Ibid. pp. 14–15.
108. Aubin (ed.), *L'Ambassade de Gregório Pereira Fidalgo*, pp. 30/31 (bilingual edition Portuguese/French).

109. Ibid. pp. 52–3.
110. Ibid. pp. 62–3.
111. Ibid. pp. 78–9.
112. Aubin (ed.), *L'ambassade de Gregório Pereira Fidalgo*, pp. 84–5; Aubin, 'Introduction', p. 22.
113. Aubin (ed.), *L'ambassade de Gregório Pereira Fidalgo*, pp. 86–7.
114. Flannery, *The Mission of the Portuguese Augustinians*, p. 96; Windler, *Missionare in Persien*, p. 273.
115. Chick (ed.), *A Chronicle of Carmelites*, vol. 1, pp. 484–5.
116. Ibid. pp. 485–6.
117. Aubin, 'Introduction', p. 22.
118. Flannery, *The Mission of the Portuguese Augustinians*, p. 97.
119. Jadid al-Islam, 'Favaʾid-i Izdivaj'. Regarding his marriage, see Jean Aubin, 'Introduction', p. 22; Windler, *Missionare in Persien*, pp. 273–4.
120. Richard, 'Un augustin portugais renégat', p. 75; Flannery, *The Mission of the Portuguese Augustinians*, p. 99.
121. Richard (ed.), *Raphaël du Mans missionaire en Perse*, vol. 1, pp. 131–2.
122. Richard, 'Un augustin portugais renégat', p. 74; Richard (ed.), *Raphaël du Mans missionaire en Perse*, vol. 1, p. 132.
123. Richard, 'Un augustin portugais renégat', p. 83.
124. Teles e Cunha, 'The Eye of the Beholder', p. 46.
125. SM, p. 56.
126. Krstić, *Contested Conversions to Islam*, p. 101; Bulliet, 'Conversion Stories', pp. 123–33; Calasso, 'Récits de conversions', p. 131. Depending on how we chose to define a narrative event, conversion narratives to Islam often spoke of dreams as moments of revelation. See García-Arenal, 'Dreams and Reason'; Tiburcio, 'Some Aspects of Conversion Narratives'. For a broader overview and genealogy of the Pauline and Augustine models, see Szpiech, *Conversion and Narrative*, pp. 30–58.
127. Krstić, *Contested Conversions to Islam*, pp. 110–14.
128. Snow and Machalek, 'The Sociology of Conversion', p. 171. See also Gooren, 'Towards a New Model of Religious Conversion', pp. 25–40.
129. Snow and Machalek, 'The Sociology of Conversion', pp. 171–2.
130. Snow and Machalek, 'The Convert as a Social Type', p. 265.
131. Juan de Persia, *Relaciones*. For an overview of the context of Don Juan's conversion (as well as that of the other Persians), see García Hernán, 'The Persian Gentelmen at the Spanish Court', pp. 283–5; Cutillas, 'Las Relaciones de Don

Juan de Persia'; Cutillas, 'Don Juan de Persia'. See also Lockhart, 'European Contacts with Persia', p. 387; Teles e Cunha, 'The Eye of the Beholder', pp. 46–7.

132. Teles e Cunha, 'The Eye of the Beholder', pp. 46–7.
133. Pourjavady and Schmidtke, ''Alī Qulī Jadīd al-Islām', n. p.
134. For critical editions of these texts, see Jadid al-Islam, 'Radd-i jama'at-i sufiyan'; Jadid al-Islam, 'Fava'id-i Izdivaj'. See also Pourjavady and Schmidtke, ''Alī Qulī Jadīd al-Islām'; Ja'fariyan, 'Muqaddimih', pp. 29–30; Tiburcio, ''Alī Qulī Jadīd al-Islām, António de Jesus', pp. 271–3.
135. Ja'fariyan, *Din va siyasat*, pp. 53–4.
136. Ibid. Pourjavady and Schmidtke, ''Alī Qulī Jadīd al-Islām'.
137. Ja'fariyan, *Din va siyasat*, pp. 53–4; Ja'fariyan, 'Muqaddimih', pp. 26–7; Pourjavady and Schmidtke, ''Alī Qulī Jadīd al-Islām'; Tiburcio, ''Alī Qulī Jadīd al-Islām, António de Jesus', pp. 268–9.
138. SM, p. 57. For more on Fazil-i Hindi, see Abisaab, 'al-Fāḍil al-Hindī'.
139. Ja'fariyan, *Din va siyasat*, pp. 53–4; Ja'fariyan, 'Muqaddimih', pp. 30–4. Pourjavady and Schmidtke, ''Alī Qulī Jadīd al-Islām'; Tiburcio, ''Alī Qulī Jadīd al-Islām, António de Jesus', pp. 269–71.

2

A Cycle of Polemics and Translation Projects

First Link: Jerome Xavier in Mughal India

The origin of the cycle to which Jadid al-Islam's main polemical work belongs can be traced back to India at the turn of the seventeenth century. At this time, Akbar the Great (r. 1556–1605) patronised religious scholars from different traditions in a quest to develop a syncretic religion, which would be called *dīn-i ilāhī* (the divine religion). Scholarship from earlier decades romanticised this project as the apex of tolerance, whereas more recent studies have convincingly highlighted its purely pragmatic nature as a way to deter factionalism in an empire as heterogeneous as Mughal India.[1] Moreover, as Audrey Truschke suggests, through this strategy, Akbar was also able to draw from different sources of knowledge to refute and condemn ideas of which he disapproved.[2] Whatever the case, Christian missionaries saw in these overtures the opportunity to proselytise; with some naively thinking that the Mughal monarch could eventually convert to Christianity. Gil Eanes Pereira, who had been previously stationed in Satgaon in Bengal, was the first priest to be entrusted with the teaching of the Gospels at the Mughal court. However, after a brief period of teaching he suggested to Akbar to seek more specialised instruction.[3] The king then sent out a delegation to Goa, which in 1580 led to the arrival at the court of the Jesuits Rodolfo Acquaviva (d. 1583), António de Monserrate (d. 1600) and Francisco Henriques. For their mission they brought with them a seven-volume Bible in Hebrew, Chaldean, Greek and Latin printed in Antwerp by the famous publisher Christophe Plantin (d. 1589).[4] Although Akbar took great pleasure in this acquisition, he remained keen on having a Persian translation of the Gospels. In 1582 he sought to contact Philip II (r. 1556–98) through Father Monserrate, requesting copies of the Holy Books in Arabic or Persian. However, due to the overload of Portuguese ships, the embassy was never able to leave the port of Goa. Facing this inconvenience, Akbar commissioned instead his court chronicler Abu'l Fazl (d. 1602) to undertake the translation project, perhaps overestimating the latter's alleged knowledge of the Pentateuch and the Gospels.[5] In 1591 Akbar saw another opportunity to recruit European specialists: profiting from the visit of the Greek sub-deacon Leon Grimon, who was passing by the court to deliver a shipload of Chinese silk, he decided to send him as an emissary to Goa in another effort to attract missionaries. This time the recruits were the Jesuits Duarte Leitão, Cristobal de Vega and Estevão Ribeiro, who left shortly after, disappointed by the king's refusal to embrace Christianity.[6]

Finally, in 1594, Akbar pursued his third attempt at recruiting priests for the translation enterprise. It was then that the Navarran Jesuit Jerónimo de Ezpeleta y Goñi – better known by his priestly name, Jerome (Jerónimo) Xavier – together with Manuel Pinheiro and Bento de Góis (d. 1607), arrived in Lahore around 1595.[7] Upon arrival, none of them had any knowledge of Persian nor Arabic. At Akbar's bequest, they established a school to teach the princes Portuguese and were assigned Muslim instructors to teach them Persian.[8] Jerome Xavier used the occasion to engage in theological discussions with courtly dignitaries. By his own admission, as of 1598 he had made little progress in his acquisition of Persian skills, but two years later he claimed to have been able to translate his works into that language. While he did indeed become well versed in Persian, he always worked in collaboration with the philosopher, theologian and chronicler ʿAbd al-Sattar Lahuri and possibly with Armenian scholars.[9] The colophons of many of Xavier's later Persian works explicitly credit Lahuri for his role in the production of these texts. Later, during Jahangir's reign (r. 1605–27) Lahuri would go on to record the courtly discussions and compiled them in what became known as the *Majalis-i Jahangiri*.[10] In any case, it is rather unclear whether Xavier (with or without Lahuri's collaboration in this case) ever managed to produce an original Persian translation of the Gospels. He mentioned his intention to undertake this project after the traveller Giovanni Battista Vecchietti (d. 1619) brought him a 1591 Arabic–Latin edition of the Gospels.[11] However, in a 1608 manuscript of the Gospels in Persian, which he offered to Akbar's successor Jahangir, he mentioned that an Armenian priest had acquired in Jerusalem a copy of a fourteenth-century Persian translation of the Gospels and that an ambassador from Shah ʿAbbas to Akbar had in turn delivered it to Manuel Pinheiro. To avoid lexical contradictions with this version, he (or his collaborators) then decided to produce only a bona fide transcription of this earlier translation.[12]

In addition to his biblical translations and transcriptions, Jerome Xavier and his collaborators produced other works in Persian with Christian content. These included the *Dastan-i Masih* (*The Life of Christ*), also known as *Mirʾat al-Quds* (*Mirror of Holiness*) and the *Dastan-i Pitru* (*The Life of Peter*).[13] For our purposes, however, the work of his that mattered the most was a polemical treatise through which he sought to refute Muslim objections to Christian dogmas such as the divine nature of Christ, the Holy Trinity and Christian ritual and devotional practices.[14] This book was conceived originally in Portuguese around 1597 under the title *Fonte de Vida* (*The Fountain of Life*). This version was lost and what survives is the Spanish one, *Fuente de Vida*, completed shortly after.[15] The structure of the book, written as a series of dialogues between a Christian priest and a Muslim philosopher, has led some scholars to speculate upon whether these dialogues might have been transcriptions of Xavier's own discussions with Akbar and other Muslim scholars.[16] Whatever the case, after completing the original version he immediately started working on a Persian translation, which he completed around 1609 under the title of *Aʾinih-i haqq-numa* (*The Truth-Reflecting Mirror*). Later on, he would also write an abridged version of this text.[17] It is precisely this work that set in motion the polemical cycle with which we are concerned.

Second Link: Ahmad al-ʿAlavi at the Court of Shah ʿAbbas I

In the early 1620s, Carmelite missionaries brought to Iran a copy of the abridged version of Jerome Xavier's *Aʾinih-i haqq-numa*.[18] In that decade, the missionaries were working in a fluctuating environment which was becoming increasingly tense. Until then Shah ʿAbbas's favourable disposition towards them had led to fruitful exchanges, even if these were motivated by diplomatic necessity. For example, in 1604, the Carmelite Juan Tadeo de San Eliseo

(d. 1634) offered him on behalf of Pope Clement VIII (papacy, 1592–1605) a parchment of the Old Testament decorated with miniature paintings.[19] In a similar fashion, in 1608 another Carmelite, Paolo Simone di Gesù Maria (d. 1643), brought him a copy of an Arabic translation of the Gospels printed in Rome by the Medici Oriental Press.[20] This edition, which Dennis Halft has called the *Roman Arabic Vulgate*, was prepared by Giovanni Battista Raimondi (d. 1614), founder of the Oriental Typography in Rome under the auspices of Pope Gregory XIII (p. 1572–85).[21] Before producing the typeset version, based on a fourteenth century manuscript of Coptic provenance now held at Spain's National Library (Biblioteca Nacional de España), Raimondi gathered a group of experts consisting of priests from the major clerical orders to elaborate an interlinear Latin translation of the Arabic manuscript, so that it could then be collated with the Latin Vulgate.[22] The latter, as it is well known, was the Latin translation of the Bible elaborated by Saint Jerome (d. 420) at the bequest of Pope Damasus I (papacy, 366–84) and adopted as the official translation of the Catholic Church following the Council of Trent in 1545. Raimondi's *Roman Arabic Vulgate* would later become the standard reference used by the Iranian ulama when seeking to engage in theological debates with missionaries.[23]

Also in 1608, as part of a diplomatic mission on behalf of Sigmund III Vassa (r. 1587–1632), Cardinal Bernard Maciejowski of Cracow (d. 1608) sent Shah ʿAbbas an illustrated Bible.[24] The Shah immediately set up a commission to translate the Latin and Hebrew annotations in it into Persian.[25] Later in 1616, Tadeo de San Eliseo, who had by then gained privileged access to the court and served as a translator, wrote enthusiastically to Rome regarding the Shah's desire to receive copies of the Bible in Persian. Tadeo himself embarked on a project to translate the Psalms and possibly the Gospels, although it is possible that – as in Jerome Xavier's case – he only coordinated the project while Jewish and Muslim collaborators were in charge of the actual linguistic work.[26]

With the expulsion of the Portuguese from Hormuz in 1622, the conditions of the missionaries began to deteriorate. As part of the retaliation against the Portuguese, the Augustinians were also ousted from Iran that same year, although they managed to return the year after.[27] Yet, hostilities against Christian groups continued, including a campaign of forced conversion of Armenians.[28] At the same time, however, both during Shah ʿAbbas's tenure and afterwards, missionaries of different orders repeatedly praised the willingness of Iranian religious scholars and political authorities to engage in theological debates in a way that could not have been possible in other realms. For instance, Niccolao Manucci (d. 1717), who travelled to the Mughal court at the time of Aurangzeb (r. 1658–1707), related from firsthand accounts that, in places like the Mughal court, Turkey, Arabia, Bukhara and Balkh 'the laws of the Mohamedans is [sic] one that, to all questions about religion put to them by Christians they should answer by the sword'. He contrasted this situation with Iran, adding: 'But in Persia you may use arguments, make inquiry [sic], and give answer in matters of religion without the least danger'.[29] It is of course possible that these praises were conceived with diplomatic intentions, but they nonetheless attest to the contextual nuances that enabled polemics to flourish: on the one hand, geopolitical and social frictions created the need to assert the legitimacy of the dominant state religion; but on the other hand, for that to be done freely in the form of written exchanges, there needed to be at least a certain degree of openness conducive to such exchanges. Thus, it was the combination of an institutional infrastructure and a cross-cultural literacy, that, despite the admittedly belligerent content of these works, facilitated the circulation of interreligious polemics in this milieu.

It was in this context that an unidentified Muslim scholar came across a manuscript of the abridged version of the *Aʾinih-i haqq-numa* at the Carmelite convent, where he worked as an Arabic instructor. Upon discovering it, he requested permission to copy it.[30] It is plausible that it was through the diffusion of this copy that Jerome Xavier's text arrived in the hands of Ahmad b. Zayn al-ʿAbidin al-ʿAlavi al-ʿAmili (d. *c.* 1650).[31] The latter served as prayer leader (*pīshnamāz*) at the court and was well versed in the study of law, philosophy and hadith, having studied under Shaykh Bahaʾi and under the famous philosopher Muhammad Baqir Astarabadi, better known as Mir Damad (d. 1631).[32] By the time that the *Aʾinih-i haqq-numa* reached his hands, al-ʿAlavi was already an experienced author of interreligious disputations. His first work of this kind, entitled *Lavamiʿ-yi rabbaniyyih fi radd al-shubah al-Nasraniyyih* (*Divine Clarifications for the Confutation of Christian Doubts*) was written in 1621 as a response to an anti-Islamic short treatise (*risāla*) from the famous traveller and polymath Pietro della Valle (d. 1652).[33] Della Valle had written his *risāla* within the context of a disputation in which he, together with the Prior of the Augustinian convent Manuel da Madre de Deus, had engaged Shiʿi clerics at the house of an Iranian nobleman by the name of Mir Muhammad ʿAbd al-Vahhabi.[34]

Having already written this work, al-ʿAlavi embarked on a refutation of Jerome Xavier's treatise, which he titled *Misqal-i safa* (*Burnisher of Purity*).[35] One of the most puzzling characteristics of this text is its numerous transcriptions of Hebrew verses in Arabic, a fact that led earlier scholarship to think that the author might have had training in Hebrew, although Dennis Halft has expressed scepticism regarding this possibility.[36] As for the reception of al-ʿAlavi's work, we know that he was presented with various Persian refutations of his opera. While most of these authors remain unidentified, he suspected them to be the same as the actual author of the *Aʾinih-i haqq-numa*, thus possibly ʿAbd al-Sattar Lahuri.[37] The most important reaction to his work would come, as we will now see, from the highest echelons of the Church in Rome.

Third Link: Guadagnoli and the Caracciolini in Rome

When Carmelite friars brought a copy of the *Misqal-i safa* to Rome, sometime around 1625, the institutional context was more than conducive to its engagement. The missionary congregation *Propaganda Fide* had been founded in 1622 under the auspices of Pope Gregory xv (papacy 1621–3), and from the outset one of its priorities had been to provide missionaries with the adequate linguistic and theological training to respond to religious controversies.[38] In the 1610s Pope Paul v (p. 1605–21) had already committed funding for the teaching of Middle Eastern languages and had entrusted the task to the Clerics Regular Minor, commonly known as Caracciolini after their founder Francesco Caracciolo (d. 1608). The order had established a school of 'Oriental languages' in Sant'Agnese in Agone in 1595 and was thus the obvious choice to take over this responsibility. The project originally fell into the hands of Giovanni Battista Raimondi, who coordinated the production of the abovementioned *Roman Arabic Vulgate*.[39] His disciple and successor, Francesco Martellotto di Martinafranca (d. 1618), a graduate of the Maronite College in Rome, embarked on the ambitious project of writing the most detailed study of Arabic grammar to date in the West, the *Institutiones linguae arabicae* (*Foundations of the Arabic language*).[40] Since he did not complete this work during his lifetime, the task was then taken over by his student Filippo Guadagnoli. Guadagnoli would later make his own contribution to the study of Arabic, through his *Breves arabicae institutiones* (*Summary of the Foundations of Arabic*) which had the particularity of offering examples of Arabic grammar tainted with a slight touch of Christian propaganda.[41] Guadagnoli went on to become one of the most prominent scholars of Middle Eastern languages in Rome. He worked together with the Maronite Sergio Rizzo (Sarkis al-Rizzi, d. 1638) in a biblical translation project which we will revisit later, and then replaced another Maronite, Abraham Ecchellensis (Ibrahim al-Haqilani, d. 1664), as teacher of Arabic at La Sapienza.[42] He also participated in the collective project of translating the *Lead Tablets of Granada* (*Laminae Granatenses*), at the time believed to have been authentic documents from the Roman period, which included fragments of the Gospels and texts about the Virgin and the Saints in Arabic. It was later revealed that the tablets had been forged to fabricate an ancient connection between Arabs and Christianity in order to persuade Muslims in al-Andalus to convert.[43] But for our purposes now, what is more important is that one of Guadagnoli's major projects was to produce a refutation of the *Misqal-i safa*.

Guadagnoli was neither the only nor the first scholar to refute al-ʿAlavi's work in Rome. Bonaventura Malvasia (d. 1666) had already done so in 1628 through an Arabic work published under the Latin title *Dilucidatio speculi verum monstrantis* (*Polishing of the Truth-Showing Mirror*).[44] However, *Propaganda Fide* set up a commission to examine Malvasia's work and the verdict was unfavourable. Guadagnoli, who had participated in the commission himself, embarked then on his own Latin refutation of the *Misqal-i safa* and published it in 1631 under the title of *Apologia pro christiana religione* (*Apology for the Christian Religion*).[45] Initially, the *Apologia* too was met with harsh criticism from Pietro della Valle, who chastised Guadagnoli for his lack of knowledge of Muslim sources and his inability to tell Sunnis and Shiʿis apart.[46] Despite this criticism, Guadagnoli obtained Pope Urban VIII's (p. 1623–44) enthusiastic support to translate the *Apologia* into Arabic. He completed this translation in 1637 and published it under the Latin title *Pro christiana religione responsio ad obiectiones Ahmed filii Zin Alabedin, Persae Asphahanensis*, also known by the Arabic title *Ijaba ila Ahmad al-Sharif bin Zayn al-ʿAbidin al-Farisi al-Isbahani* (*Response to Ahmad al-Sharif bin Zayn al-ʿAbidin al-Farisi al-Isbahani*).[47] This edition was also criticised, this time by Abraham Ecchelensis, who reproached Guadagnoli for trying to address complex theological subtleties in ways that were not easily comprehensible to Arabic readers and potential converts.[48] In 1649, perhaps seeking to amend these problems and seeking to attenuate the various *ad hominem* attacks on Muhammad that he had originally included in his work, Guadagnoli published a revised Arabic version of the *Ijaba* under the Latin title, *Considerationes ad Mahometanos cum responsione ad obiectiones Ahmed Filii Zin Alabedin* (*Considerations against Mohammedans as a Response to the Objections of Ahmad b. Zayn al-ʿAbidin*).[49] The most notable addition here was a final chapter in which he tried to persuade his Muslim readers that the Gospels and the Qur'an did not contradict each other.[50] In adding this section, Guadagnoli sought to make the work more effective as a missionary text as the new edition would allegedly be more persuasive and less confrontational. However, not all the higher authorities in Rome were convinced by his approach, as demonstrated by the fact that the *Considerationes* was censored by *Propaganda Fide* and the Holy Office. A Carmelite censor went as far as to consider the work useless. He argued that if the book was meant to circulate in a Christian context, then there was no point in defending the Qur'an, and added that he did not think that the book could circulate in Muslim lands without being burned. The Holy Office established then yet another commission to re-examine the *Considerationes ad Mahometanos*. To Guadagnoli's fortune, among the censors were some of his collaborators in the translation of the *Lead Tablets*. These included Ludovico Marracci (d. 1700), who would eventually succeed him as Arabic teacher at La Sapienza and undertake a Latin translation of the Qur'an, and the famous Jesuit polymath Athanasius Kircher (d. 1680). Their evaluation was favourable to Guadagnoli's work, albeit with some reservations.[51] Later on, already in the eighteenth century, the story of Guadagnoli's work became the object of legendary accounts, some of which went as far as to claim that he had managed to have Ahmad al-ʿAlavi baptised and had him become a passionate defender of the Christian faith.[52]

Aside from these refutations by Malvasia and Guadagnoli, the work of Ahmad al-ʿAlavi was also read by the Franciscan Dominus Germanus of Silesia

(d. 1670). He first had access to a copy of the *Misqal-i safa* during his studies in Rome in 1645, and then to the *Lavami'-yi rabbani* during a short stay in Isfahan around 1650, from where he was hoping to embark for Samarqand before Rome gave orders to abort the mission.[53] Like Marracci, Germanus also translated the Qur'an into Latin, and like Guadagnoli, Malvasia and Della Valle, he also wrote a treatise defending Christian concepts. His major work was the *Veni-meco ad Mohammedanos ex Alcorano contra Alcoranum, pro defensione Evangelicae Veritatis* (*Response to Mohammedans from within the Qur'an against the Qur'an to Defend the Truth of the Gospels*),[54] which he translated (or perhaps had someone translate) into Persian as *Maqalat ya tasnif-i mukhtasar* (*Short Essay or Breviary*).[55] According to Francis Richard, this book cannot really be considered a fully-fledged polemic but rather a presentation of Christian concepts from a philosophical point of view and without many scriptural references.[56]

A Half-link: Aimé Chézaud and the Jesuits under Shah 'Abbas II

While it is unclear how widely read Guadagnoli's *Apologia* was in Iran, the French Jesuit Aimé Chézaud was at the forefront of whatever diffusion it did have. Chézaud had been a candidate for establishing the Jesuit mission in Iran from its early stages. His experience in Aleppo during the 1640s and his interaction with Muslim Iranians and Armenians made of him a perfect fit for the task. However, as was mentioned in the previous chapter, the mission was instead entrusted to François Rigordi in 1647 and then to Alexandre de Rhodes, during a brief hiatus in which Rigordi had to leave Iran. When Rigordi returned in 1652, Chézaud arrived with him as part of his retinue. Chézaud and Rigordi were welcomed at the court as part of a diplomatic mission whereby France promised to build a new anti-Ottoman military alliance with Iran.[57] Rigordi left Iran soon after and the Jesuits began to experience their first obstacles: on the same year of his arrival in Isfahan, the newly appointed Primate of New Julfa, Dawit Julayeci, accused the missionaries of trying to convert Muslims. One of New Julfa's *kalāntars*, who happened to be an Armenian favourable to the Catholics, hosted Chézaud briefly at his house, but was forced to evict him shortly after for fear of reprisals from the Primate. Thus, Chézaud had no other option than to temporarily stay at the Carmelite convent.[58] As Francis Richard has suggested, it was most likely there that he first had access to a manuscript of the *Misqal-i safa* around the year 1653.[59] Chézaud would then refuse to leave New Julfa as long as other orders – notably the Capuchins – were allowed to stay. As the Armenian faction led by Dawit Julayeci accused the missionaries of trying to convert Muslims, a royal decree was promulgated ordering the expulsion of all missionaries from New Julfa in 1654.[60]

Despite these troubles, the Jesuits would eventually regain access to the court and were able to engage the Shiʿi ulama in debates. In 1656 Chézaud contributed to the cycle of refutations with which we are concerned, through the completion of his *Mash-i misqal-i safa-yi Aʾinih-i haqq-numa* (*Wiping of the Burnisher of Purity of the Truth-reflecting Mirror*), which is to a certain degree an abridged Persian version of Guadagnoli's *Apologia*.[61] In it, he accused Ahmad al-ʿAlavi of not having read the work of Jerome Xavier directly nor completely. He argued that had he read it, he would not have omitted a series of key references that were essential to Jerome Xavier's argument:

> It was a surprise for me [to see] that this eloquent and honourable Mulla [ʿAlavi], as these two books of his [show], clearly did not read the *Aʾinih-i haqq-numa*, but rather chose to read a summary of it. [. . .] If he had seen, read and understood [a series of references from Jerome Xavier's text], he would have included them in his refutation. But since he wrote two books claiming that [other] Divine religions have corrupted the shariʿa, and continued to [claim] this after reading the Truth [revealed by] the *Aʾinih-i haqq-numa*, it became a duty for me to write a treatise (*risālih*) or a short piece (*maqālih*) about this Truth.[62]

Despite the rather harsh tone of his refutation, he dedicated his book to Ahmad al-ʿAlavi's son Mirza Hasib.[63] According to a missionary source, Chézaud presented his text to the grand vizier Muhammad Beg, who received it with good disposition and gathered a group of Muslim scholars to debate Chézaud. At the beginning, the grand vizier had refrained from praising the Jesuit for fear of appearing biased towards a Christian, but ended up siding with Chézaud for 'being a man of sense, capable of grasping and discerning arguments put forward'.[64] One of the scholars to debate Chézaud was a former Rabbi who had embraced the Muslim faith. He argued that the Torah contained some signs of the veracity of Islam.[65] The presence of this argument is anything but banal. As I will explain in the next chapter, the use of Jewish and Christian scriptures as proofs of the prophecy of Islam was a genre in and of itself and this anecdote attests to its recurrence in oral debates, even beyond the few surviving written treatises. According to this same source, a group of Armenians were so impressed by Chézaud's ability to defend the tenets of the Christian faith against Muslims, and so disappointed in their bishops for failing to do so, that they called for a union with the Church of Rome. However, Chézaud refused to discuss the differences between the Catholics and the Orthodox in the presence of the ulama, a fact for which the Armenian Patriarch thanked him.[66] On another occasion, Chézaud managed to save an Armenian who had been forced to become a Muslim, by negotiating an agreement with the authorities: Chézaud would be asked a series of complex theological questions and if he were able to answer them, the man would be then set free. Chézaud victorious outcome in this debate allegedly played a role in securing a royal edict giving the Jesuits a house to settle in New Julfa.[67]

Fourth Link: Jadid al-Islam and the Translation Projects at the Court of Shah Sultan Husayn

It was in response to Guadagnoli's *Apologia* that Jadid al-Islam conceived his *Sayf al-muʾminin*. It is hard to determine whether he gained access to this work already in Iran or during his previous appointments. In any case, European travelogues offer some clues regarding the circulation of these kinds of texts and their possible social impact. For instance, the famous traveller Jean Chardin (d. 1713), who visited the country in the late 1660s and 1670s devotes a great deal of detail in his memoirs to presenting the tenets of the Muslim faith as he understood them. Among other things, he notes the importance of the Islamic interpretation of the Paraclete in the Gospel as a sign of the coming of Muhammad:

> Mohammedans [sic] pretend that Muhammad is [the one] being announced in this passage, and when one explains to them how these explanations are forced and far-fetched (*tirées des cheveux*), they agree, but they say that this is because of the malice of Christians and Jews, who have falsified and truncated from their Holy Books all the prophecies related to Muhammad.[68]

Closer to Jadid al-Islam's time, the missionary Nicolas Sanson (d. after 1695) who arrived in Iran in 1683 and stayed for a decade (thus, before the arrival of Padre António), also speaks of the ongoing religious debates between the ulama and the missionaries. He discusses the question of the falsification of the Scriptures, saying: '[Muslims] object to the missionaries, who employ against them the authority of the Divine Scriptures that it is Christians who have falsified them'.[69] And then, he also adds a reference to the theme of the Paraclete:

> They say, for example, that in chapter XIV of Saint John, where Jesus said to his disciples: the Paraclete, the consoler that my Father will send unto you, will teach you everything. [They said that] Christians had effaced the name of Muhammad, who they take to be the Paraclete promised by Jesus Christ.[70]

Since neither Chardin nor Sanson explicitly mention any Muslim author in connection with this otherwise widespread thesis, it is unclear to what extent they had access to written contemporary or near-contemporary debates on the matter or whether they relied only on reports and were familiar with these tropes because of their prevalence in more classical sources. In the next chapter, we will see in more detail how these motifs were recurrent in polemical discussions. For now, what matters is that their presence in other kinds of documentation suggest that while the readership of theological polemics remained the domain of small scholarly circles, their major tropes permeated the shared cultural references of broader audiences, often being quoted by laymen who did not necessarily had access to the actual texts.

It was thus not in isolation that the cycle started by Jerome Xavier found fertile ground in the Iran of the late seventeenth century when the apostate Jadid al-Islam entered the debate. Before his *Sayf al-mu'minin*, Jadid al-Islam had already ventured into the genre of polemics through his *Hidayat al-zallin*. This treatise is divided into four parts: *Radd-i usul-i din-i Nasara va isbat-i usul-i din-i Islam az ru-yi kitabha-yi ishan* (*Refutation of Christianity and the Proofs of the Principles of Islam According to their Books*); *Radd-i furu'-i din-i Nasara va isbat-i furu'-i din-i Islam az ru-yi kitabha-yi ishan* (*Refutation of the Branches (furu') of Christianity and Proofs of the Branches of Islam*); *Isbat-i payambari va khatmiyyat az kitabha-yi ishan* (*Proofs of the Prophecy of Muhammad and the Seal of the Prophecy*); and *Isbat-i imamat va mahdaviyyat az kitabha-yi ishan* (*The Proofs of the Imamate and of the Coming of the Mahdi*).[71]

The *Sayf al-muʾminin* builds on this project and in many instances makes explicit reference to it.[72] In both works, the author seeks to bring forward proofs for the validity of Islam and to refute Christianity. The *Sayf al-muʾminin*, however, combines these classical tropes of polemical literature with other elements. Among these are his explicit response to some of the claims made in Guadagnoli's *Apologia* and a biblical exegesis and a translation of the *Book of Genesis* based on the Latin Vulgate and an Arabic Bible. At the end of the book, he adds an appendix containing what he claims to be his Persian translation of Imam ʿAli's own Arabic translation of forty 'Suras' of the Torah.

Jadid al-Islam's translation enterprise, however, was not an isolated case in Shah Sultan Husayn's court. Close to the time of his conversion, in 1697, the prominent cleric Mir Muhammad Baqir Khatunabadi (d. 1715) – who would then go on to become the first bearer of the tile of *mullā-bashī* (chief scholar) in 1712, having refused earlier the post of Shaykh al-Islam and having taught some time at the newly founded *Madrisih-i Sultani*[73] – had already translated the Gospels into Persian.[74] In Khatunabadi's case, he worked exclusively with the Arabic translation of the Gospels, since he had no knowledge of Latin to access the Latin Vulgate, let alone Hebrew or Greek, to access the original sources. He claimed, however, to have consulted extensively with specialists on the biblical sources and to have read relevant commentaries.[75] As Dennis Halft has shown, Khatunabadi used the aforementioned Medici edition of the *Roman Arabic Vulgate*, although he also drew from other Arabic versions to produce his translation.[76] In his introduction, Khatunabadi explains the aims and structure of his project, admitting to an extent the shortcomings of working with the Arabic text and recognising the potential room for improvement:

> It so happens that a Christian that has commented on the Gospels in Arabic, was not very well acquainted with Arabic syntax and structure, and in some cases used foreign terms and non-Arabic words in his terminology as well as unfamiliar combinations and disjointed sentences. Therefore, understanding what he meant is impossible without referring to the original Gospel

> – which is not Arabic – and without finding many subjects based on stories and terms which have to be learned from outside the text. [This translation] is based on some of their [Christians'] own trusted books and treatises which have found their way into this land, and I researched and studied, and consulted with people who are knowledgeable about the original biblical source. I translated whatever [parts] where the intended [meaning] is clear, and whatever is based on stories. In addition, [special] terminology and complex phrases are clarified in the commentaries. I did not write the explanation on the original source in order not to contravene the laws of translation. Wherever there were arguments against faulty Christian claims, or contradictions that would benefit Islam, they have been also mentioned briefly, so that the seeker of truth and righteousness can find some benefit from it. I do hope that those who command eloquence, the initiates and the wise masters who demand perfection would be so generous as to study all [this text] before pointing fingers at it and before raising objections. Thus, after having looked at it carefully, if they come across any oversight or error, they will proceed to amend it with a forgiving and lenient pen.[77]

The translation is followed by a relatively brief commentary, which as Franco Ometto has noted, was informed by unreliable or fabricated Christian sources.[78] For example, in one section he makes reference to a story that appears in the *Legenda aurea* (Golden Legend), a work by the thirteenth century archbishop of Genoa, Jacobus da Voragine (d. 1298).[79] In it, Adam falls sick after being expelled from the Garden of Eden. When his son Seth tries to re-enter the Garden to get help, the Angel Gabriel intercepts him and gives him a tree branch which he then instructs him to put on Adam's chest. After Adam recovers, they bury the branch, which remains under the ground until the reign of Solomon.[80] Aside from this, Khatunabadi also engages in more common discussions within Muslim–Christian polemics, such as the question of scriptural falsification (*taḥrīf*), which I will also discuss in Chapter three.[81] In any case, the scope of his commentary is relatively circumscribed and does not constitute a fully-fledged theological treatise.

In contrast, Jadid al-Islam's *Sayf al-muʾminin* was of a much larger scale. Although it is possible that he might have had access to the Medici *Roman Arabic Vulgate* like many of his contemporaries in Iran, since his project was not based on the Gospels but on the Pentateuch, his main object of engagement was another Arabic Bible that began to circulate in Iran in the late seventeenth century. Rasul Jaʿfariyan has identified this as being the *Biblia Sacra Arabica*, an Arabic–Latin edition printed by *Propaganda Fide* between 1671 and 1673.[82] The idea behind the elaboration of this latter Bible was the brainchild of Pope Gregory XIII, who in 1578 entrusted Cardinal Antonio Carafa (d. 1591) with the task of setting up a commission of experts to assemble and collate Arabic Bible manuscripts to get the best possible version of it in print. This Bible would be used as a missionary tool in the Near East, in sharp contrast to other Arabic and Polyglot Bibles, which were more geared towards a European scholarly audience. For the initial attempts of the project, missionaries collaborated with Maronites in the Levant, leading to the 1584 establishment of the Maronite College. While some progress was made during these early stages, it was only after the foundation of *Propaganda Fide* that the project could count on the institutional backing needed for its completion. Thus, in the 1620s the initiative was entrusted to Sarkis al-Rizzi, who in turn assembled another group of experts, with Guadagnoli among them.[83] During Sarkis al-Rizzi's time, only the Pentateuch was completed. Abraham Ecchellensis was in charge of coordinating the completion of the Old Testament, which was achieved in 1647. The complete Bible was finished between 1671 and 1673, long after the passing of Ecchellensis and Guadagnoli.[84]

The *Biblia Sacra Arabica* rapidly replaced the *Roman Arabic Vulgate* in Iran in the last decades of the seventeenth century.[85] Although little is known about the exact history of its arrival and circulation, a study on the inventory of the missionary library of Isfahan by Dominque Carnoy-Torabi makes reference to the availability of the Latin Vulgate and of some French editions of the Bible, but does not mention any Arabic Bibles.[86] Thus, although it is hard to determine whether Jadid al-Islam had acquired this Bible before his arrival in Iran, what is clear is that he made use of it for his polemic *qua* biblical commentary. In his introduction, our author describes what he sees as the problems of the Arabic Bible translation and its contribution to the dissemination of the allegedly corrupted contents of Christian canonical scriptures:

> It so happened that a Christian priest translated the Torah and the Books of the Prophets from Latin into Arabic, and the alterations (*taghīyrāt*),

> falsifications (*taḥrīfāt*), and the abundant hyperboles and understatements (*ziyādih va naqṣān-i farāvānī*), which he included in the Arabic translation in accordance to his own beliefs, were put into print (*bar qālib zadih būd*). People who were introduced to the contents of the Torah through this Arabic translation are not to blame for pursuing the wrong path, since they presumed that the Truth would come forward through its pages. However, every time our ulama (may God be pleased with them) have sought to refute Christians, they have faced the need to argue against their books and to affirm the Truth of the religion of Islam. Yet, since they were not well versed in the Latin language, they have had to rely on this Arabic translation to provide their proofs. But since the Arabic translation was written in a way that would be acceptable to Christians, whenever Christians studied the objections and the arguments of the Muslim ulama, they despised them and expressed their lack of knowledge about them. Therefore, since this humble servant (*kamtarīn*) was acquainted with the language of the Christians and knew the sorts of deceits they have resorted to – with the fire of honour (*ātish-i ghayrat*) and the zeal of the clear religion (*ḥamiyyat-i dīn-i mubīn*) blazing [inside him], and clinging to the zeal of the pious ulama (*ta'ṣṣub-i 'ulamā'-yi abrār dāman-gīr shudih*), he wanted to translate this Arabic translation into Persian, and to collate (*muqābilih*) it with the source of the Torah which is in Latin, and to provide an exegesis and interpretation (*tafsīr va tā'vīl*) of its terminology (*'ibārāt*). [In so doing, this humble servant seeks] to scrap (*pārih gashtan*) the repeated snares (*dām-hā*) and traps (*farīb*) of the Christian ulama, so that they can no longer hunt with them.[87]

Here we begin to see what will become the leitmotif of the Jadid al-Islam's work, namely the question of Scriptural falsification (*taḥrīf*). In the next chapter, we will delve more into its implications and its relationship with the Latin Vulgate of Saint Jerome. For now, let us concentrate on how Jadid al-Islam describes his text as a tool that could potentially serve the ulama in theological debates. To distinguish his work from that of other Muslim scholars, he emphasises his knowledge of the original biblical corpus:

> The goal of this translation is to collate the source of the Arabic Torah, which is a Latin translation, and then to translate it [into Persian] and interpret it so that it can serve as a proof to overcome the enemy. Should

> there be any apparent discrepancies between the terminology used in this translation and interpretation and that of the Arabic translation, [I ask] my brothers in the faith to be forgiving. [This is because] the source [of the Arabic Torah], the Latin Torah – which is itself a translation from the Hebrew Torah – contains many instances of tampering (*taḥrīf*) that resulted from the licenses (*taṣarrufāt*) taken by the impure [Saint]Jerome, and because the Arabic translation too differs a great deal from the Latin one. [Therefore,] somebody who is not familiar with the Latin terminology may not realise, from [reading] the Arabic translation, the degree to which the Christian priests have tainted it with impurity. Thus, in translating the Arabic Torah, this humble servant has translated every single term that is not false and that is translatable. Otherwise, I have done this [translation of the] Torah so that, from now on, whenever someone challenges the Christians using this Arabic Torah, he can also collate its terminology with that of the translation that I have made based on the Latin Torah, so that the Christians cannot transgress its content.[88]

Thus, Jadid al-Islam's project is somehow complementary to Khatunabadi's in that it seeks to satisfy the need for a biblical translation that can refer back to the Latin Vulgate. In addition, however, his work also aspires to serve a corrective function regarding the original – and therefore, uncorrupted – Scriptures. This is clear from the author's brief introduction to the appendix containing his translation of ʿAli's rendition of the forty Suras of the Torah:

> To demonstrate to Jews and Christians, in view of the facts (*ḥasab al-vāqiʿ*), the extent to which their books have been corrupted by ignorants like Jerome and his high priests, this humble servant [found it] fitting to translate into Persian and to include in this book the forty Suras from the Torah, which the Leader of the religion of Islam, the Guide of Men and Jinn, the Angel Commander of the Faithful ʿAli b. Abi Talib (pbuh) translated from the original Hebrew sources into Arabic. [I have done this] so that any Jew or Christian that so wishes can collate them with the terminology and contents of the translation that the accursed Jerome made for them, to see how different the true and the false (*ḥaqq va bāṭil*) and the corrupted and the uncorrupted (*muḥarraf va ghayr-i muḥarraf*) are from each other.[89]

The idea of ʿAli translating the Torah is of course substantiated here by the belief that the Imams knew all the revealed scriptures. More specifically, a hadith that appears in Muhammad Baqir Majlisi's collection *Bihar al-anwar* (*Seas of Light*) and in Muhammad b. Hasan al-Fattal al-Nisaburi's (d. 1114–15) *Rawdat al-waʿizin* (*The Garden of the Preachers*) portrays the Prophet transmitting to ʿAli the Holy Scriptures, from the Torah to the Qurʾan, emulating how biblical prophets transmitted to their successors the parts of the revelation they were given.[90] As we will see later in this study, Jadid al-Islam displays a profound knowledge of Shiʿi hadith collections throughout his work. It is thus hardly surprising that he would subtly elaborate on ideas taken from the hadith and incorporate them in the broader thematic configuration of his book. Needless to say, Jadid al-Islam's Persian rendition of ʿAli's Torah is taken from his revision and reinterpretation of the Latin Vulgate and the *Biblia Sacra Arabica*. What is more important, however, is that by adding ʿAli's Torah to his biblical commentary, our author sought to redeem the original uncorrupted sources of the revelation, an endeavour that, as we will see throughout the rest of this book, proved essential for the larger aims of his exegetical project.

Reception in the Qajar Period and other Polemical Exchanges

It is hard to assess the impact of Jadid al-Islam's work in terms of readership. The fact that three manuscripts survive shows that it had at least a certain degree of circulation, although this was most likely circumscribed to select scholarly circles. The *Chronicle of Carmelites* mentions that Father Basil de Saint Charles (d. 1711) requested permission from Rome to write a refutation of an attack on Christianity written by a renegade, which is almost certainly a reference to Jadid al-Islam.[91] However, it is unclear whether he ever wrote such refutation and if so, whether it survived. In the late eighteenth century, an anti-Christian and anti-Jewish piece written by Aqa Muhammad ʿAli Bihbahani Kirmanshahi (d. 1801) made reference to another one of Jerome Xavier's polemical works, the *Havarinamih* (*The Book of the Disciples*), as well as to Ahmad al-ʿAlavi's *Lavamiʿ-yi rabbani* and to Jadid al-Islam's *Hidayat al-zallin*.[92] Already in the nineteenth century, under the tenure of Fath ʿAli Shah (r. 1797–1834) and at the time when the Russo–Persian frontier wars were stirring up confessional sensibilities, a new influx of missionaries came to Iran. The recruits of the French Lazarist Eugène Boré (d. 1878) constituted the bulk of an important Catholic retinue. Yet, as far as the history of polemics is concerned, it was the presence of two Protestants, the German-born Karl Gottlieb Pfander (d. 1865) and the British Henry Martyn (d. 1812) that had a more tangible effect. Pfander first drafted a polemical treatise in German of which he immediately wrote a Persian version by the title of *Mizan al-haqq* (*The Measure of the Truth*). This work was immediately translated into various languages including Turkish, Armenian and Urdu, and was the object of several refutations in Persian.[93]

However, it was Martyn who would go on to become the most influential missionary ever to visit Iran, given the sheer number of responses his work attracted. Having spent time in India, Martyn arrived in Shiraz in 1811 where he spent eleven months. He first set out to work on a translation of the New Testament into Persian in collaboration with an Iranian translator by the name of Mirza Sayyid ʿAli Khan.[94] He would then go on to engage in oral and written debates with the ulama. Of these exchanges, the most notable were his two responses to an attack on Christianity written in Arabic by Mirza Muhammad Ibrahim Husayni Fasaʾi (1839).[95] Martyn's polemics would then attract at least twenty-eight responses. Among these we can count one by Mirza Muhammad Hashim Asaf, author of the famous chronicle *Rustam al-hukamaʾ* (*The Rustam of the Philosophers*). Another such refutation, the *Irshad al-muzillin* (*Guidance for Those Who Were Led Astray*) written by the jurist Mulla Muhammad Riza Hamadani, became – according to Abbas Amanat – perhaps the first work of a living Persian-speaking author to be translated into a European language.[96] The renowned philosopher Mulla ʿAli Nuri (d. 1831) also contributed to the corpus of refutations against Martyn, writing what became his longest piece in Persian, the *Hujjat al-Islam ya burhan al-millih* (*The Proof of Islam or the Proof of the Nation*), also known as *Radd-i padiri* (*Refutation of the Priest*).[97] More importantly for our purposes, however, was the refutation written by the famous mujtahid Mulla Ahmad b. Mahdi al-Naraqi (d. 1829) entitled *Sayf al-ummih va burhan al-millih* (*The Sword of the Community and the Proof of the Nation*), given that it quotes directly from Jadid al-Islam's *Sayf al-muʾminin*, particularly in his discussion on the theme of *taḥrīf*.[98] In his work, Naraqi reproduces Jadid al-Islam's critique of the validity of

Saint Jerome's Vulgata, a central component of the latter's work, as we will discuss in more detail in the next chapter.

Independently from the abovementioned cycle, another key contributor to Muslim–Christian polemics in the mid-seventeenth century was Zahir al-Din Tafrishi (d. before 1702), a scholar of a highly prestigious intellectual pedigree, who spent some time as *pīshnamāz* in Georgia. His major contribution to the genre was the *Nusrat al-haqq* (*The Victory of the Truth*), of which he produced both an Arabic and a Persian version. This work was written in response to a *risāla* by the Capuchin missionary Gabriel de Chinon (d. 1668), whom he debated in Georgia. The Persian versions of the *Nusrat al-haqq* also include details of Tafrishi's debate with the Greek Melkite Patriach of Aleppo, Makarios III b. al-Zaʿim (d. 1672).[99] From the biblical quotations used in Tafrishi's work, it has been proven that he drew from the *Roman Arabic Vulgate*.[100] Much later, the famous traveller and scholar Shaykh Muhammad ʿAli Hazin-i Lahiji (d. 1766), who produced an important amount of his work in India after the fall of the Safavid dynasty, wrote a short piece by the title *Risalih dar basharati ba zuhur-i Hazrat-i Khatm al-Anbiyaʾ az kutub-i asimani* (*Treatise on the Good Tidings of the Appearance of the Seal of the Prophets from the Holy Books*). This piece is too short and his use of tropes too formulaic to give us a clear idea of the extent of his biblical knowledge. However, the fact that he talks about what he found 'in other manuscripts' (*dar baʿż-i nusakh-i dīgar*), reveals that he did have access to written sources.[101] Given the period, I suspect his source could have been the *Biblia Sacra Arabica*, but to my knowledge, this has not been studied in detail. Aside from this, in his *Safarnamih* (*Travelogue*), Hazin-i Lahiji mentions that he studied the Torah with a rabbi and the Gospels with Khalifih Avanus, a highly ranked Armenian orthodox priest who was well versed in Persian and Arabic.[102] This is most likely a reference to Yovhannes Mrkuz Julayeci (d. 1715), a renowned theologian and painter who wrote a treatise in defense of the Armenian Church and engaged in theological discussions with the Shah himself.[103] It is likely that it was in response to this latter work that a scholar by the name of Muhammad Khalil Qaʾini (d. 1723–4) conceived his *Radd-i Nasara* (*Refutation of the Christians*). This work remains unpublished and we know relatively little about its author, aside from the fact that he studied under Aqa Razi Khvansari (d. 1702) and that he fled to Qazvin after the Afghan invasion of Isfahan in 1722.

More importantly for our purposes, Ebrahim Ashk Shirin has observed that Qaʾini's *Radd* contains a refutation of the validity of Saint Jerome's Vulgata similar to that of Jadid al-Islam.[104] Although this could suggest that Qaʾini could have read Jadid al-Islam; as we will see in the next chapter, the theme of the *taḥrīf* of vernacular translations also had earlier proponents. Future scholarship will have to determine whether Qaʾini's argumentation is only thematically similar to Jadid al-Islam, or indeed a verbatim quotation of him, like in the case of al-Naraqi's abovementioned example.

In addition to these examples, Francis Richard has written briefly about a short *risāla* by an Armenian renegade priest, known as Muhammad ʿAli Jadid al-Islam, who converted during the first year of Sultan Husayn's reign (1694). However, this work is not a polemical treatise but a translation of the ritual of the Eucharist, intended for 'Muslims to know its sense (*de manière qu'ils* [Muslims] *en connaissent le sens*)'. [105] Finally, in addition to Muslim–Christian disputes, there is evidence that Jewish scholars also participated in polemical debates. A well-documented case is that of the rabbi Yehudah b. Elʿazar , who in 1686 wrote a treatise by the title of author of *Hobot Yehudah* (*The Duties of Judah*).[106] Vera Moreen has suggested that this book, which was heavily modelled on Maimonides's (d. 1204) *Dalalat al-haʾirin* (*Guide for the Perplexed*), might have been motivated by the hardships experienced by Iranian Jews in the seventeenth century.[107] In it, Yehudah argues that it is not possible to apostatise from Judaism and attacks the 'erroneous' beliefs of Christians and Muslims.[108] Moreen notes that, as with most classical polemics, Yehudah's work was primarily an intellectual exercise.[109] However, the author's context did manifest itself indirectly, as Yehudah referred to all Christians indiscriminately as 'Armenians'.[110] These kinds of examples notwithstanding, it is clear that the impact of the Christian–Muslim (and specifically Shiʿi) exchange was much larger, as evidenced by the roughly hundred and sixty Shiʿi refutations of Christianity written after the seventeenth century that have been identified.[111] What they had to add as a whole to the overall history of interreligious polemics, however, is something that would require a more thorough and – ideally – case-by-case examination. The rest of this book seeks to take us a step further in this direction.

Notes

1. For the classical referent for the romanticised vision of Akbar's religious project, see Roychoudhury, *The Din-i-Ilahi or the Religion of Akbar.* For more nuanced approaches, see Rizvi, *Religious and Intellectual History of the Muslims in Akbar's Reign*; Nizami, *Akbar and Religion.* For the most up-to-date study on the question, see Azfar Moin, *The Millennial Sovereign.*
2. Truschke, *Culture of Encounters*, p. 14.
3. Gulbenkian, *Translation of the Four Gospels into Persian*, pp. 21–3; Alam and Subrahmanyam, 'Frank Disputations', pp. 462–4.
4. Gulbenkian, *Translation of the Four Gospels into Persian,* pp. 23–4; Camps, *Jerome Xavier S.J. and the Muslims of the Mogul Empire*, pp. 4–5, 59.
5. Gulbenkian, *Translation of the Four Gospels into Persian,* pp. 25–6.
6. Gulbenkian, *Translation of the Four Gospels into Persian,* p. 26; Camps, *Jerome Xavier S.J. and the Muslims of the Mogul Empire*, pp. 4–5.
7. Camps, *Jerome Xavier S.J. and the Muslims of the Mogul Empire*, p. 5. For an overview of Jerome Xavier's career, see Didier, 'Jerome Xavier'; Didier, 'Jerónimo Xavier, un Navarro en la India'.
8. Gulbenkian, *Translation of the Four Gospels into Persian,* p. 27.
9. Gulbenkian, *Translation of the Four Gospels into Persian,* p. 29; Alam and Subrahmanyam, 'Frank Disputations', pp. 468–9.
10. Alam and Subrahmanyam, 'Frank Disputations', pp. 468–9.
11. Gulbenkian, *Translation of the Four Gospels into Persian,* pp. 29–32.
12. Gulbenkian, *Translation of the Four Gospels into Persian,* p. 9. See also Fischel, 'The Bible in Persian Translation', pp. 20–1; Richard, 'Les frères Vecchietti, diplomates, érudits et aventuriers', p. 16; Richard, 'Les manuscripts persans rapportés par les frères Vecchietti', pp. 291–300. See also Bernardini, 'Giovan Battista and Gerolamo Vecchietti in Hormuz', pp. 280–1.
13. Camps, *Jerome Xavier S.J. and the Muslims of the Mogul Empire*, pp. 14–16; Alam and Subrahmanyam, 'Frank Disputations', p. 470; Khan, 'Late 16th- and Early 17th-Century Contestations', pp. 66–7. For a detailed study of the first source in question, see Moura Carvalho, *Mir'at al-quds (Mirror of Holiness).*
14. Camps, *Jerome Xavier S.J. and the Muslims of the Mogul Empire*, pp. 16–17.
15. Camps, *Jerome Xavier S.J. and the Muslims of the Mogul Empire*, pp. 16–17. For a modern edition of this source, see Xavier, *Fuente de Vida.*
16. Camps, *Jerome Xavier S.J. and the Muslims of the Mogul Empire*, pp. 20–1. Didier, 'Jerónimo Xavier, un Navarro en la India', p. 151.

17. Camps, *Jerome Xavier S.J. and the Muslims of the Mogul Empire*, p. 21.
18. Richard,'Le père Aimé Chézaud', p. 8.
19. Ometto, 'Khatun Abadi, the Ayatollah who Translated the Gospels', p. 61.
20. Halft, 'The Arabic Vulgate in Safavid Persia', pp. 69–70.
21. Pizzorusso, 'Filippo Guadagnoli, i Caracciolini e lo studio delle lingue orientali', p. 249.
22. The original manuscript, which served as the template (*Vorlage*), was identified by Francisco Guillén Robles. See Halft, 'The Arabic Vulgate in Safavid Persia', pp. 52–3. For details on the collation of the Arabic version and the Vulgate, as well as its process of evaluation, see also pp. 57–9.
23. Halft, 'The Arabic Vulgate in Safavid Persia', pp. 69–70.
24. Richard, 'Le père Aimé Chézaud', p. 16.
25. Ibid. p. 16.
26. Halft, 'The Arabic Vulgate in Safavid Persia', pp. 79–81.
27. Matthee, *Persia in Crisis*, p. 163. For an overview of Portuguese missionary activities after 1622, see Jean Aubin, 'Introduction'.
28. Matthee, *Persia in Crisis*, pp. 180–1.
29. Manucci, *Storia do Mogor*, vol. 1, p. 41.
30. Halft, 'The Arabic Vulgate in Safavid Persia', pp. 123–5.
31. For a detailed study of his polemical works, see Halft, 'Schiitische Polemik gegen das Christentum im safawidischen Iran', pp. 273–334.
32. Richard, 'Le père Aimé Chézaud', p. 8. For details on the curricula that al-ʿAlavi pursued with his teachers, see Halft, 'The Arabic Vulgate in Safavid Persia', pp. 100–2.
33. Richard, 'L'apport des missionnaires européens', p. 261; Richard, 'Le père Aimé Chézaud', p. 13; Halft, 'The Arabic Vulgate in Safavid Persia', p. 88; Ometto, 'Khatun Abadi, the Ayatollah who Translated the Gospels', p. 60.
34. Halft, 'Pietro della Valle', pp. 518–19.
35. Richard, 'L'apport des missionaires européens', pp. 260–1; Haʾiri, 'Reflections on the Shiʿi Responses', pp. 155–6.
36. Halft, 'Hebrew Bible Quotations in Arabic Transcription in Safavid Iran', pp. 239–44.
37. Halft, 'The Arabic Vulgate in Safavid Persia', pp. 113–14.
38. Pizzorusso, 'Filippo Guadagnoli, i Caracciolini e lo studio delle lingue orientali', pp. 248–50; Pizzorusso, 'La preparazione linguistica e controversistica dei misionari', pp. 260–1; Girard, 'Teaching and Learning Arabic in Early

Modern Rome', pp. 191–3; Girard, 'Des manuels de la langue entre mission et erudition orientaliste', pp. 279–81. For an overview of Guadagnoli's career, see Tiburcio, 'Filippo Guadagnoli'. For a more general overview of Guadagnoli's institutional environment, see also Piemontese, 'Leggere e scrivere Orientalia'. See also Bevilacqua, *The Republic of Arabic Letters*, p. 52.

39. Pizzorusso, 'Filippo Guadagnoli, i Caracciolini e lo studio delle lingue orientali', pp. 249–50; Pizzorusso, 'La preparazione linguistica e controversistica dei misionari', pp. 257–8.
40. Pizzorusso, 'Filippo Guadagnoli, i Caracciolini e lo studio delle lingue orientali', pp. 253–4; Girard, 'Teaching and Learning Arabic in Early Modern Rome', 196; Girard, 'Des manuels de la langue entre mission et erudition orientaliste', p. 280.
41. Hamilton, 'The Qur'an as Chrestomathy in Early Modern Europe', p. 219. For more on Guadagnoli's use of Christian examples in his grammar, see Girard, 'Des manuels de la langue entre mission et érudition orientaliste', pp. 287–8.
42. It was formerly believed that he had also taught Syriac. See Pizzorusso, 'Filippo Guadagnoli, i Caracciolini e lo studio delle lingue orientali', pp. 257–9; Girard, 'Teaching and Learning Arabic in Early Modern Rome', p. 195.
43. Pizzorusso, 'Filippo Guadagnoli, i Caracciolini e lo studio delle lingue orientali', p. 258. For details on Guadagnoli's involvement in the translation of the tablets, see García-Arenal and Rodríguez Mediano, *Converted Muslims, the Forged Lead Books of Granada*, p. 31.
44. Pizzorusso, 'Filippo Guadagnoli, i Caracciolini e lo studio delle lingue orientali', p. 263; Richard, 'Le père Aimé Chézaud', p. 13.
45. Pizzorusso, 'Filippo Guadagnoli, i Caracciolini e lo studio delle lingue orientali', p. 263. For a detailed study of this work, see Trentini, 'Guadagnoli, controversista e islamologo'.
46. Pizzorusso, 'Filippo Guadagnoli, i Caracciolini e lo studio delle lingue orientali', p. 263
47. Ibid. See also Trentini, 'Guadagnoli controversista e islamologo', p. 300.
48. Pizzorusso, 'Filippo Guadagnoli, i Caracciolini e lo studio delle lingue orientali', pp. 264–5.
49. Ibid., p. 266; Trentini, 'Guadagnoli controversista e islamologo', p. 300.
50. Pizzorusso, 'Filippo Guadagnoli, i Caracciolini e lo studio delle lingue orientali', pp. 266–7; Trentini, 'Guadagnoli controversista e islamologo', pp. 310–11; Bevilacqua, *The Republic of Arabic Lettters*, p. 56.

51. Pizzorusso, 'Filippo Guadagnoli, i Caracciolini e lo studio delle lingue orientali', pp. 267–72. For a study on Marracci's Qur'an translation, see Glei and Tottoli, *Ludovico Marracci at Work*. See also Bevilacqua, *The Republic of Arabic Letters*, pp. 50–5. For more on the censorship of the Considerationes, see Heyberger, 'Polemic Dialogues between Christians and Muslims', p. 507.
52. Alam and Subrahmanyam, 'Frank Disputations', p. 507. For the legend of al-ʿAlavi's conversion, see Nicéron, *Mémoires pour servir à l'histoire des hommes illustres*, vol. 7, p. 276.
53. Richard, 'Le Franciscain Dominus Germanus de Silésie', pp. 92–5.
54. Ibid. pp. 95–8.
55. Ibid. pp. 100–1.
56. Ibid. p. 104.
57. Richard, 'Le Père Aimé Chézaud', pp. 7–9; Matthee, 'Poverty and Perseverance', pp. 468–70; Richard, 'L'apport des missionnaires européens', p. 255.
58. Matthee, 'Poverty and Perseverance', p. 471.
59. Richard, 'Le Père Aimé Chézaud', p. 8.
60. Matthee, 'Poverty and Perseverance', pp. 471–2.
61. Richard, 'Un augustin portugais renégat', p. 78; Richard, 'L'apport des missionaires européens', pp. 260–1.
62. Jaʿfariyan and Sadiqi, 'Padiri-yi Aimé Chézaud', pp. 50–1; Tiburcio, 'Aimé Chézaud', p. 596.
63. Richard, 'Le père Aimé Chézaud', pp. 13–14 ; Tiburcio, 'Aimé Chézaud', p. 596.
64. Wilson (ed. and trans.), 'History of the Mission of the Fathers of the Society of Jesus', p. 690.
65. Ibid. p. 690.
66. Ibid. pp. 693–4.
67. Ibid. pp. 697–701.
68. Chardin, *Voyages du Chevalier en Perse*, vol. 6, pp. 284–5.
69. Sanson, *Voyage*, p. 203.
70. Ibid. pp. 203–4.
71. Jadid al-Islam, *Hidayat al-zallin*, f. 6; Schmidtke and Porujavady, 'ʿAlī Qulī Jadīd al-Islām'; Tiburcio,'ʿAlī Qulī Jadīd al-Islām, António de Jesus', pp. 268–9.
72. SM, p. 62. Consider also the fact that, in both works, the author makes use of analogical language to refer to Christian theological and ritual matters in

Islamic terms. The *Sayf al-muʾminin* classifies the belief in the Trinity and the Holy Conception, the incarnation and the Passion of the Christ, his decent to the underworld (*jahanam*) to the release the souls of the old prophets, his resurrection, his ascension to heaven and his return on the Day of Judgement within the *uṣūl al-dīn* (principles of religion) of Christianity. In contrast, the seven sacraments – Baptism, Confirmation, Confession, Communion, Ordination, Matrimony and Extreme Unction – are classified as the *furūʿ al-dīn* (ramifications of religion). See SM, pp. 208–13.

73. Moazzen, 'Institutional Transformation or Clerical Status Quo?', pp. 74–6. See also Arjomand, 'The Office of *Mulla-Bashi* in Shiʿite Iran', pp. 135–8.
74. Ometto, 'Khatun Abadi, the Ayatollah who Translated the Gospels', pp. 60–3; Moazzen, 'Institutional Transformation or Clerical Status Quo?', p. 67. For an overview of Khatunabadi's career and of the institutional context in which he worked, see Moazzen, *Formation of a Religious Landscape*, pp. 65–76.
75. Ometto, 'Khatun Abadi, the Ayatollah who Translated the Gospels', p. 65.
76. Halft, 'The Arabic Vulgate in Safavid Persia', p. 169.
77. Khatunabadi, *Tarjumih-i Anajil-i arbaʿa*, pp. 4–5.
78. Ometto, 'Khatun Abadi, the Ayatollah who Translated the Gospels', p. 71; Moazzen, 'Institutional Transformation or Clerical Status Quo?', p. 68.
79. Butler, 'Legenda Aurea', pp. 8, 130.
80. Khatunabadi, *Tarjumih-i Anajil-i arbaʿa*, p. 275.
81. Ibid. p. 230.
82. Jaʿfariyan, *Safaviyyih*, vol. 3, p. 1017; Halft, 'The Arabic Vulgate in Safavid Persia', pp. 172–3.
83. Vollandt, 'Che portono al ritorno quì una Bibbia Arabica integra', p. 413.
84. Ibid. pp. 413–14.
85. Halft, 'The Arabic Vulgate in Safavid Persia', pp. 172–6.
86. Carnoy-Torabi, 'A biblioteca esquecida dos missionários do Ispaão', p. 103.
87. SM, p. 56.
88. Ibid. p. 57.
89. SM, p. 730.
90. Majlisi, *Bihar al-anwar*, vol. 35, p. 22; Nisaburi, *Rawdat al-waʿizin*, p. 84.
91. Chick (ed.), *A Chronicle of Carmelites*, vol. 2, p. 813.
92. Pourjavady and Schmidtke, 'Muslim Polemics against Judaism and Christianity in 18th Century Iran', pp. 85–6; Halft, 'The Arabic Vulgate in Safavid Persia', p. 120.

93. Pourjavady and Schmidtke, 'Muslim Polemics against Judaism and Christianity in 18th Century Iran', pp. 75–6. For an overview of Pfander's career and of the composition of his *Mizan al-haqq*, see Powell, *Muslims and Missionaries in Pre-Mutiny India*, pp. 132–57. See also Green, *Terrains of Exchange*, pp. 137–8.
94. Amanat, '*Mujtahids* and Missionaries', pp. 249–51. For more details on Martyn's collaboration with Mirza Sayyid ʿAli Khan, see Green, *Terrains of Exchange*, pp. 114–15. For a broader overview of Martyn's career in India, see Powell, *Muslims and Missionaries in Pre-Mutiny India*, pp. 107–14.
95. Amanat, '*Mujtahids* and Missionaries', pp. 251–2. Rizvi, 'Mullā 'Alī Nūrī', pp. 153–4.
96. Amanat, '*Mujtahids* and Missionaries', pp. 256–7. See also Green, *Terrains of Exchange*, p. 116.
97. Rizvi, 'Mullā 'Alī Nūrī', pp. 153–5.
98. al-Naraqi, *Sayf al-ummih va burhan al-millih*, pp. 313–19. For more on the circumstances of the composition of this book, Amanat, '*Mujtahids* and Missionaries', pp. 257–8. Rizvi, 'Mullā 'Alī Nūrī', p. 154.
99. Richard, 'Trois conférences', pp. 254–5. Halft, 'The Arabic Vulgate in Safavid Persia', pp. 146–8; Haʾiri, 'Reflections on the Shiʿi Responses', p. 159. For an overview of this work, see Rashtiyani, 'Muqaddimih'. There seems to have been some degree of enmity between Chinon and Chézaud, since the latter declared that he would not stay in Julfa as long as Chinon remained there. For more on this, see Richard (ed.), *Raphaël du Mans missionaire en Perse*, vol. 2, p. 216.
100. Halft, 'The Arabic Vulgate in Safavid Persia', 149.
101. Hazin-i Lahiji, *Rasaʾil-i Hazin-i Lahiji*, p. 118.
102. Hazin-i Lahiji, *Tarikh va Safarnamih-i Hazin*, pp. 171–2.
103. Richard, 'Le père Aimé Chézaud', p. 18; Richard, 'L'apport des missionaires européens', p. 262. For an overview on this character, see Halft, 'Hovhannēs Mrkʿuz'. For more on this treatise see Ghougassian, *The Emergence of the Armenian Diocese of New Julfa*, p. 144. For more on the author's discussions with the Shah, see p. 160, and for his career as a painter see pp. 183–5.
104. Ashk Shirin, 'Muḥammad Khalīl Qāʾinī', pp. 274–7. See also Jaʿfariyan, *Din va siyasat*, p. 311.
105. Richard, 'Un augustin portugais renégat', pp. 80–1.
106. Moreen, 'A Seventeenth-Century Iranian Rabbi's Polemical Remarks', p. 158.
107. Ibid. pp. 158–60.
108. Ibid. pp. 162–6.
109. Ibid. p. 166.

110. Ibid. p. 163.
111. The list was elaborated by Hamid Naji Isfahani in an edition of the *Misqal-i safa* used by Len Harrow, and cited by Flannery. See Flannery, *The Mission of the Portuguese Augustinians*, p. 106.

3

Jadid al-Islam and the Signs of the Prophecy

The Genre of *Dalāʾil al-nubuwwa*

Jadid al-Islam's magnum opus, the *Sayf al-muʾminin fi qital al-mushrikin*, is written following established conventions of polemical writing. The major characteristic of this work is that it treats biblical passages as signs that foretell the coming of Islam. This argumentative theme dates back to the Abbasid period (750–1258) and is intrinsically linked to the history of Muslim engagement with the Bible more broadly. According to scholarly consensus, no biblical translations predated the advent of Islam.[1] Moreover, the first ones to be made were conceived by, and for the use of, Christians.[2] Embellished stories of the biblical prophets appeared indeed very early in the Islamic tradition in the form of the popular tales of the prophets (*qiṣaṣ al-anbiyāʾ*), which set out to provide a narrative background to the rather schematic portrayal of the prophets in the Qurʾan.[3] However, as Hava Lazarus-Yafeh noted, literal biblical quotes are rare in this kind of literature as well as in early Muslim historiography. It is thus likely that the popular storytellers (*quṣṣāṣ*) and early Muslim historians only knew of biblical excerpts through the oral tradition or at most through abridged Arabic translations.[4] This seems to have also been the case for early Muslim scholars who ventured into biblical exegesis and refutations, and hence why they cited the same set of biblical verses throughout generations.[5]

In contrast, converts were usually well acquainted with the Bible, either through the original Hebrew and Greek sources or through Syriac, Coptic and Arabic translations. Some of them became *quṣṣāṣ*, as they could draw from their biblical expertise in a way that a Muslim-born storyteller usually could not.[6] Others, as we will see throughout this chapter, would go on to produce the most representative works of polemical literature. As Lazarus-Yafeh observed, it was oftentimes they who contributed the most to 'biblical misinformation' in Islam through intentional misquotations: from Saʿid b. Hasan of Alexandria (date of conversion, 1298) extrapolating the name of Ismael into various passages of the Old Testament, to the Maghrebi Jewish renegade ʿAbd al-Haqq al-Islami (d. fourteenth century) playing with phonetics and altering the vowels of Hebrew words to make them sound like references to the trilateral root 'ḥ-m-d', and hence to Muhammad.[7] In the ninth century CE, the Nestorian convert ʿAli b. Rabban al-Tabari (d. 870) and his contemporary Abu Muhammad ʿAbd Allah b. Muslim Ibn Qutayba (d. 889) became the first Muslim scholars to write lists of biblical signs predicting the coming of the Prophet Muhammad. They thus inaugurated a branch within a larger theological genre known as *aʿlām* (or *dalāʾil*) *al-nubuwwa* (signs of the prophecy), which consists of providing scriptural proofs of the prophecy.[8] Although Jewish and Christian theologians also had exegetical traditions which were roughly equivalent to the *dalāʾil* genre, it was Islam which, as a newcomer to the Abrahamic faiths, bore the burden of proof. As we will see later in this book, the *dalāʾil* genre did not exclusively draw from biblical references, nor was it only concerned with interreligious polemics.[9] However, we should now direct our attention to this branch of biblical proofs in light of Jadid al-Islam's text.

The genre continued to evolve as Muslim knowledge of the Bible became deeper: Ibn Hazm of Cordoba, whose *Kitab al-fisal fi-l-milal wa-l-ahwaʾ wa-l-nihal* (*Book of Opinions on Religions, Sects and Heresies*) became one of the classics of this tradition, boasted a high degree of familiarity with Arabic translations.[10] The same can be said of the Maliki jurist Shihab al-Din al-Qarafi in his response to an anti-Islamic polemic written by the Melkite Bishop Paul of Antioch (d. 1180),[11] and of the Cairene Najm al-Din al-Tufi (d. 1316), author of an extensive biblical commentary.[12] Others, like the *mufassir* (Qurʾanic exegete) Ibrahim b. ʿUmar al-Biqaʿi (d. 1480) began to use the Bible as a tool of *tafsīr* (Qurʾanic exegesis), which signified a rupture with the purely polemical approach to the Bible.[13] However, this did not mean that the *dalāʾil al-nubuwwa* genre disappeared as such. In the fifteenth century, the Majorcan Anselm Turmeda (ʿAbd Allah al-Tarjuman after conversion) became one of the best known convert-polemicists of all time, through the writing of his *Tuhfat al-arib fi-l-radd ʿala ahl al-salib* (*The Gift to the Intelligent for Refuting the Arguments of the Christians*), which has ever since attracted a significant amount of scholarly attention among Romance philologists and Islamicists alike.[14] In the Ottoman Empire, some examples of polemics that also follow the conventions of *dalāʾil* literature were penned by Jewish renegades, such as ʿAbd al-Salam al-Muhtadi al-Muhammadi and Ahmad Mustafa Tashkubrizade (d. 1561).[15] However, the most notable polemicist of this realm was the Hungarian convert Murad b. ʿAbd Allah (d. *c.* 1586), whose trajectory resembles Jadid al-Islam's in that he too worked as a translator at the royal court, in his case under Süleyman the Magnificent (r. 1520–66).[16] To make matters more interesting, Tijana Krstić has pointed out structural and thematic similarities between his work and Turmeda's.[17] This of course raises questions regarding the transmission and authenticity of these texts, as Turmeda's work has itself been a target of suspicion, given its relative resemblance with that of ʿAli al-Tabari.[18]

As for the milieu that concerns us here, Safavid Iran, Ahmad al-ʿAlavi was the pioneer of the genre through his response to Jerome Xavier. As Dennis Halft has noticed, al-ʿAlavi's work uses a rather standard pool of biblical quotations, and contrary to what Henri Corbin suggested in earlier scholarship, it is unlikely that he had any knowledge of Hebrew and consequently any knowledge of the original texts.[19] Jadid al-Islam, however, had the particularity of being the only convert in the cycle of refutations originated by Jerome Xavier. And although he was not the only convert in this milieu to have left a testimony – given the existence of ʿAli Akbar Armani's memoir, as we have seen in Chapter one – he was indeed the only of his kind to produce systematic theological treatises. It is hard to verify whether he was familiar with the classics of the genre, particularly with those by converts like ʿAli al-Tabari and Turmeda. Thematic continuities suggest he could have probably been, although this would be hard to prove. In any case, like them, he too would claim to have an expertise in the tradition he was converting from, which was deeper than that of Muslim-born scholars like al-ʿAlavi. As we have warned, however, his convert background did not preclude the possibility of intentional misrepresentation of the Bible. Yet at a discursive level, his background infused him with an authoritative status and an intellectual capital that made him more relevant among his scholarly Muslim peers, patrons and potential readership.

Scriptural Falsification or *Taḥrīf*

One of the historical leitmotifs of interreligious polemics has been the idea held by theologians of different faiths that their counterparts in other traditions had falsified the Holy Scriptures. This notion can be traced back at least to Late Antiquity (2nd to 8th centuries AD), when Sabians, Samaritans and Christians discredited the authenticity of each other's books.[20] With the arrival of Islam and the subsequent engagement between Muslims and the People of the Book, this theme became one of the pillars of theological polemics. In the Qurʾan the idea of scriptural falsification by Jews and Christians, referred to in Arabic as *taḥrīf*, has its scriptural support in verses like 4:46: 'Some Jews distort the meaning of [revealed] words from their [proper] usages (*min alladhīna hādū yuḥarrifūna al-kalima ʿan mawāḍiʿihi*)'.[21] Other verses point towards the same implications, albeit with different terminology and with different nuances. In *Surat al-Baqara* (2:42) we can find the command 'Do not mix the truth with falsehood (*lā talbisūna al-ḥaqq bi-l-bāṭil*)', as well as (2:79): 'So woe to those who write something down with their own hands and the claim, 'This is from God'(*fa-waylun alladhīna yaktubūna al-kitāb bi-ayadihim thumma yaqūlūna hadhā min ʿindi-llāh*)'.[22] Since many early Muslim scholars believed that Jews and Christians had exercised *taḥrīf* on the Bible, thus making it a corrupted source, and since the Qurʾan was in and of itself sufficient for Muslims as a proof (*ḥujja*) of Islam, Muslims had in theory no need to use Christian and Jewish scriptures for guidance. In reality, as we have previously seen, Muslims scholars have referenced the Bible since the early centuries of Islam for two seemingly contradictory purposes: on the one hand, they wanted to prove that the coming of the Prophet Muhammad had been foreseen in it; and on the other, they wanted to expose what they saw as the falsities contained therein.[23]

Throughout the history of Muslim–Christian (and Muslim–Jewish) polemics, *taḥrīf* has been understood in two different ways. The first, *taḥrīf al-naṣṣ* (or *taḥrīf al-ḥarf* or *tabdīl*) (falsification of the text or the letter), refers to the idea that the biblical text itself had been corrupted by the People of the Book. This could imply that certain passages were added to the text, which were not based on true revelation, or that key passages were suppressed from it or obscured in their wording to conceal certain aspects of the revelation. The second, *taḥrīf al-maʿnā* (or *taʾwīl*) (falsification of the meaning or the sense), implies that it was not the text itself that had been corrupted, but rather the way Jews and Christians have interpreted it.[24] Examples of both understandings of *taḥrīf* can be found throughout the history of *dalāʾil al-nubuwwa* literature. Among the proponents of the notion of false interpretation were ʿAli al-Tabari, al-Qasim b. Ibrahim (d. 860) and Fakhr al-Din al-Razi (d. 1210), whereas the idea of textual corruption started with al-Jahiz (d. 870).[25] As Gabriel Said Reynolds has noted, the fact that certain authors gave more weight to *taḥrīf al-maʿnā* does not mean that they believed that the text itself was uncorrupted, nor that they favoured the use of the Bible as a source of guidance.[26] Further, oftentimes polemicists combined both understandings of *taḥrīf* in their work: Ibn Hazm and Ibn Taymiyya (d. 1328), for example, recognised both, but accorded a higher weight to the allegedly corrupt interpretation.[27] Likewise, Tufi went to great lengths to point out the kind of *taḥrīf* that could be found in each specific biblical passage.[28]

As a general rule, few Muslim polemicists ever proposed any kind of historical genesis of the falsification. Among the few who did was the Muʿtazili scholar and judge ʿAbd al-Jabbar. According to a passage from his *Tathbit dalaʾil al-nubuwwa* (*Confirmation of the Proofs of the Prophecy*), a group of Christians living side by side with Jews were persuaded by the Romans to change their doctrine in exchange for preferential treatment over the Jews. When they brought forward their proposal to their community, they were met with resistance. The Romans then suppressed the group that remained faithful to its original doctrine, but as a result of the conflict, the group which had adopted Roman ways lost access to their original scripture. Eventually, this pro-Roman group went on to become today's Christians, whereas the original Christians eventually received the final revelation and became Muslims.[29] Another one to propose a historical genesis for *taḥrīf* was the aforementioned Murad b. ʿAbd Allah, who attributed it to the translations into vernaculars.[30] As we will shortly see, Jadid al-Islam's approach to this theme corresponds to this latter take.

Taḥrīf in the *Sayf al-muʾminin*

As would be expected of any work of *dalāʾil al-nubuwwa*, Jadid al-Islam's *Sayf al-muʾminin* reserves a prominent role for the theme of *taḥrīf*. While our author does allude to alleged hermeneutical errors made by the People of the Book, which would correspond to the idea of *taḥrīf al-maʿnā*, the notion of *taḥrīf al-naṣṣ* is more dominant throughout his text. As in the aforementioned example of ʿAbd al-Jabbar, Jadid al-Islam's treatment of the subject has the unusual characteristic of attempting to historicise the genesis of *taḥrīf*. Like Murad b. ʿAbd Allah, he also links the genealogy of *taḥrīf* to the moment of translation into vernaculars. In this sense, he does not seem to attribute the falsification to the original biblical books themselves, but rather to the canonical translations made throughout the process of institutionalisation of the Church. This seemingly redemptive approval of the original biblical text is not, however, without limits. Closely associated with the theme of *taḥrīf* is another historical motif of polemics, namely the notion that Saint Paul was the forger of what would eventually become canonical Christian doctrine. This would of course invalidate the Pauline letters, but also other parts of the Bible, as we will later see. This idea, recurrent throughout the Islamic tradition, and inspired to an extent by Jewish polemical texts such as the *Toledot Yeshu* (*The Life of Jesus*), appears not only in theological polemics strictly speaking, but also in other kinds of texts.[31] For instance, Sayf b. ʿUmar al-Tamimi (d. ca. 796), a chronicler of the early wars of apostasy and conquest writing during the Abbasid period, portrayed Saint Paul as a fake convert who, among other things, abolished the obligation of defending the faith through the waging of Holy War. Al-Qarafi will later reproduce a similar version of this story in his own work.[32] In the early modern period, an Ottoman text known as *Gurbet-name-yi Sultan Cem* (*The Book of the Exile of Sultan Cem*) portrayed Paul as an old Jewish man who faked his conversion in order to infiltrate Christian circles and lead them astray.[33] In contrast with these accounts, Jadid al-Islam introduces the figure of Saint Paul in the *Sayf al-muʾminin* without a very detailed narrative of his motivations or his background, limiting himself to explaining that Christians recognised him as a disciple of Christ, and condemning him as an 'accursed one who leads to perdition (*malʿūn-i gumrāh-kunandih*)'.[34] Throughout this study, we will see how Jadid al-Islam refers frequently to the Pauline theme in many sections of his work, using it in conjunction with other motifs and arguments. For now, let it suffice to say that he introduces this theme in the context of a much broader account of his historical genesis of *taḥrīf.*

The narrative in question starts with the history of the assembly and translation of the Greek Septuagint under Ptolemy II Philadelphus (d. 246 BCE), reproducing a story similar to the one recounted in the famous – yet almost certainly apocryphal – *Letter of Aristeas.*[35] Jadid al-Islam recounts how seventy different scribes worked on the project, noting that each of them had access only to a small part of the corpus, ignoring therefore the context surrounding their assigned excerpts and being unaware of each other's work. He then mentions that the Greek Hellenistic scholar Theodotion (d. 200 CE) translated the Greek version into Latin, and that his translation was in turn used by Origen (d. 253/4 CE), in an obvious reference to the latter's *Hexapla.*[36] This is of course not precise, since Theodotion translated the Hebrew Bible into Greek and Origen's *Hexapla* contains collations of different Hebrew versions and Greek translations.[37] Finally, our author refers to the elaboration of the Latin Vulgata by Saint Jerome under Pope Damasus I.[38] Since the Vulgata became the canonised version of the Church of Rome following the Council of Trent in 1545, Jadid al-Islam makes Saint Jerome the main target of his accusation of *taḥrīf.* Having laid out his genealogy, Jadid al-Islam provocatively asks:

> Who can base a religion on a book that has been grappled with by so many ignorant hands (*dast-hā-yi jāhilān*) and [how can] the prophecy come forth in all these numerous translations and falsifications (*taḥrīfāt*) from the language of Jerome, who Christians consider [to have been] the seat of the inspiration of the Holy Spirit (*maḥal-i ḥulūl-i Rūḥ-i Quds*) and assisted (*mu'ayyad*) [by God]?[39]

He then reproaches the Arabic translators of the *Biblia Sacra Arabica* for purposely omitting Jerome's prologue to the Pentateuch in order to conceal these falsifications:

> If he [the translator] had rendered it [Jerome's prologue] into Arabic and published it (*qālib mī zad*), everyone would have become aware, [by

reading] this prologue, of the trickeries (*bāzīchih*) of the books and ways (*ṭarīqih*) of the Christians.[40]

Jadid al-Islam's major claim to authority was, after all, his first-hand knowledge of the Latin Vulgata, at a time when his contemporaries among the ulama were working with the Arabic translations.

To further substantiate his case, Jadid al-Islam reproduces a fragment of the prologue in question. In it, Jerome explains his motivations for undertaking his translation, at the request of a certain Desiderius. Among other things, Jerome disapproves of some word choices from the seventy translators and argues against the authenticity of the books of Hosea, Zechariah, Isaiah and Proverbs. He suggests that Ptolemy could have ordered this falsification, possibly motivated by Platonist ideas, which rejected notions like the Trinity and the dualistic nature of Christ.[41] Jadid al-Islam rebukes the premise behind Saint Jerome's alleged need for a new translation and reproaches him for omitting these books. However, while claiming that Jerome's omission was intended to hide the dualistic elements espoused by current Christian dogma, he does not speak approvingly of Ptolemy either, whose Platonic monotheism he sees as closely related to the pantheism of the Sufi concept of *waḥdat al-wujūd* (unity of existence).[42] In concluding this discussion, our author reproaches Desiderius for accepting Jerome's project uncritically:

> But if Desiderius had not been ill-intentioned (*marż nadāsht*) and had been indeed interested in finding the Truth; how come [having read] the original sources of these books, all of which are in Hebrew, or the translations that the seventy [aforementioned scholars] made into Greek, or those of Theodotion and Origen into Latin, he did not come to the conclusion that Jerome should be chastised for further corrupting the scriptures (*dū-bārih kharāb kardan-i kutub*)?[43]

He closes by adding that the acceptance of the canonicity of Jerome's Latin translation would be akin to recognising that Christians (and Jews before them) would have lived in misguidance throughout all previous centuries:

> If it were impossible to find the Truth in the original Hebrew sources, and if Jerome's Latin translation were an entry point into the true faith; this would imply that throughout a long period, the religion of Moses (pbuh),

> and the religion of Jesus throughout the 380 years before Jerome's translation came into the picture, would have been incomplete (*nātamām*) and indeed false (*bāṭil*). [This would imply] that everyone who had adhered to the religion of these Noble men (*Ḥażrat*) would have been lost (*gumrāh*) and confused (*ḥayrān*).[44]

Other Tropes of *Dalāʾil al-nubuwwa* in the *Sayf al-muʾminin*

Jadid al-Islam's major theological preoccupations throughout the *Sayf al-muʾminin* correspond not only to the standard motives of the *dalāʾil* genre, but also to a certain extent to recurrent themes within the cycle started by Jerome Xavier and to his own rejection of Islamic mysticism (*taṣawwuf* and *ʿirfān*) and scholastic philosophy. We will look at these latter aspects more closely in the forthcoming chapters, but for now let us consider some examples of his use of biblical proofs.

One of the most recurrent motifs in Jadid al-Islam's work and throughout the history of *dalāʾil al-nubuwwa* more broadly is that of the *fārqālīṭ*, the Arabic rendering of the Greek Paraclete. This figure appears in John's Gospel, in quotes such as *John* 15:26: 'When the Advocate [Paraclete] comes, whom I will send to you from the Father—the Spirit of truth who goes out from the Father—he will testify about me'.[45] In the Christian tradition, the Paraclete is associated with the Holy Spirit.[46] In the Islamic tradition, the first one to argue that the Paraclete should be identified with Muhammad was the Qurʾanic exegete Muqatil ibn Sulayman (d. 767), although in his case without citing the Gospel as a proof.[47] The first Islamic reference to the Paraclete to include the biblical citation is in Ibn Hisham's (d. 833) reconstruction of Ibn Ishaq's (d. *c.* 767) *al-Sira al-nabawiyya* (*The Biography of the Prophet*).[48] Ibn Ishaq accused the Jews of withholding information regarding the prophecy of the Paraclete, which is why – according to this line of reasoning – he is only mentioned in the New Testament. The term that Ibn Ishaq used for Paraclete was translated into Arabic from the Syriac *Munaḥanma*, which he believed to be a concealed reference to Muhammad.[49] In specifically polemical works, occurrences of this trope appear as early as in Ibn Qutayba's own *Aʿlām al-nubuwwa*, in which the author also proposes an etymological analysis to link the term to the trilateral Arabic root ḥ-m-d, shared by the name of the Prophet.[50]

Following these conventions, Jadid al-Islam introduces the subject by providing his rendition of *John* 16:8:

> It is in your advantage (*maṣlaḥat-i shumā dar ān ast*) that I leave, for if I do not leave, the Paraclete cannot come. When it is the time for him to come to the world, he shall convince it about three things: about sin (*gunāh*), about righteousness (*ḥujjat*) and about judgement (*qiyāmat*): about sin, given that they did not have faith in me, about righteousness given that I will leave you to join my father [in Heaven] after which you will not want to see me [the third element of the quotation is omitted].[51]

He then follows the quote with his interpretation:

> [There is] a clue to recognise him [Muhammad] in this passage from the Gospel, [which indicates] that it is better not to interpret the Paraclete as [being] Jesus. Whenever you see Jesus announcing the Paraclete, know that he is referring to our Prophet [Muhammad]. You should believe what this noble man [Saint John] says in the chapter of the rapture of Jesus. That is, when Jesus says that he is going to meet with his father, he means that he will be lifted by God, not that he will be killed [crucified], like [Christians] say.[52]

Jadid al-Islam's interpretation of this passage has some important traits. First, the fact that he claims that Christians see the Paraclete as an interpretation of Jesus, as opposed to the Holy Spirit. Second, it begins by subscribing to the notion of *taḥrīf al-maʿnā*, with the emphasis put on the faulty interpretation rather than on the corruption of the text. However, as the text continues, it moves on to include an accusation of *taḥrīf al-naṣṣ* against Saint Jerome, who our author accuses of falsifying the text to speak of the resurrection.

> Be aware that what Jerome narrates in Chapter 16 (of John's Gospel) is a lie. [The passage] says: 'After being killed, Jesus came to his disciples. Some of them though he was one of the jinn but others recognised him. He said to them: "I have been given authority over heaven and earth. Go throughout the world and preach to the people in the name of the Father, the Son and the Holy Spirit."' It was not Jesus who said this, but rather Satan who

> inspired Jerome to write this. If Jesus had indeed said this, it would then be necessary to believe that the statement 'I will go where my father is, and after that you will not see me anymore' was a lie.[53]

Finally, in a different section, which also brings about the theme of the Paraclete, Jadid al-Islam also recurs to a faux etymological argument to substantiate his reading. In his case, rather than referring back to the alleged Syriac roots of ḥ-m-d as in earlier Muslim texts, he draws from the lexicographical work of the sixteenth century Augustinian monk Ambrogio Calepino (d. 1510), author of a Latin Dictionary and of the multilingual *Dictionarium Septem Linguarum* (*Seven Language Dictionary*).[54] In this context, Jadid al-Islam draws from Calepino when discussing the subtle implications of the term *angelus* (angel):

> Ambrogio Calepino, who knew Greek, Hebrew, and six other languages, and who is well reputed among Christians, says [in his lexicon in the entry for] the letter 'a', which is [the equivalent of] 'alif', that *angelus* means angel, and that angel means the bearer of a message (*payghām-āvarandih*) from God. Therefore, anyone who brings a message from God can be called an angel, and there is evidence for this everywhere [in the Scriptures]. Thus, following this line of reasoning, since Jesus brought a message from God Almighty through the Paraclete, then he [the Paraclete] can also be called an angel. [Therefore,] this angel of the covenant, of whom Almighty God said 'he is the ruler of the House of God (*farmān-farmā-yi bayt-i Allāh*)' is the Prophet Muhammad (pbuh). When he was still living in this insignificant world (*ʿālam-i ẕarrih*), God said to him: 'am I not your Lord (*a-lastu bi-rabbikum*)'? [Then,] God Almighty took a vow from him to affirm the unity of God (*vaḥdāniyyat-i Khudā*), the faith on the prophethood (*īmān bih nubuvvat*) and the leadership of all the creation (*pīshvāyī-yi hamih-i makhlūqāt*). [And He would entrust him] to deliver this message to men and jinn.[55]

In his use of Calepino's work, Jadid al-Islam clearly does not deny its authoritative scholarly status, but rather uses it to turn its authority against the arguments of the Christian tradition, a strategy that he will pursue in many instances using other Christian sources, as we will see later in this book.

Other common motifs incorporated by Jadid al-Islam's work, which can be found in earlier works of *dalāʾil al-nubuwwa*, function more as refutations of Christian tenets than as proofs of the prophecy strictly speaking. One that is particularly illustrative of this is the discussion surrounding the figure of Melchizedek, the archetypical first priest in history mentioned in *Genesis* 14 and in Saint Paul's *Letter to the Hebrews* 7. Like other Muslim polemicists before him, including the aforementioned al-Qarafi,[56] Jadid al-Islam believes that Melchizedek's existence was a fabrication intended to circumvent Mosaic Law and justify Christian rituals: Melchizedek's offering of bread and wine, which Christians consider as an antecedent of the Eucharist, is seen by Muslim scholars as a violation of the rules of sacrifices, which require that only animals be offered.[57] Later in this book, I will more closely analyse the implications of emphasising the adherence to Mosaic Law in the discussion of these kinds of passages. For now, let us note a more poignant aspect of Jadid al-Islam's treatment of the subject. Our author observes that in the *Book of Genesis* Melchizedek is not said to have any place of origin or kin. This would imply that the character in question would share the attribute of perennial life with the Divine. This would of course be unacceptable to Muslims, who would recognise in this an example of polytheism (*shirk*):

> This Melchizedek, who Paul calls the High Priest of God (*pīshvā-yi Khudā*), the King of Righteousness and Justice (*pādishāh-i ḥujjat va ʿadālat*), had no mother and no father, no offspring (*nasl*) and no lineage (*nasab*), and his days had no beginning nor his life had any end. That is, he is and was always alive, and was thus like a descendant (*farzand*) of God. Christians consider him a person that we should still know about. However, theologians (*Khudā-shināś*) of all nations (*millat*), including Christians, [know] that no one other than God can be characterised (*mawṣūf*) with these attributes (*ṣifāt*) which Paul the hypocrite (*munāfiq*) has ascribed to Melchizedek. For it is the essence of the necessary existence (*ẕāt-i wājib al-wujūd*) not to have mother nor father, offspring nor lineage, beginning nor end.[58]

In describing the nature of God – to which Melchizedek's is compared – Jadid al-Islam reveals his familiarity with classical Islamic philosophical terminology through the use of the Avicennian concept of necessary existence (*wājib al-wujūd*).[59] He then continues to elaborate on the matter, focusing on the theological implications of Melchizedek's ritual offering of bread and wine, beyond the mere transgression of Mosaic Law:

> And if Christians, out of shamelessness and effrontery (*bī-sharm va ḥayāyī*) and [in adherence to] the [doctrine of] the unity of existence (*waḥdat-i mawjūd*) which is part of the beliefs of their spiritual leaders (*iʿtiqād-i pīrān-i īshān*), say that Melchizedek was God, this would necessarily imply that the God of the World (*Khudāvand-i ʿālam*) would be rendering permissible to consider this exalted [figure] (*subḥānih*) [that is, Melchizedek] as the High Priest of another God, who would be higher [in status] [than God]. Otherwise, for whom would this bread and wine be offered in sacrifice?[60]

Thus, if describing Melchizedek in terms proper to the Creator was already a heresy that equated him with God, the fact that he is then said to have offered a sacrifice to a higher being would imply the existence of an even more powerful entity, whose attributes would transcend those of the *wājib al-wujūd*. In other words, if a Godlike figure – as Melchizedek is portrayed as being – prays to a higher entity, the latter would then have to be higher than God Himself, which would be a clearly blasphemous idea for all monotheists.

A Shiʿi Take on Biblical Signs

If Jadid al-Islam's treatment of common tropes from the *dalāʾil al-nubuwwa* tradition already demonstrates his subtle treatment of what would otherwise be commonplaces, this is made even clearer in his use of biblical proofs to promote a specifically Shiʿi agenda. In the next chapter, I will elaborate on an offshoot of *dalāʾil* literature, which seeks to provide proofs for the legitimacy of the tenets of Shiʿism. The works that comprise this archive usually bear titles containing some variation of the term *dalāʾil al-imāma* (signs of the imamate). Given their decidedly intra-Muslim orientation, these works draw from purely Muslim sources – primarily hadith – rather than from biblical proofs. As we will see, Jadid al-Islam also draws from the hadith in the *Sayf al-muʾminin*, but for now let us see how he applies a Shiʿi reading to biblical quotations. The best examples of our author's Shiʿi exegesis of the Bible can be found in his approach to eschatological themes. Islamic readings of biblical passages on the Day of Judgement can also be found in Sunni works of *dalāʾil al-nubuwwa*, as Krstić has shown in her study of Ottoman cases. However, in the examples she has studied, the Messiah of the Day of Judgement is alternatively identified with Jesus, Muhammad or even the Mahdi himself, but without the Shiʿi connotation of his being the Twelfth Imam returning from occultation.[61] In contrast, Jadid al-Islam's exegesis of these kinds of passages does adhere to a decidedly Shiʿi interpretation, as we will now see.

Let us begin with the example of a section devoted to discussing the covenant of *Isaiah* 59:21, which our author translates thus:

> This is what your Lord has said: 'know that the covenant (*mīs̱āq*) that I have made with them [says]: "my spirit is with you, and the words that I have put in your mouth, will remain in your mouth through the intercession of the Spirit (*bih tavassuṭ-i ān rūḥ*), and in your children's mouths, and in the mouths of the children of your children, from now until forever"'.[62]

In his interpretation of the passage, the author speaks of the coming of a later covenant, which would eventually supersede this earlier one:

> This covenant follows [another] covenant, which God Almighty had taken from his people at the beginning of the leadership [Imamate] (*imāmat*) of the sons of Aaron. Since by the time God Almighty had brought the message to Isaiah, both Moses and Aaron, and all of Aaron's children had already passed away, then the covenant that God had made at the beginning of the leadership [Imamate] of the sons of Aaron had reached its term (*bih ʿamal āmadih būd*). It would thus follow that this [new] covenant of which God talks about [here] would be different from that [old] covenant, and that this religion (*dīn*) and its leaders [Imams] (*imāmān*) would be different from those of [the religion of] Moses. [However], the religion and the prophecy of Jesus is excluded by what is stipulated in the statement (*az ḥukm-i ān ʿibārat bīrūn mī ravand*): 'I would never abandon your sons nor the sons of your sons from now until forever'. It is evident that [Christians] are not the intended recipients [of this covenant], since according to both Christians and Muslims Jesus had no descendants, nor were the sons of Simon designated as leaders [Imams] among the Christians (*bih imāmat dar miyān-i Naṣārā mashhūr nashudih-and*), nor are there any names [of possible leaders] mentioned in the Scriptures.[63]

Aside from the use of the word *Imamate* (*imāmat*) applied to the leadership of Moses and Aaron, the reader is confronted with the question of who the beneficiaries of the new covenant would be. Then Jadid al-Islam begins to draw the reader's attention to the key clue to this question, namely the fact that the number of followers (*khulafā*) of Jesus was twelve. He then resorts to the *Fourth Book of Ezra* (or *Second Book of Esdras*), from which he quotes an excerpt in which God reprimands the Israelites for their lack of faith after been released from captivity. In the excerpt, Ezra sees some enigmatic people 'who come from the East (*kih az ṣamt-i mashriq mī āyand*)' and upon whom God would bestow the government and the kingship (*ḥukūmat va pādishāhī*).[64] Jadid al-Islam offers his interpretation about who these characters were:

> [There were] fifteen people in the following order: Abraham, Isaac, Jacob, Oseas, Amos, Micheas, Joel, Abadias, Jonas, Nahum, Habacuc, Sophonias, Aggeus, Zachary and Malachy, which is also the name of an Angel. Thus, it is both evident to reason and revealed by the text (*muwāfiq-i ʿaql va naql maʿlūm mī shavad*), that this king that appears among these fifteen people must be the Prophet of the End of Times, Muhammad Mustafa (the Chosen One, pbuh), and that the other kings would be the twelve successors of the religion (*khalīfih-hā-yi dīn*), and the remaining two would be Isaac and Ismael.[65]

Clearly then, these twelve *khalīfih-hā-yi dīn* would have to be the Shiʿi Imams, and Jadid al-Islam defends his univocal interpretation by adding that this could only be so, 'since there are a few thousand prophets among the Sons of Israel, all of them should have been mentioned and not specifically these twelve'.[66]

However, to better substantiate the idea of a rupture between the recipients of the old and the new covenants, our author needs to establish that these 'people from the East' were not from the Bani Israel, thus dispelling any potential Christian pretension to the covenant. Here, Jadid al-Islam resorts to *Matthew* 5:17, another commonly used quotation in the genre, in which Jesus declares not to have come to abrogate (*naskh kardan*) Mosaic Law.[67] In the context of this passage, the continuity between Christianity and Judaism expressed in the Gospel precludes the possibility of Christians being the heirs of the new covenant. Further proof of the rupture comes from *4 Ezra* 2:33–34:

> I, Esdras, have received an order from the Almighty on Mount Oreb [asking me] that to go [and preach] to the children of Israel. But when I came to them, they rejected what I had to say and did not accept my message, [so now] I shall say to you: 'listen up, oh people, what I have written in this book by God's command. You should wait for the Shepherd (*chūpān*), who is your Messenger, for He will grant you everlasting rest, for He who will come at the end of times is already near'.[68]

Anticipating objections for his use of the non-canonical book of Ezra, Jadid al-Islam complements his proof with *Genesis* 49:10, where Jacob summons his tribe on the day of his departure. Jadid al-Islam's rather loose translation of it reads:

> The crown of prophethood (*tāj-i nubuvvat*) shall not depart from the head of the tribe of the Judah, nor shall the robes of rulership [Imamate] (*libās-i imāmat*) fall from their bodies until the coming of He who God Almighty will send, for He is the one that all nations (*ummat-hā*) await.[69]

This quotation, too, was recurrent in works of *dalāʾil*. Ibn Hazm, for example, said about it that it was historically inaccurate because the sceptre had departed from Judah long before the coming of the awaited one.[70] In contrast, the convert from Judaism, Samawʾal al-Maghribi (d. 1180), used it show that Jews had rejected Muhammad in the same way they had rejected Jesus before him.[71] In contrast, Jadid al-Islam's take on this quote concentrates more on the genealogical and ethnic information it provides to establish the identity of the 'awaited one':

> This Judah is the same Judah son of Jacob into whose tribe Christians claim that Jesus (pbuh) was born, just as they say every time they cannot prove something with their books. Thus, since Jacob said that until God sends the one who all humankind awaits, the crown of prophethood and rulership [Imamate] (*tāj-i nubuvvat va imāmat*) will not depart from the tribe of Judah; it thus follows that the character of which Jacob talks about here – and the coming of whom Esdras announces in the [previously] cited passage – is not Jesus, of whom Christians speak and who they invoke in place of the one [mentioned in the Prophecy]. Nor is he one of the sons

> of Aaron, of whom Jews say that he was the awaited Messiah, since this character [the Messiah] cannot come from the people of Israel.[72]

The text arrives here at the predictable conclusion that the 'awaited one' would be the Prophet Muhammad, with only the previous reference to the twelve enigmatic characters from *Ezra/Esdras* as an explicitly Shiʿi interpretation of the passage.

The motif of the old covenant of Abraham reappears, however, in other sections where the sectarian twist is emphasised more thoroughly. The section in question starts with the standard Muslim argument in favour of Ismael as the legitimate heir of the covenant. The author centres his argument around the idea that, although prophets were to be found among all branches of the descendants of Abraham, Ismael's kin should have precedence based on the principle of primogeniture:

> Christians say that this covenant [implied that] Abraham (pbuh) would have many children, among which there would be prophets and lawgivers (*ṣāhibān-i sharāʾīʿ*), all of whom would worship God. [They say] that this covenant was fulfilled (*bih ʿamal āmad*) through the religion and prophecy of Moses, Aaron and of all the prophets of the House of Israel, and was terminated (*bih itmām rasīdih*) and then resumed (*mustamir*) through the religion of Jesus (pbuh). However, the refutation of this interpretation is [the following]: whenever there is any mention about the amount of children that Abraham had, or about the religion professed by the prophets that hailed among them, it [says that] there would be prophets among the children of Isaac, Abraham's youngest son, and that the religion would be entrusted to them. But by the same token, there would have to be prophets among the children of Ismael, who was also son of the friend of God [Abraham]. However, since the latter was the eldest son, we should pay more attention to him, because there would have to be prophets also among his descendants. Each of these [prophets] would adorn their worshipping rituals (*ʿibādat*) and those of the rest of God's servants with the ornaments of religion (*va har kudām bih zuyūr-i dīnī rū-yi ʿibādat-i khūd va sāyir-i bandigān-i Khudā rā biyārāyand*). God Almighty does not specifically mention every single son of Abraham, but says in general terms (*bih lafẓ-i ʿām*) that 'this covenant which I now settle between you and me, will be [valid]

> for you and for your children after you until the end of times'. It thus follows that, according to this doctrine, whatever is born into the offspring of Isaac, will also be born into the offspring of Ismael. Yet, both Christians and Jews have denied this interpretation, arguing that no religion and no prophecy have come out of Ismael's offspring. They have thus denied the honour and grandeur of Ismael, to the point of concluding that he should not even be counted among the pious. It is thus clear from this interpretation that Christians make of the covenant, there is no place for these two lineages [Isaac's and Ismael's] in the eyes of this evil sect (*mazhab-i kharāb*). However, if they indeed adhered to this interpretation, [they would see that] the foundations of their evil sect would become ruined, even more so than that of their neighbours of the Jewish sect, to the point of coming close to falling into disbelief (*az bī-mazhabī dar bi-dar khvāhand āftād*). Therefore, they should renounce this sect and recognise the falsity of this interpretation that they have made [of the covenant].[73]

The author then turns to consider the question of what the geographical limits of the Promised Land would be, given its status as Moses's rightful domain according to the covenant. While Christians believed that only the tribe of Moses was entitled to the entire Levant, our author contends that this was the right of all the descendants of Abraham. He further adds that *Deuteronomy* 34 demonstrated that the Levant was not intended for Moses, since the passage shows God comforting him in the enigmatic land of Moab.[74] Up to this point, the exegesis of the passage lacks any sectarian undertones. However, as the passage approaches more eschatological territories, the adherence to the Shiʿi conception of Mahdi surfaces:

> According to the People of the True Sect (*ahl-i mazhab-i ḥaqq*), meaning the partisans (*shīʿiyān*) of the Viceroy of God (*Vali-yi Khudā*), ʿAli b. Abi Talib; [they] have gotten a voluminous exegesis (*tāʾvīl-i ganjā*) from this guide of theirs, of whom it is written that he shall be the guide of the people of all religions (*hādī-yi ahl-i har dīnī*) and the honour of the People of the House [of the Prophet] (*ahl-i bayt*). According to the religion of the Shiʿa, from the time when God Almighty made the covenant with Abraham (pbuh) until today, and from today until the Day of Resurrection, the Earth has never been, nor will it ever be, deprived from a proof (*ḥujjat*) or

> from a leader (*pīshvā*) from the kin of Abraham. Thus, [the Shiʿia] believe with absolute faith (*īmān-i tamām*) and firm devotion (*ikhlāṣ-i muḥakam*) that at this moment, the Mahdi, the Lord of the Age (*Ṣāḥib al-Zamān*) stands by Abraham's side guarding his place (*qāʾim-maqām*[75]) and standing on God's soil (*dar rū-yi zamīn-i Khudā-st*). And although he remains in occultation (*dar ghayb ast*), he will [return] to rule over everyone on this land (*ṣāḥib-i ikhtiyār-i hamih rū-yi zamīn mī bāshad*). Thus, the promise that God Almighty has made is that every land is Canaan. In chapter thirteen of this same book [*Genesis*], God Almighty promised to Abraham that all the land of the inhabitable quarter [of the Earth] would be given to him and to his children. And according to what this humble servant [Jadid al-Islam] has been able to prove from the notes on this thirteenth chapter in numerous documents on the Christian Scriptures; it is clear that at the time of the appearance of the government of the Lord of the Age – that is, the Mahdi (pbuh) – every pious person who died in exile since the [time of] the children of Abraham – that is, anyone who had died during the time of the *fitra* – will be resurrected, and the entire Earth will be at the service of its Master and under his domain, and – God willing – an age of well-being will come to Earth.[76]

The interpretation acknowledges thus the universal appeal of the prophetic mission, but makes its redemptive message conditional to the proper adherence to Shiʿi doctrine: it is only through Imam Mahdi that the realm of Abraham can be expanded and transcend the specificity of its Jewish origin.

Having thus set the tone for his Shiʿi reading of this passage, Jadid al-Islam proceeds to discuss the implications of the circumcision of Abraham, another common topic in Muslim–Christian discussions.[77] While he acknowledges its validity as a sign of the covenant, he reintroduces the idea of the distinction between the old and the new covenants. The circumcision would thus correspond to the covenant of *Genesis* 9. He rebukes the Christian claim that circumcision was not practised before Abraham, given the lack of references to this custom before the biblical passage in question. He lays another accusation of *taḥrīf* against Jerome for what he sees as the forging of *Genesis* 17:26, where Abraham and Ismael are circumcised at ninety and thirteen respectively, since this would imply that the standard practice of circumcising boys seven days after birth had not yet been established. Had this been the case, the circumcision would have been a sign of a rupture with the covenant of Noah, and thus the new covenant would have been sealed at that moment and the Jews would have remained its eternal beneficiaries:

> We seek refuge from this [statement of] infidelity (*naʿūẕu bi-llāh az īn kufr*) that this accursed man [Saint Jerome] has written. According to Christian beliefs, prophets before Abraham did not circumcise, because it would imply that this covenant, which is the same as the one that God had made with Noah and his sons, would have required the circumcision of Noah and his sons. It is thus clear [to Christians] that this [other] covenant [meaning, Noah's] did not entail any circumcision.[78]

However, our author then notes that there were no indications in the Scripture suggesting that the covenant of Abraham had been abrogated:

> In none of the Christian books do we read at any point that God transferred the covenant that He had made with the family of Abraham to anyone else. Instead, the meaning that appears to be proven (*s̱ābit*) and alluded to (*maḥkūm bihi*) throughout the entire *Book of Genesis* is [the following]: if this circumcision [were to] be different from the [old] covenant, this would [imply that] by rejecting (*maḥrūm gashtan*) both the [old] covenant and [the covenant of] the circumcision, because of their malicious disposition (*ṯaynat-i khabīs̱*) and of the evil sect (*maẕhab-i badī*) that they have created, Christians would be departing from God's command.[79]

Having thus concluded that the covenants of Noah and Abraham were one and the same, Jadid al-Islam defends the standard Muslim position of the duty to circumcise, although with clearly ʿAlid undertones, saying that its avoidance would attract the wrath of God and of the fourteen immaculate ones (*maʿṣūm*; meaning the Prophet, Fatima and the Twelve Imams).[80] He concludes by condemning Christians for believing that Jesus had abrogated this duty, alluding to the notion of legal continuity between Judaism and Christianity expressed in *Matthew* 5.[81] The section closes with another sectarian innuendo, with our author drawing a parallelism between the defeat of the Pharaoh in *Ezekiel* 32 and that of the Caliph ʿUmar at the hands of ʿAli. In his interpretation of the passage, Jadid al-Islam considers ʿUmar and his followers to be the target of God's condemnation in the passage on the fall of Edom and the uncircumcised:

> You too will perish among the uncircumcised. There lies Edom and all of his kings and princes, who despite their power perished by the sword. You will join Rome and its kings and all of those who did not practice this custom [circumcision] in the bottom of hell.[82]

As we see then, in addition to the substantial interpretation of the biblical text through a Shiʿi lens, the passage reaffirms its sectarian character by adding the layer of the condemnation of Sunnism, which we will revisit in other chapters.

Finally, Jadid al-Islam devotes another section to provide biblical proofs for the return (*rajʿa*) of the Twelfth Imam. He finds the first of such proofs embedded in an excerpt from *Daniel* 12, which reads: 'But on that day, the Great Prince Michael will rise'.[83] The commentary that follows analyses the implications of the use of the term 'prince':

> It is understood by [the use of] the term 'prince' (*shāhzādih*) that the name of the Mahdi should have been used instead of [the name of] Michael, because the former is the real prince that will rise at the end of times, and not Michael, who is not known to have been a prince. He [Michael] is not [part] of humankind, but rather an angel, sitting by the side of the Almighty (*firishtih-i muqarrab dar gāh-i kibriyāʾ-st*). Nowhere in the Holy Books is the name of Michael mentioned as being among the sons of Adam, nor [does it say] that he will rise at the end of times.[84]

In this case, the alleged *taḥrīf* would have consisted of substituting the name of the Mahdi with that of the Archangel Michael. As the passage develops, the author calls the reader's attention to the enigmatic book the archangel brings with him:

> It had to be that either [Saint] Jerome or someone else who, for his own benefit and following Satan's advice, substituted the name of the Mahdi with that of Michael. The same happens [in the passage] where Daniel is told: 'on that day the Great Prince Michael, ruler and lawgiver of your nation, will rise. When that time [comes] it will be unlike any other time

> since the creation of mankind, and at that time there will be a list of everyone from your nation whose name has been written in the book'.[85]

Jadid al-Islam then moves on to inquire what the reference to this book could be concealing. In his interpretation, he sees in this book a reference to the Preserved Tablet (*al-Lawḥ al-Maḥfūẓ*), which is said to contain the record of all human actions. He also alludes to the more specifically Shiʿi notion that the accurate Qurʾan and the list of human deeds are written in the *Book of Fatima* (*Muṣḥaf*), which was given to the Mahdi to protect until the end of times:

> This book must certainly be the Holy Qurʾan. Therefore, the meaning of this section is that 'on that day everyone from your nation who is mentioned in the Qurʾan as having done good deeds will be free from any torment, both in this world and in the afterlife'. This could have also been a reference to the Book (*Muṣḥaf*) of Fatima (pbuh), in which the Commander of the Faithful wrote down the message from the Angel Gabriel. This is because according to a hadith from the family of the Prophet, the name of every believer and every disbeliever, and all their deeds from the beginning until the end of times and the day of resurrection are written in this text. This text is now under the custody of the Master of Authority (*Ṣāḥib al-Amr*), the Mahdi. Thus, the interpretation of the terms from [the passage from] Daniel [would be]: 'on that day, anyone from your nation whose name is mentioned in this book – which the Almighty graciously delivered to the most honourable of women (*sayyidih-i zanān*), Fatima Zahra, to comfort her heart through the intercession of Gabriel, [God's] intermediary – will be released from the torment and will see goodness in both worlds [here and the hereafter]'. Or it could also be that this book is the Preserved Tablet (*Lawḥ-i Maḥfūẓ*), which represents three books: for anyone who is mentioned in the *Lawḥ-i Maḥfūẓ* as a good-doer, will also be mentioned as such in the Holy Qurʾan and in the Book of Fatima, and [the same will apply] in the opposite sense [meaning, that evil-doers will be considered as such in all three books]. [86]

Finally, Jadid al-Islam concludes his discussion on *rajʿa*, drawing from the *Book of Revelation*, which he calls the *Book of John* (*Kitāb-i Yūḥannā*), after the disciple to whom it is attributed. From it, he quotes an excerpt from chapter nineteen in which the apostle sees an enigmatic and redemptive figure riding a white horse and describes him with the epithets of *faithful* (*amīn*) and *truthful* (*rāst*). In his interpretation, Jadid al-Islam resorts to the same kind of etymological proof that we previously saw being used in the context of proving the prophethood of Muhammad, but this time applied to the fulfillment of the Mahdi's mission:

> This knight would have to be the Master of Authority (*Ṣāḥib al-Amr*). According to a hadith from the Messenger [of God], he [the Prophet] said: 'at the end of times, someone from my progeny (*az z̲urriyyih-i man*) will come, and his name will be my name'. And since *Amīn* [Faithful] was the epithet (*laqab*) of the Messenger and has since been commonly used (*musta'mal*) [in association] with the name of the Prophet, to the point that he is often referred to as 'Muhammad Amin', according to this hadith the name of this holy person will also be 'Muhammad Amin'. And John added: 'he will ride a white horse and his name will be *Amīn*, and he will pass judgement so that the proof be fulfilled (*bih ḥujjat tamām shudih dīvān mī kunad*), and will step forward in the Holy Fight (*bih jihād iqdām mī namāyad*) and his eyes will be filled with fire'. This is a metaphor (*kināyih*) of the anger and embezzlement (*khishm va ghaṣb*) and of the frankness (*rukī*) that this holy person will display at the time of his appearance. [The phrase] 'And on his head he will have many crowns' alludes to the fact that, when he rises, this king will rule over all other kings and will reign over every kingdom on earth. 'And there was a name written down which nobody knew other than himself' must be [a reference to] the magnificent name of God Almighty which nobody will know on that day other than this noble person. 'And he will be dressed in an outfit full of blood stains' is a sign of the great amount of executions that he will have to carry out on the day of his coming. 'He made the word of God be mentioned (*nāmīdih mī shud kalām-i Allāh*)' means that this noble person is the Speaking Qur'an (*Qur'ān-i nāṭiq*). 'And every army in heaven followed him', means that an army of angels will be there to assist him in his auspicious stirrup (*rikāb*) on the day of his appearance, and it can also indicate the coming of Jesus and his disciples, all of whom will be at the service of the Master of Authority (*Ṣāḥib al-Amr*) (pbuh) on that day.[87]

It is therefore in the enigmatic passages on the Day of Judgement that Jadid al-Islam finds it more suitable to promote his Shiʿi reading of biblical signs. Apart from the thematic specificity of this passage, here we can begin to see how the author makes recourse to hadith, which he freely interlaces with biblical proofs. Throughout the next chapter, we will delve more into our author's use of this other archive, to see how he draws from it to add complexity to his arguments, further legitimising his spiritual commitment and his intellectual authority before his new coreligionists.

Notes

1. Griffith, *The Bible in Arabic,* pp. 97–106. For a detailed overview of the rise of Arabic Bible translations, see Vollandt, *Arabic Versions of the Pentateuch*, pp. 40–60.
2. Lazarus-Yafeh, *Intertwined Worlds*, p. 115; Griffith, *The Bible in Arabic*, pp. 106–10.
3. Saleh, 'A Fifteenth-Century Muslim Hebraist', pp. 632–3. For more detailed study of the genre and its relation to other forms of religious literature and to the portrayal of biblical prophets in the Qur'an, see Tottoli, *Biblical Prophets in the Qur'ān*, pp. 138–57.
4. Lazarus-Yafeh, *Intertwined Worlds*, pp. 112–14, 118.
5. Lazarus-Yafeh, *Intertwined Worlds*, pp.118–19; See also Griffith, *The Bible in Arabic*, pp. 179–82.
6. Tottoli, *Biblical Prophets in the Qur'ān*, pp. 91–2.
7. Lazarus-Yafeh, *Intertwined Worlds*, pp. 124–5.
8. Schmidtke, 'The Muslim Reception of Biblical Materials', p. 250. See also Vollandt, *Arabic Versions of the Pentateuch*, pp. 91–2, 97–8; Griffith, *The Bible in Arabic*, p. 181; Thomas, ''Alī l-Ṭabarī', pp. 669–74; Thomas, 'Ibn Qutayba', pp. 816–18.
9. For a comprehensive overview of *dalāʾil* literature beyond the use of biblical proofs, see Stroumsa, 'The Signs of Prophecy', pp. 101–14.
10. Lazarus-Yafeh, *Intertwined Worlds*, pp. 122–3. Vollandt, *Arabic Versions of the Pentateuch*, pp. 106–7. For a detailed study of Ibn Hazm, see Adang, Fierro and Schmidtke (eds), *Ibn Hazm of Cordoba.*
11. Sarrió Cucarella, *Muslim-Christian Polemics across the Mediterranean*, pp. 1–5.
12. Demiri, *Muslim Exegesis of the Bible in Medieval Cairo*, pp. 25–7.
13. Saleh, 'A Fifteenth-Century Muslim Hebraist', p. 633.

14. For the most complete study on Turmeda's work, see Epalza, *La Tuḥfah, autobiografía y polémica islámica contra el Cristianismo.* (Reprinted as *Fray Anselmo Turmeda (Abdallāh al-Taryumān) y su polémica islamo-cristiana*). For details on Turmeda's life, see Epalza, 'Nuevas aportaciones a la biografía de fray Anselmo Turmeda', pp. 87–158. For more recent studies, albeit less comprehensive, see Benigni, 'The Many Languages of the Self in the Early Modern Mediterranean', pp. 194–221; Álvarez, 'Anselmo Turmeda: Visionary Humanism of a Muslim Convert and Catalan Prophet', pp. 172–91. See also Krstić, *Contested Conversions to Islam*, p. 102.
15. Adang, 'Guided to Islam by the Torah', pp. 61–2; Adang and Schmidtke, 'Ahmad b. Mustafa Tashkubrizade's (d. 968/1561) polemical tract against Judaism', p. 81.
16. Krstić, *Contested Conversions to Islam*, pp. 98–9.
17. Ibid. pp. 100–6.
18. For a discussion on the authenticity of Turmeda's work, see Epalza, 'Fray Anselmo Turmeda', p. 97; Beier, 'Una coincidència textual entre la Tuḥfa d'Anselm turmeda', pp. 83–8. A famous example of a convert narrative that attracted a large amount of scepticism was that of 'Hermann the Jew'. See Schmitt, *La conversion d'Hermann le Juif*, pp. 33–44; see also Tiburcio, 'Some Aspects of Conversion Narratives', pp. 368–9.
19. Halft, 'Hebrew Bible Quotations', p. 244; Corbin, 'Annuaire 1976–1977', p. 169.
20. Lazarus-Yafeh, 'Some Neglected Aspects of Medieval Muslim Polemics against Christianity', p. 64; Griffith, *The Bible in Arabic*, pp. 175–6.
21. For studies on *taḥrīf* that refer to this quote, see Said Reynolds, 'On the Qur'anic Accusation of Scriptural Falsification', p. 190; Demiri, 'Taḥrīf in der vormodernen muslimischen Literatur', pp. 24–5. For the Qur᾽anic quotation, I use M. A. S. Abdel Haleem's translation; *The Qur'an*, p. 55.
22. Said Reynolds, 'On the Qur'anic Accusation of Scriptural Falsification', 192; Demiri, 'Taḥrīf in der vormodernen muslimischen Literatur', p. 5. Qur᾽anic translation by Abdel Haleem, *The Qur'an*, pp. 8, 10.
23. Saleh, 'A Fifteenth-Century Muslim Hebraist', pp. 630–2.
24. Demiri, 'Taḥrīf in der vormodernen muslimischen Literatur', p. 33; Sarrió Cucarella, *Muslim-Christian Polemics across the Mediterranean*, p. 224; Said Reynolds, *A Muslim Theologian in a Sectarian Milieu*, p. 84. For more comprehensive studies on the term and its recurrence in Muslim texts, see Gaudeul and Gaspar, 'Textes de la tradition musulmane concernant le *taḥrīf*'; Thomas,

'The Bible in Early Muslim Anti-Christian Polemics'. For an overview of the genealogy of the study of *taḥrīf* in Western academia, see Scheffner, 'The Bible through a Qur'ānic Filter', pp. 39–41.

25. Urvoy, 'Le sense de la polémique anti-biblique', p. 486; Behloul, 'The Testimony of Reason', p. 458.
26. Said Reynolds, 'On the Qur'anic Accusation of Scriptural Falsification', pp. 189–90.
27. Sarrió Cucarella, *Muslim-Christian Polemics across the Mediterranean*, pp. 224–5; Uvoy, 'Le sense de la polémique anti-biblique', pp. 485–6; Behloul, 'The Testimony of Reason', pp. 457–9.
28. Demiri, *Muslim Exegesis of the Bible in Medieval Cairo*, pp. 60–1.
29. Said Reynolds, *A Muslim Theologian in a Sectarian Milieu*, pp. 86–8; Stern, ''Abd al-Jabbār's Account of how Christ's Religion was Falsified', pp. 128–85. Said Reynolds, 'On the Qur'anic Accusation of Scriptural Falsification', pp. 190–1.
30. Krstić, *Contested Conversions to Islam*, pp. 84–5.
31. For an overview on Jewish discourse on Paul, see Bammel, 'Christian Origins in Jewish Tradition', pp. 330–4.
32. Sarrió Cucarella, *Muslim-Christian Polemics across the Mediterranean*, pp. 197–9; Bammel, 'Christian Origins in Jewish Tradition', p. 332.
33. Krstic, *Contested Conversions to Islam*, p. 86.
34. SM, p. 61.
35. SM, pp. 58–61. For a study on the *Letter of Aristeas*, see Pelletier, *Lettre d'Aristée à Philocrate.*
36. SM, p. 58. He mistakenly calls him Theodosius (Tiyādāziyūs).
37. Fenlon, 'Hexapla'.
38. SM, p. 58.
39. SM, p. 59.
40. Ibid. p. 59.
41. Jerome, *Preface to Genesis*. For more background on Saint Jerome's disagreements with the Hellenistic translations, see also Fenlon, 'Hexapla'.
42. SM, p. 60.
43. Ibid. p. 62.
44. Ibid. pp. 62–3.
45. *John* 15:26. [From here on, the biblical quotes that are not a direct translation of Jadid al-Islam's own rendition will be from the New International Version].
46. Kiefer, 'John', p. 224.
47. Sarrió Cucarella, *Muslim-Christian Polemics across the Mediterranean*, pp. 226–7.

48. Amir-Moezzi, 'Muhammad the Paraclete', p. 48; Lazarus-Yafeh, *Intertwined Worlds*, pp. 77–8; Griffith, *The Bible in Arabic*, p. 179.
49. Lazarus-Yafeh, *Intertwined Worlds*, pp. 77–8.
50. Schmidtke, 'The Muslim Reception of Biblical Materials', p. 256.
51. SM, p. 75.
52. Ibid. p. 75.
53. Ibid. p. 75.
54. Calepino, *Dictionarium Latinum*; Calepino, *Dictionarium Septem Linguarum*. See also Dubray, 'Ambrogio Calepino'.
55. SM, p. 124. Calepino, *Dictionarium Latinum*, n. p. [entry on Angelus]; Calepino, *Dictionarium Septem Linguarum*, p. 53.
56. Sarrió Cucarella, *Muslim-Christian Polemics across the Mediterranean*, pp. 189–91.
57. SM, pp. 246–7. For a history of the Christian interpretation of The Sacrifice of Melchizedek as a predecessor of the Eucharist, which goes back to Clement of Alexandria (d. 215), see Grypeou and Spurling, *The Book of Genesis in Late Antiquity*, pp. 225–6.
58. SM, p. 243.
59. For more on this concept, see Hourani, 'Ibn Sina on Necessary and Possible Existence'.
60. SM, p. 243.
61. Krstić, *Contested Conversions to Islam*, pp. 91–5.
62. SM, p. 249.
63. Ibid. p. 249.
64. Ibid. p. 251.
65. Ibid. p. 251; Biblical reference from *2 Esdras* (or *4 Ezra*) 1:39–40.
66. Ibid. p. 252.
67. Ibid. p. 253.
68. Ibid. p. 253.
69. Ibid. p. 254.
70. Lazarus-Yafeh, *Intertwined Worlds*, pp. 98–9.
71. Ibid. pp. 99–100.
72. SM, p. 254.
73. Ibid. pp. 318–19.
74. Ibid. p. 319.
75. This term can also be translated as 'Lieutenant'.
76. Ibid. p. 320.

77. For a good overview of circumcision in Islam and Christianity and its relation to the theme of the covenant, see Kueny, 'Abraham's Test', pp. 164–70.
78. SM, p. 320.
79. Ibid. pp. 321–2.
80. Ibid. pp. 323.
81. Ibid. pp. 325.
82. Ibid. p. 326. Jadid al-Islam alters the second part of the quotation slightly. The part that reads 'you will join Rome and its kings (*khvāhī būd tū va Rūm va pādishāhān-i ū*)' is not included in the biblical quote.
83. Ibid. p. 298.
84. Ibid. p. 298.
85. Ibid. p. 298.
86. SM, p. 298. For more on the *Book of Fatima* and a discussion about its status in Shiʿism, see Sindawi, 'Fāṭima's Book'.
87. SM, pp. 299–300.

4

Appropriating Shiʿi Tradition and Engaging Christian Sources

As we have seen in the previous chapter, converts played a leading role in the history of religious polemics. Among them, those boasting formal training in their religion of origin found in the tradition of *dalāʾil al-nubuwwa* a useful way to apply their knowledge of the Bible. However, this was not the only manner in which they could use their backgrounds to their advantage. They also incorporated historical and theological knowledge from both ends of their spiritual transition beyond the Holy Scriptures. For instance, in his *Al-radd ʿala al-Nasara* (*Refutation of the Christians*) ʿAli al-Tabari discussed at some length issues pertaining the Nicene Creed.[1] In a similar fashion, Turmeda incorporated into his *Tuhfa* citations from a wide array of Christian sources,[2] and in one of his minor works in Catalan, the *Disputa de l'ase* (*Dispute of the Donkey*), he drew from texts from the mystical brotherhood *Ikhwan al-safaʾ* (*Brethren of Purity*).[3]

As we will see shortly, Jadid al-Islam too makes use of a rich corpus of sources beyond the biblical text. In discussing the similarities between Jadid al-Islam's work and the classics of the polemical genre regarding his treatment of biblical signs, I have already raised the question of his possible familiarity with earlier works of *dalāʾil*. This question is also relevant when considering his use of extra-scriptural materials, although less so because of the specific choice of sources than because of the fact that they served as a rhetorical resource, as we will now see.

Hadith in the *Dalāʾil al-nubuwwa* Genre

While *dalāʾil al-nubuwwa* literature necessitated an engagement with the biblical corpus in order to reclaim it as a tool for Islamic hermeneutics, the genre was not historically circumscribed only to interreligious polemics. An entire branch of *dalāʾil* texts developed in parallel which was more concerned with providing proofs for the prophecy from *within* Islamic sources and for the purpose of engaging in intra-Muslim theological discussions. From the earliest developments of the genre, scholars of different schools of thought specialising in different disciplines of Islamic learning drew upon a wide variety of sources to use them as argumentative tools. Scholars as diverse and antithetical as the Muʿtazilites al-Jahiz and ʿAbd al-Jabbar al-Hamadhani (d. 1025) on the one hand, and scholars with Ashʿarite tendencies, like Abu al-Hasan al-Mawardi (d. 1058) on the other, produced works which could be classified as belonging to this tradition.[4] Thematically speaking, these works focused on the charisma and the figure of the Prophet. It is thus hardly surprising that the study of the *al-Sira al-nabawiyya* was intimately linked to the development of the genre, and that Ibn Ishaq, the author of the best known account of the *Sira*, was also among the earliest to venture into this strain of *dalāʾil* literature.[5]

Likewise, the study of hadith constituted another major source of *proofs*, with a whole branch of *dalāʾil* literature consisting in the compilation of thematically relevant hadith collections. The earliest works of this kind were produced by scholars like Maʿmar b. Rashid (d. 770), who drew from narrations that would later be included in the canonical *Sahih* of al-Bukhari (d. 870) and Ibn Saʿd (d. 845) and who made use of the *Sira* and the hadith.[6] As the tradition developed, later authors expanded their pool of texts and used different methodological criteria in their compilations. Abu Nuʿaym al-Isfahani (d. 1038), for example, excluded details from the *Sira* that were not central to the notion of *proofs*, and compiled only hadith that served this specific purpose; even if that meant including reports from non-canonical collections, from so-called weak (*ḍaʿīf*) traditions, and from the *Israʾiliyyat*.[7] Abu Bakr al-Bayhaqi (d. 1066), on the other hand, was more thematically comprehensive in his selection and produced the most detailed biography of the Prophet to be written within this tradition.[8] In a similar fashion, works that were primarily concerned with the biography of the Prophet also included hadith-based subsections on *dalāʾil al-nubuwwa*, like in the case of the *Sharaf al-mustafa* (*The Honour of the Chosen One*) of al-Waʿiz al-Khargushi (d. *c.* 1016).[9] The most recurring themes of *dalāʾil*-themed hadith include passages on the annunciation of the prophecy of Muhammad to biblical prophets and reports on the quasi-miraculous circumstances surrounding his birth.[10]

While some of the hadith included in the early *dalāʾil*-themed collections may have displayed a certain degree of devotion towards the family of the Prophet or towards figures revered by the Shiʿa, such as Salman al-Farisi (d. *c.* 656),[11] the nature of these works was decidedly nonsectarian and rather entrenched within the Sunni tradition. However, as we anticipated in the previous chapter, there is also a significant corpus of texts that invoke the notion of *dalāʾil al-imāma* through examples taken primarily from Shiʿi hadith collections. The most famous book of this kind is that of Muhammad b. Jarir al-Tabari al-Saghir (d. eleventh century), unambiguously invoking in its title the concept in question.[12] Other notable contributors to this subgenre include the canonical compiler of Shiʿi hadith Ibn Babawayh (d. 991), as well as ʿAbd al-Karim b. Tawus al-Hilli (d. 1294) and Muhammad ʿAli b. Ahmad b. ʿAli al-ʿAmili al-Makki.[13]

In accordance with this latter strain of *dalāʾil al-nubuwwa* and of *dalāʾil al-imāma*, Jadid al-Islam also integrates hadith into his work, sometimes as free-standing proofs and sometimes interwoven with biblical proofs like the ones we have seen so far. A close look at the corpus of hadith he draws from is necessary for at least three reasons: first, as has been noted before, there are more documentary gaps than clues regarding the depth of our author's training in Islamic sciences. We know that the prominent mujtahid Fazil-i Hindi encouraged him to write the *Sayf al-muʾminin*, but we do not have any explicit indications regarding any other teachers he might have had, nor what curriculum he might had pursued. Thus, a careful consideration of these sources can shed light on this and, by extension, on the degree to which the ulama of Isfahan were capable of fully integrating (at least some) convert scholars into their own circles of high learning. Second, beyond the case of Jadid al-Islam himself, analysing the corpus of hadith in the *Sayf al-muʾminin* can indirectly enrich our understanding of the circulation of knowledge among the ulama at the time and of the nature of their engagement with this corpus. This is essential given the centrality of discussions surrounding the self-sufficiency (or lack thereof) of hadith as a source of legal and theological truth throughout the history of Shiʿi thought. This was especially relevant at the end of the seventeenth century, at the height of the feud between the Akhbaris (traditionists or traditionalists) and Usulis (rationalists). The former camp sought to circumscribe legal rulings to matters for which textual precedents could be extracted from the hadith, whereas the latter advocated an extended use of reason (*ʿaql*) and of legal hermeneutical thinking (*ijtihād*) to derive rulings.[14] The hadith in the work of Jadid al-Islam should not be taken as a sign of his allegiance to any of these trends. Nevertheless, it is important to keep this context in mind when considering some of the intellectual authorities from which he quotes.

The third and most important aspect of our author's use of hadith is that his choice of corpus may very well be one of his – or that of the Safavid polemicists – most original contributions to the interreligious strain of *dalāʾil* literature: by blending the corpus and the themes of *dalāʾil al-nubuwwa* and *dalāʾil al-imāma*, Jadid al-Islam infuses his interreligious polemics with a specifically Shiʿi character. As we will see, the value of Jadid al-Islam's use of hadith does not reside in the rarity of the traditions he cites – on the contrary, many of these were fairly well-known – nor is his interpretation of them particularly original. What matters instead is the way he intertwines these narrations with other more common elements of interreligious polemics and of the *dalāʾil al-nubuwwa* genre as a whole.

Hadith in the *Sayf al-muʾminin*

Although quotations from the hadith and the *riwāyāt* (hadith that trace their line of transmission to the Imams) appear in relatively few instances within the *Sayf al-muʾminin*, they play an important structural and thematic role in certain key passages. Jadid al-Islam does not always reveal the hadith collections he uses, and it is difficult to identify a systematic reason – if any at all – for why he does choose to do so in some few cases. He also does not quote any of the texts in Arabic. However, it is possible to trace back his sources by comparing his Persian rendition to the body of the text (*matn*) of the different versions of these hadith and *riwāyāt*. In some cases, the versions are too similar to determine which one he is drawing from, but in other cases there are key words that point towards a particular version.

In the previously mentioned section devoted to the discussion of the *taḥrīf* of Saint Jerome, Jadid al-Islam makes a passing reference to Ibn Babawayh's *ʿUyun akhbar al-Rida* (*The Source of Traditions of Imam al-Rida*). In the narration he refers to, Imam Riza brings forward the proofs of the prophecy from the Torah and the Gospels respectively to a Jewish Exilarch (*Rāʾs al-Jālūt*) and an Orthodox Christian Katholikos (*Jāthlīq*). Both religious dignitaries are convinced by the proofs and embrace Islam after being 'released from the darkness of disbelief (*az ẓulumāt-i kufr kufr bīrūn āvardih*)'.[15] Jadid al-Islam does not elaborate here on the nature of the proofs presented, nor does he quote the passages verbatim. What he does instead is to draw a parallel between the conversion of the hierarchs and his own, by saying that he too was persuaded to convert by scriptural proofs:

> From the moment I had the good fortune to join in the this laudable path (*ṭarīqih-i marżiyyih*) through the guidance of the People of the House of the Prophet of God (pbuh), I have taken upon myself to hit the books [of Christians] with my hand (*dast bih kutub-i īshān mī zanam*), [hoping] that through divine grace (*luṭf-i ilāhī*) and through the Light of the People of the House of the Noble [Bearer] of the Concealed Message (*nūr-i ahl-i bayt-i Ḥażrat-i risālat-i panāhī*) (pbuh) [i.e., Muhammad], they will be released from the darkness of disbelief (*ẓulumāt-i kufr*) and brought into the kingly path of faith (*shāhrāh-i īmān*).[16]

In this case, the function of the story is to reinforce the notion of the validity of extracting proofs of Islam from the Scriptures of the People of the Book. In other words, the Islamic text serves as a validation of the use of Christian Scriptures against potential Muslim objections. Thus, the use of hadith and, by extension, of Islamic revelation, is interdependent here with that of the validation of previous Scriptures. In other passages, however, the hadith are treated as self-sufficient proofs, which are only linked to Christian Scriptures through analogy – and by the fact of their being mutually intertwined within the structure of the text – rather than through intertextual referencing.

In the section devoted to the discussion of the Paraclete, Jadid al-Islam recurs to various hadith to support the notion of Muhammad's predestined mission. He quotes from *al-Anwar fi mawlad al-nabi* (*The Lights in the Birth of the Prophet*) of Abu Hassan al-Bakri, a teacher of the famous Shiʿi theologian and martyr Zayn al-Din al-ʿAmili, al-Shahid al-Thani (the Second Martyr) (d. 1558). These same hadith are quoted verbatim in the *Bihar al-anwar* of Muhammad Baqir Majlisi. The latter, as we have seen in Chapter one, was Jadid al-Islam's contemporary and one of the most influential scholars of the late seventeenth century, often associated with hostility against religious minorities. As we will see, in addition to explicitly mentioning Majlisi in certain points, many of the hadith cited in the *Sayf al-muʾminin* also appear in the *Bihar al-anwar*. This raises the question of whether Jadid al-Islam had direct access to all of the hadith collections he quoted from (including al-Bakri's) or whether in some cases he relied solely on the quotations from Majlisi. Speculation in this regard is inevitable, but given that his sources were important Shiʿi collections, it is not unlikely that he read them directly. More important however is the evidence of Jadid al-Islam's direct knowledge of Majlisi's work. Since Majlisi did not live to see his project completed, some scholars of the stature of Yusuf al-Bahrani (d. 1772) only had access to the first volumes of the *Bihar*, even well into the eighteenth century. However, others like al-Hurr al-ʿAmili (d. 1693), who were closer to him, were able to draw from relatively later volumes of the collection in their own work.[17] Therefore, the fact that Jadid al-Islam could display a fairly detailed knowledge of Majlisi's work bears witness to his integration into influential circles of knowledge in Isfahan.

The hadith from the *al-Anwar al-mawlad al-nabi* (and from the *Bihar al-anwar*) in this section revolve around the creation myth, and trace their chain of transmission back to ʿAli. There are other similar versions of this myth, including one in the *Nahj al-balagha* (*The Peak of Eloquence*), the book of sayings attributed to ʿAli and compiled by al-Sharif al-Radi (d. 1015).[18] However, the sequence and the details in Jadid al-Islam's narrative, and in this case his own explicit mention of al-Bakri, clearly indicate that our author used either al-Bakri's text directly or through Majlisi. The passage in question starts by recounting that the *Light of Muhammad* (*nūr-i Muḥammadī*) was created before all things. God calls it 'the intention and the purpose (*murād va maqṣūd* [in Jadid al-Islam's text]/ *al-murād wa-l-murīd* [in al-Bakri and in Majlisi])"and the "chosen one (*bar-guzīdih* [Jadid al-Islam]/*khayra* [al-Bakri/Majlisi])' of creation, without whose existence He would not have created the world.[19] The Light grows into a flame, from which God creates twelve tents (*ḥijāb*), corresponding to power (*qudra*), might (*'aẓima*), glory (*'uzza*), awe (*hayba*), omnipotence (*jabrūt*), mercy (*raḥma*), prophecy (*nubuwwa*), grandeur (*kibriyā'*), exaltation (*manzila*), highness (*raf'a*), supremacy (*sa'āda*) and intercession (*shafā'a*). God orders the Light to enter each tent and to spend twelve thousand years in the first one, eleven thousand in the second one, and so forth until reaching one thousand years in the 'tent of intercession' (*ḥijāb al-shafā'a*).[20] God then creates twenty seas from the same Light, corresponding to glory (*'uzza*), patience (*ṣabr*), modesty (*khushū'*), humility (*tawāḍi'*), satisfaction (*riḍā*), loyalty (*wafā'*), forbearance (*ḥilm*), abstinence (*par-hīz-kārī* [Jadid al-Islam]/ *taqā* [al-Bakri/ Majlisi]), fear (*khashiyya*), repentance (*ināba*), well-doing (*'amal*), generosity (*mazīd*), rightful guidance (*hidāya*), conservation (*ṣiyāna*) and diffidence (*ḥayā*).[21] From the water of these seas, God creates the prophets. He then creates a gem (*jawhar*) from the Light and divides it in two. From one half comes sweet water and from the other comes heaven (*'arsh*). Next, God builds a throne (*kursī*) in heaven and orders a pen (*qalam*) to write down the proclamation of His unity (*tawḥīd*). The pen asks in what terms this should be expressed, to which He responds by reciting the Muslim proclamation of faith (*shahāda*): 'There is no God but God, and Muhammad is His Prophet (*lā ilāha illā Allāh wa Muḥammad Rasūl Allāh*)'. Upon hearing the name of Muhammad, the pen takes a bow and asks who this person was. God responds:

> If it were not for Him, I would not have created you. It is only for him that I have created my creation (*Agar ū namī būd tūrā khalaq namī kardam va nayāfarīdam khalq-i khūd rā magar az barā-yi ū* [Jadid al-Islam]/ *fa-lāwlahu mā khalaqtuka wa lā khalaqtu khalqī illā li-ajlihi* [al-Bakri/ Majlisi]).[22]

God goes on to create the world and its creatures and illuminates half of heaven with the light of erudition (*faḍl*) and the other half with the light of justice (*'adl*). From erudition He derives reason (*'aql*), knowledge (*'ilm*), forbearance (*ḥilm*) and benevolence (*sakhā'*); and from each of these He derives other qualities: from reason – fear (*khawf*), from knowledge – satisfaction (*riḍā*), from forbearance – cordiality (*mawdda*) and from benevolence –

affection (*maḥabba*). All these constitute attributes of the Prophet and his family. The passage closes with the creation of Adam, who raises his sight towards heaven and sees the *shahāda* written on it.[23] Having quoted this hadith, Jadid al-Islam provides his interpretation, once again going back to biblical parallelisms to argue that it was with this same primordial spirit of Muhammad that John the Baptist was baptised.[24]

The choice of a passage on the *nūr-i Muḥammadī* in this section serves both as a scriptural and thematic complement to the biblical theme of the Paraclete: in his quest to demonstrate the scriptural continuity between the biblical premonition and Islamic tradition, Jadid al-Islam recurs to a hadith that evokes the idea that the essence of the Prophet (and hence his mission) pre-existed the rest of the creation. However, religious scholars have historically disagreed on what the trope of the *nūr-i Muḥammadī* entailed, with some arguing that the pre-destination of the prophetic mission of Muhammad should not be confused with his pre-existence.[25] Within Shiʿism, the Imams are considered as representatives of the *nūr*, the transmission of which, in the words of Mohammad Ali Amir-Moezzi, 'probably constitutes the most important element of the capital notion of *waṣīya* (viceregency)'.[26] Thus, the choice of the trope of the *nūr* carries with it a subtle ʿAlid component that reaffirms the Shiʿi character of the text, not only because of the sectarian adherence of the compilers of the narration, but also because of the elements in its content. Further, the fact that this hadith is not necessarily among the most commonly used in reference to the theme of the *nūr* (nor is al-Bakri's work for that matter)[27] attests to Jadid al-Islam's knowledge of Shiʿi tradition beyond the most common pool of scriptural references.

While the above section was concerned with the qualities of the prophethood and the premonition of Muhammad's mission, another hadith-rich section of the *Sayf al-muʾminin* is devoted to the nature of the Imamate and to the sacrifice of Husayn in Karbala. The section in question, which appears in the context of Jadid al-Islam's commentary on the sacrifice of Isaac, is more elaborate in its way of intertwining the hadith with the biblical references, and draws from more collections. Consistent with commonly held Islamic views on the matter, our author argues that it was not Isaac but Ismael that Abraham was asked to sacrifice before being offered the sacrificial lamb as a substitute. He builds his case by pointing to the presence of the word *unigenitus* in the Latin Vulgate in reference to the son that was prepared for sacrifice. He then provides the definition given by Ambrogio Calepino in his lexicon, this being of course someone without siblings (*farzand-i yigānih* [Jadid al-Islam]/*filius qui unic est* [Calepino]).[28] He then notes that in *Genesis* 18, in the passage in which Ismael is circumcised at the age of thirteen, Isaac had not been born yet. Therefore, Ismael could be said to have been *unigenitus* until that moment, whereas Isaac never was.[29]

Up to this point the argumentative resources are circumscribed to biblical proofs, with the notion of *taḥrīf* once again being brought up in reference to the alleged interchanging of the names of the sons of Abraham. But Jadid al-Islam then builds a bridge between his refutation of the biblical text and the hadith we are concerned with, by establishing a link between the sacrifices of Ismael and Husayn. He starts by quoting reports that show that biblical prophets were admonished about Husayn's fate in Karbala beforehand. In one of them, Zacharias asks God to tell him the names of the family of the Prophet (*ahl al-bayt*). The Angel Gabriel descends upon him and recites the names. While hearing the list, Zacharias is moved to tears every time he hears the name of Husayn. He asks why this name had such an effect on him, and Gabriel tells him the story of Husayn's martyrdom. Zacharias is then told the esoteric meaning of the Arabic letters *kāf*, *hā*, *yā*, *ʿayn*, *ṣād*: *kāf* stood for Karbala, *hā* for *halāk* (the destruction that would fall upon the Prophet), *yā* for Yazid, who would inflict injustice (*ẓulm*) on Husayn, *ʿayn* for *ʿaṭash* (thirst), and *ṣād* for *ṣabr* (patience). Upon hearing this, Zacharias secludes himself for three days lamenting the fate of the family of the Prophet. In response to his prayer he is granted a son, John (Yahya), who like Husayn, is born after six months of gestation.[30] This tradition appears in *al-Ihtijaj* (*The Contention*) of Ahmad b. Ali b. Abi Talib al-Tabrisi (d. twelfth century)[31] and is quoted also in Majlisi's *Bihar al-anwar*.[32]

Following the same thematic line, the next hadith, which appears in Ibn Babawayh's *al-Amali* (*The Dictations*) and again in Majlisi's *Bihar al-anwar*, shows Jesus and his disciples approaching a group of grazing gazelles while walking in Karbala. As the gazelles start crying, Jesus sits down and joins in their lamentation. The disciples ask him why he cries, and he replies that it was in that land that the son of Ahmad would be killed.[33] Traditions similar to the latter were recurrent in Shiʿi discourse. Linking Husayn to

Jesus is a thematic commonplace in Shiʿi literature, in which we can find stories about Husayn praising God while still being in Fatima's womb – a pun on the Qurʿanic passage in which Muhammad speaks from the cradle (19:29–33)– or claims that Husayn ascended to heaven like Jesus in the Christian tradition.[34]

As the section progresses, Jadid al-Islam cites another hadith, this time explicitly revealing its source: al-ʿAllama al-Hilli's (d. 1325) manual of prayer *Minhaj al-salah fi ikhtisar al-misbah* (*The Way of Wisdom through a Succinct Light*). The fact that he reveals this source explicitly perhaps implies that he recognises in it a higher weight in terms of its authoritative status. Al-Hilli's figure is of course of utmost significance for various reasons: firstly, he is considered one of the founding pillars of a distinctive Shiʿi theology and was the first scholar to bear the title of *Āyat Allāh* (*Sign of God*).[35] Because of his involvement at the court of the Ilkhanid ruler Muhammad Khudabandih Uljaytu (r. 1304–17), he was once credited for the conversion of the latter to Shiʿism.[36] Secondly, while al-Hilli's most significant contributions were of a theological nature, he also produced major contributions to the genre of apologetics, writing works in defense of the tenets of Imami Shiʿism, which would become a target of refutations: the most important of this was his *Minhaj al-karama fi maʿrifat al-imama* (*The Miraculous Way of Konwledge of the Imamate*), which was refuted by Ibn Taymiyya in his *Minhaj al-sunna al-nabawiyya* (*The Way of the Prophetic Tradition*).[37] Likewise, his *Nahj al-haqq wa kashf al-sidq* (*The Way of Rightness and the Unveiling of the Truth*), dedicated to Uljaytu, became the target of a refutation by the historian and scholar Fazl Allah Ruzbahan Khunji Isfahani (d. 1521), a fierce opponent of the Shiʿitisation of Iran.[38] And thirdly, and perhaps more importantly, al-Hilli represented one of the main historical pillars of the evolution of the concept of *ijtihād*. During Jadid al-Islam's time, al-Hillī was seen – somehow a posteriori – as a foundational figure of the Usuli trend in Shiʿi jurisprudence, which as mentioned before, advocated for widening the scope of *ijtihād* to derive legal judgements and opinions.[39] As such, his work was targeted by Muhammad Amin Astarabadi (d. 1626–7), whose *al-Fawaʾid al-Madaniyya* (*The Medinese Benefits)* was one of the pillars of Akhbari thought.[40] One can only speculate regarding the depth of Jadid al-Islam's knowledge of al-Hilli's work. It is conceivable that he could have studied it with Fazil-i Hindi, whose

Kashf al-litham (*The Lifting of the Veil*) was itself a detailed study of al-Hilli's *Qawaʿid al-ahkam* (*Principles of Legal Rulings*).[41]

The work of al-Hilli from which Jadid al-Islam quotes, the *Minhaj al-salah*, contains one of al-Hilli's most commonly copied passages, its eleventh chapter (*al-Bab al-hadi ʿashar*)[42], which was originally conceived as an independent piece.[43] Jadid al-Islam, however, quotes from a different section, thus showing that he did have access to the work in its entirety and not only to this excerpt. The section is question is the one devoted to 'what corresponds to the month of Muharram' (*fi-ma yataʿallaq bi-shahr Muharram al-Haram*). In this hadith, the Prophet visits Fatima in the presence of ʿAli, Hasan and Husayn. While performing the prayer, the Prophet is moved to tears and immediately after bursts out laughing. Perplexed, ʿAli asks him what the source of his affliction was, to which he responds that the Angel Gabriel had come to him during his prayer and had given him the news about their martyrdom:

> Your daughter will be the first one among your relatives to join you after injustice (*ẓulm*) is done against her and after her right is taken away from her and after the inheritance of Fadak is taken from her and after injustice is done against her husband and after they crush the bones of her flank. Injustice will be done against your nephew, he will be prevented from his right to the Imamate and he will be killed. There will be injustice done against Hasan, and he will be deprived from his right and he will be killed with poison. Husayn too will be deprived from his right and he will be slaughtered and carried away with horses, and his dwelling place will be plundered and his daughters will be captured and strangers will pollute him with burial blood.[44]

The fact of quoting al-Hilli should of course not be taken as an indication of Jadid al-Islam's allegiance in the Usuli–Akhbari dispute, especially given the nature of this quote. At most, this suggests that Jadid al-Islam could not have been staunchly pro-Akhbari, given al-Hilli's stature among the Usulis, but neither can it be taken as an unequivocal declaration of commitment to the latter trend. I will revisit this question later in this book, in the context of our author's stance on Sufism. To my knowledge, there are no clear indications in his work suggesting that he developed a position on the matter. What this does signal, however, is once again the depth of our author's exposure to texts beyond the most basic and canonical hadith collections.

As the text goes on, Jadid al-Islam continues to develop the theme of the premonition of Husayn's martyrdom through other narrations. In one of them, which appears both in al-Kulayni's (d. 940) *Kitab al-kafi (The Sufficient Book)* and in Ibn Qawlawayh's (d. 977) *Kamil al-ziyarat* (*The Complete Guide to Pilgrimage*), the Angel Gabriel greets the Prophet and tells him that Fatima will have a son who will be slayed by his community. The prophet replies that he does not need such a descendant, but the angel comes to him once again and tells him that this son of Fatima will bear the imamate, the command (*wilāya*) and the vice-regency (*waṣīyya*). Upon hearing this, the Prophet is satisfied.[45] A series of hadith then follow which enforce the notion of the divine guidance of the Imams and of the family of the Prophet. One of them alludes to the well-known theme of the tablet (*lawḥ*) of Fatima. There are many versions of this hadith, but Jadid al-Islam's rendition is closer to the version that appears in the *al-Fada'il* (*The Virtues*) of Shadhan b. Jibra'il al-Qummi (d. 1261–2). In it, one of the companions of the Prophet, Jabir b. 'Abd Allah Ansari (d. 697) comes to Fatima's house and finds her holding a green tablet with white letters. He asks her what the tablet was, and she answers:

> This is a tablet that God has given to the Prophet. On it are the names of my father, my husband and my two sons, as well as those of my extended progeny. My father gave it to me as sign of good tidings (*tā bashārat dahad marā bih ān* [Jadid al-Islam]/ *li-yubashiranī bi-dhalika* [Jibra'il al-Qummi]).[46]

She then hands him the tablet so that he can read an inscription that says:

> This is a book [given] from God, the Powerful (*'azīz*) and Wise (*ḥakīm*) to the Prophet Muhammad, His light, His messenger, His veil (*ḥijāb*) and His sign (*dalīl*), brought to him by Gabriel [in Jadid al-Islam's version /by the Holy Spirit (*Ruḥ al-Amīn*) in Jibra'il al-Qummi] from the abode of the Lord of the Universe (*Rabb al-'ālamīn*).[47]

Another tradition, recorded in Ibn Babawayh's *al-Amali*, combines the theme of the premonition of Husayn's death with that of the quasi-miraculous nature of his childhood. In it, the Prophet goes to Umm Salama's (d. 596) house and asks her not to let anyone approach him. However,

Husayn, a toddler at the time, runs towards him. Umm Salama chases the child to prevent him from disturbing the Prophet, but when she reaches him, the Prophet is already carrying him in his arms. Muhammad then shows her something he is carrying in his hand and says:

> This is Gabriel, who has told me that Husayn will be killed. And this is the dust upon which he will be killed. I will keep this dust close to me so when it turns into blood, [I will know] my beloved [Husayn] has been killed (*har vaqt kih munqalab bih khūn gardad, ḥabīb-i man bih qatl rasīdih bāshad* [Jadid al-Islam]/*fa-idhā ṣārat damman fa-qad qutila ḥabībī* [Ibn Babawayh]).[48]

Jadid al-Islam then refers to another popular tradition, which is intended to demonstrate the quasi-miraculous nature of Husayn even before his birth. This appears in Ibn Qawlawayh's *Kamil al-ziyarat*[49] as well as in Nisaburi's *Rawdat al-wa'izin*.[50] This narration tells the story of Fitrus, an angel God had punished by cutting off his wings and exiling him to an island in the middle of the ocean. One day, the Angel Gabriel is sent to Muhammad to summon him upon God's presence. As he is on his way, Gabriel passes by the island, where he finds the fallen angel. Fitrus asks Gabriel to take him along, hoping that Muhammad would intercede on his behalf. When he hears this, Muhammad orders Fitrus to touch the cradle of Husayn. Upon doing so, the angel's wings grow again.[51]

Finally, in an example that deviates from Jadid al-Islam's pattern of references until then, he cites a source, which he in fact misattributes. He claims to be quoting from the *Kitab Sulaym b. Qays*, an early Shi'i text, which has long been debated by scholars, because of reasonable doubts surrounding the historicity of its alleged author.[52] What he presents instead is a hadith recorded in Ibn Babawayh's *al-Amali* and reproduced in Nisaburi's *Rawdat al-wa'izin* and in Majlisi's *Bihar al-anwar*. This tradition shows the Prophet's aunt and companion Safiyya b. 'Abd al-Muttalib (d. *c.* 640) handing Husayn to the Prophet at the moment of his birth. The Prophet carries the baby and introduces his tongue into his mouth. When the baby starts to suck, Safiyya tells the Prophet that he should only be fed honey and milk. The baby then urinates and the Prophet kisses his forehead, hands him to Safiyya, and cries out loud, saying: 'May God curse the folk that will kill you [oh son] (*laʿnat kunad Khudā bar qawmī kih kushandih-i tū-and* [Jadid al-Islam]/*laʿn Allāh qawman hum qātalūka yā bunaya* [Ibn Babawayh, Nisaburi, Majlisi])'. Safiyya asks who could do such a thing, and the Prophet replies that it would be someone from the Umayyad family.[53]

Different versions of this story were used recurrently in Shiʿi literature as a proof of the predestined mission of Husayn and of the quasi-miraculous circumstances of his birth. For example, Mahmoud Ayoub has identified another hadith in which the Prophet suckles Husayn with his tongue or with his thumb.[54] As Ayoub has shown, many of these narrations (and of similar ones) have played a pivotal role in the imagery of Shiʿi folk devotionalism. Thus, their inclusion in Jadid al-Islam's text is not so much a resource to provide his Muslim audience with little-known hadith evidence for the validity of Islamic revelation – and of specifically Shiʿi tenets. Rather, these citations serve as a thematic bridge through which potential Muslim readers could draw parallels between the biblical signs the author presents and other motifs, which are more recognisable in their tradition. In this sense, the recourse to the hadith in the text serves a quasi-performative function similar to that of a sermon: the audience is presumed to have a certain degree of familiarity with the scriptural passages and examples evoked, but must reaffirm its devotion through the re-enacting and remembrance of episodes of symbolical significance, such as the events of Karbala. This could also explain Jadid al-Islam's choice to neither explicitly reveal most of his sources nor to cite the excerpts in Arabic, as his potential readers are likely to have heard at least some version of the stories. However, the precision of the quotes, which correspond so closely to the Arabic originals, also suggests that Jadid al-Islam was working with those texts directly at the moment of writing or had at least studied them before with a certain degree of depth and rigor.

Engaging Christian Sources

In parallel to his use of Muslim sources, Jadid al-Islam also references a series of works that can be grouped under the umbrella term of 'Christian sources'. By this I do not simply mean Christian scripture, but rather books on the history of the Catholic Church, and even one by a Protestant scholar written in response to Jerome Xavier. While some of the works Jadid al-Islam uses were well-known classics of Church history from preceding periods, others were written closer to his own time. It is possible to gain a rough idea of the materials he could have had access to in Isfahan during his time as a missionary. In her study of the inventory of the missionary library in Isfahan from the sixteenth to the eighteenth centuries, Carnoy-Torabi has identified around 780 titles and 850 exemplars. Four hundred and forty of these are known to be from the seventeenth century, of which 198 were in Latin, with Italian and French having also an important presence in the collection, and with Rome and Venice representing the place of origin of the largest number of books. The library was not exclusively composed of 'religious literature'. The collection also housed exemplars of the works of Cicero, the life of Richelieu, as well as books on medicine and geography. Dictionaries of various languages, including Middle Eastern ones, were also an important part of the collection.[55] However, the most important clues for our purposes come from the collection of religious works: the Latin Vulgate was the most commonly used Bible, although French biblical translations were also available. Other important titles included Aquinas' *Summa Theologica*, an exemplar of the work of Saint Augustine, various versions of the lives of Christ and the saints and the works of more recent theologians such as the Jesuits Cornelius Cornelii a Lapide (d. 1637), Leonardus Lessius (d. 1623), Tomás Sánchez (d. 1610), Saint Robert Bellarmine (d. 1621), the work of the cardinal and church historian Caesar Baronius (d. 1607) and a series of compendiums of the proceedings of Church councils.[56] Unfortunately, Carnoy-Torabi does not disclose the full list of titles available at the library and therefore it is not possible to verify whether all of Jadid al-Islam's 'Christian' references were included in the collection.

As we will see shortly, through the subtle hints included in his references, our author's critique of Christianity, while presented through the lenses of a purely Muslim critique, also reveals a degree of awareness of intra-Catholic disputes surrounding the Council of Trent. In contrast with his use of Muslim sources, Jadid al-Islam's treatment of Christian texts is rather schematic: while in the case of the abovementioned hadith he makes use of extended quotations, for the Christian sources he mostly references the titles and provides short paraphrases of key passages. It is plausible that by the time Jadid al-Islam was working on his polemics, he no longer had access to the original sources and was relying solely on memory. This could explain some imprecisions, as we will see shortly. However, it could also be that he considered it less necessary to be precise in his quotations of Christian literature in a book intended for a mostly Muslim audience. Thus, while of a relatively minor philological value, these references play a symbolic and authoritative function within the embroidery of the text, because they allow Jadid al-Islam to position himself as a figure of authority in the knowledge of the Christian tradition.

The section that best illustrates our author's use of Christian sources is the one devoted to contesting the legitimacy of Saint Peter as the successor of Christ and by extension of the Church of Rome as Christ's institutional heir. Here, Jadid al-Islam seeks to show his Muslim readers that the question of legitimate authority and the succession of Christ was a matter of contention between Christian factions. To illustrate his point, he refers to a critique made by the Dutch scholar Ludovicus de Dieu (d. 1642) against two of Jerome Xavier's works, the *Mirʾat al-Quds* and the *Dastan-i Pitru*. A minister of the Dutch Reformed Church and a son of a Calvinist minister, De Dieu studied Oriental languages at Leiden. His interest in Persian was triggered partly after coming across a Jewish–Persian translation of the Pentateuch by Rabbi Yaʿqub b. Taʾus. Upon discovering Jerome Xavier's Persian texts, perhaps during his sojourn in India, he published them in Leiden in 1639 under the titles *Historia Christi Persice* and *Historia S. Petri*. The publication contains a Latin commentary refuting what he saw as Catholic propaganda and the misrepresentation of the spirit of the Scripture.[57] Jadid al-Islam most likely possessed or had access to a copy of De Dieu's works at the moment of writing, as suggested by the precision of his reference in which he even provides a page number, which contrasts with his general treatment of the rest of his Christian sources. By using De Dieu's work, that is, by bringing forward the arguments of another Christian, Jadid al-Islam seeks to present his critique as unbiased. This becomes all the more pertinent when anticipating criticism for his newly acquired Muslim zeal, as evidenced by the way he presents this text, saying that he does it:

> [. . .] in case Christians do not accept what I have said against these Papists, [saying] it is a mere conjecture (*amā az barā-yi ān kih īn guftār-i marā kih dar bārih-i īn Rīm-Pāpāyān-i kuffār dar īnjā taqrīr kardam Naṣārā napandārand kih maḥẓ-i adʿā-st*).[58]

Jadid al-Islam then proceeds with some references to heretics from Classical and Medieval sources. He starts by alluding to Tertullian (d. 240 CE), from whose letter against Marcion of Sinope (d. 160 CE) he allegedly gets the story of Marcion's excommunication by Pope Zephyrinus (papacy 199–217 CE). This story, however, does not appear either in Tertullian's *Adversus Marcionem* (*Against Marcion*) or in the much later Pseudo-Tertullian's *Adversus Omnes Haereses* (*Again all Heretics*).[59] The story can be traced, however, to Saint Optatus of Milevis (d. fourth century) in his *Contra Schismate (Against the Schismatics)* together with a reference to Tertullian,[60] and thus it is possible that Jadid al-Islam was working from memory or with other sources that also report the same information. More accurate is Jadid al-Islam's next reference, which concerns the cases of Pope Liberius (p. 352–66 CE) and the anti-pope Felix II (p. 355–65 CE), taken from Saint Jerome's *Chronicon*.[61]

Once the lack of unanimity on the authority of the Church of Rome has been established, Jadid al-Islam goes on to provide evidence for the existence of contradictory opinions even within the hierocracy of the Catholic Church. For this, he starts with a reference to Eusebius of Caesarea (d. *c.* 339–40 CE). While our author does not specify from which of Eusebius's books he is drawing his information, it is obvious that it would have to be from his *Historia Ecclesiastica* (*Ecclesiastic History*), a history of the popes up to the fourth century. Jadid al-Islam has Eusebius saying that Pope Marcellinus (p. 296–304 CE) was removed from the papacy after offering sacrifices to idols. However, the only thing the *Historia Ecclesiastica* says about Pope Marcellinus is that he was overtaken by persecution, after succeeding Pope Caius (p. 283–96 CE).[62] There are however two sources that talk about Pope Marcellinus's idolatry. One is an addendum that appears in only one manuscript of the *Liber Pontificalis* (*Pontifical Book*), a compilation of biographies of the popes assembled throughout various centuries.[63] The other is a document known as the *Passio Marcellinis* (*The Passion of Marcellinus*). These two allude to the Council of Sinuessa, an event that almost certainly never occurred,[64] at which it was said about Marcellinus:

> And after a few days a synod was held in the province of Campania in the city of Sessana [Sinuessa], where with his own lips he professed his penitence in the presence of 180 bishops. He wore a garment of haircloth

> and ashes upon his head and repented, saying that he had sinned. Then Diocletian was wroth and seized him and bade him sacrifice to images. But he cried out with tears, saying, 'It repenteth me sorely for my former ignorance', and he began to utter blasphemy against Diocletian and the images of demons made with hands. So, inspired by penitence, he was beheaded.[65]

The origin of this accusation against Marcellinus comes from the Donatist bishop Petilian (d. fifth century), and was the object of a refutation by Saint Augustine in *Contra Litteras Petiliani* (*Against Petilian's Letters*).[66] This implies that our author, well acquainted with the work of Saint Augustine, the eponym of the religious order to which he had belonged, would be ascribing in this passage an authoritative status to a source he had initially been trained to refute or dismiss.

But there is yet another source that reproduces this portrait of Pope Marcellinus, which also happens to be the source that Jadid al-Islam uses immediately after in this section.[67] As another example of sinful popes, our author references the work of the Polish Dominican friar Martin of Opava (d. 1278) and his depiction of Pope Sylvester II (p. 999–1003) engaging in magic and in 'other Satanic [or mischievous] [activities] (*ākhar-i shayṭānī*)'.[68] This appears indeed in Opava's *Chronicon Pontificum et Imperatorum* (*Chronicle of Pontifices and Emperors*), a chronicle on the popes which enjoyed a great degree of popularity in the Middle Ages.[69] The story of Sylvester II, a French polymath also well-known by his pre-pontifical name, Gerbert d'Aurillac, had wide circulation in medieval times. One of the earliest accounts of this legend is the one by William of Malmesbury (d. 1143) in his *Gesta Pontificum Anglorum* (*The Deeds of the Bishops of England*).[70] Both Malmesbury and Opava worked as editors of the *Liber Pontificalis* at some point in their lives.[71] Both Opava's *Chronicon* and the *Liber Pontificalis* claim that Silvester II consulted the devil on various matters. These sources even mention that the devil helped him become bishop and pope and assured him that his papacy would last for as long as he did not hold a mass in Jerusalem, a transgression he would inadvertently commit by officiating at the Church of Jerusalem in Latran.[72] The popularity of this story as an archetypical example of a sorcerer-pope makes its appearance in Jadid al-Islam's text unsurprising. And once again, as with the case of the *Adversus Marcionem*, our author ascribes here an authoritative status to a legend he would have had to refute as a Catholic missionary.

In continuing with the examples of theological disagreements between popes, Jadid al-Islam mentions how some papal theological positions were abrogated by succeeding pontifices. For this, he draws from the *Vitae Pontificum* (*The Lives of the Popes*) by the Renaissance humanist Bartolomeo Platina (d. 1481). From the latter he references the case of Pope John IX (p. 898–900), who rejected every judgement from Stephen VI (p. 896–7), who himself had rejected every judgement made before him;[73] as well as that of Pope Formosus (p. 891–6) rejecting the judgements of John VIII (p. 872–82) and Sergius II (p. 844–7). [74] And finally, our author cites Cesar Baronius's *Annales Ecclesiastici* (*Ecclesiatic Annals*) in reference to Gregory VII (p. 1073–85), who he accuses of disbelief, and to John XX (p. 1276–7).[75] When using these latter sources, our author commits a couple of minor imprecisions, which although banal, strengthen the hypothesis that he no longer had access to them at the time of the composition of his treatise: first, the entries for post-1227 popes such as John XX were completed by Odorico Rinaldi (or Raynaldi, d. 1671), not by Baronius himself. And second, Pope John XX, although indeed the twentieth pope of his name, had to assume the name John XXI due to an administrative confusion.[76] As with the case of Pope Sylvester II and Marcellinus, both John XXI and Gregory VII were also the objects of unfavourable portrayals in certain legends, with both being accused of necromancy.[77] In addition, accusations against Gregory VII became widespread among Protestant polemicists through the work of the Puritan English theologian John Foxe (d. 1587).[78] Thus, the inclusion of these popes in Jadid al-Islam's text are also part of a standard pool of references to heretical popes and a valuable, although not necessarily novel, tool to further undermine the holiness of the institution of the papacy from *within* Christianity.

One reference in Jadid al-Islam's text, however, is of particular significance, given that it subtly hints at some of the most crucial debates on the canonical status of the Latin Vulgate among sixteenth-century Catholic theologians, including many based in the Iberian Peninsula. When alluding to the apostasy of Pope Honorius I (p. 625–38) and of Stephanus VI (p. 896–7), our author refers to a certain Malikyar and to his book *Contraria*. While it is difficult to identify this title, the character is most certainly the Spanish theologian Melchor Cano (d. 1560), who does indeed refer to these popes in one of his minor works.[79] But more important than Cano's mentioning of these popes *per se* is the fact that he was a critic of some of the major theological consensus of the Council of Trent. In his *De Locis Theologicis* (*On Theological Matters*), Cano addressed the question of whether Saint Jerome's Vulgata could be used as an authoritative source or whether it was necessary to refer back to the original Hebrew and Greek sources of the Bible. He argued in favour of recurring to the original sources to resolve disputations on matters of faith and custom. This position contradicted the consensus reached during the Council, which accorded the Vulgata an authoritative status on such questions. Cano was of course careful not to imply that the Vulgata was subjected to falsification as such, especially after being elevated to such canonical status. He also encountered criticism for being too close to Judaism for defending the higher status of the Hebrew text.[80] Further, in his *Consultatio Theologica* (*Theological Consultation*), written for Philip II, Cano questioned the dogma of the infallibility of the pope and advised the king to curtail the encroaching power of the Church, warning that the popes could take over the political power in Spain.[81]

From his short reference to Cano in the *Sayf al-muʾminin*, we cannot determine the extent to which Jadid al-Islam was acquainted with his opera. However, it is unlikely that he would have only known him from the minute reference to the popes in the abovementioned quote. It is, on the other hand, surprising that he would not elaborate more on Cano's scepticism towards the Vulgata in a work in which one of the leitmotifs is precisely the alleged corruption of the latter. At the risk of falling into the trap of a historiographical fallacy, I would argue that this reference to Cano suggests that Jadid al-Islam's choice to focus on the *taḥrīf* of the Vulgata was informed by his awareness of intra-Catholic debates such as this one. Jadid al-Islam's genealogy of *taḥrīf* as originating at the moment of assembly, but mostly at the moment of translation, of the original biblical sources, with Saint Jerome as the primary culprit, is a way of taking Cano's scepticism about the consensus of Trent to its logical and radical conclusion. This hypothesis is reinforced by the fact that Jadid al-Islam then also makes a passing reference to what he calls *Kitab-i Kunsiliyarun*, an obvious reference to the summaries of the conciliar proceedings which Carnoy-Torabi has identified in the catalogue of the missionary library of Isfahan, as we have previously seen.[82] Moreover, as we have also seen in Chapter three, in the Ottoman realm, Murad b. ʿAbd Allah also traced the moment of *taḥrīf* to the assembly and translation of the Bible into vernaculars, which shows that this particular understanding of *taḥrīf* was not uncommon in the early modern period.[83] What is less clear, however, is whether Jadid al-Islam could have also had access to works like Murad d. ʿAbd Allah's. Speculation on this matter is inevitable, but our author – and other polemicists of this period, for that matter – could have very well been influenced by both conciliar debates as well as by the use of polemical tropes in previous works.

Appropriating Shiʿi Tradition *while* Engaging Christian Sources

Finally, in a section devoted to discussing the institution of the Inquisition, Jadid al-Islam combines Muslim and Christian references in a way reminiscent of his overall treatment of both kinds of corpus throughout the text. He starts his discussion by alluding to the letter of Saint Jerome to Pope Damasus I (p. 366–84 CE). This well-known document was written as a preface to Jerome's translation of the Gospels.[84] As seen in Chapter three, Jadid al-Islam continues to develop the accusation of *taḥrīf* against Jerome by pointing out that, according to his own confession, he had only acquired reading knowledge of Hebrew late in his life.[85] He then adds another layer to the history of scriptural falsification and of the tenet of the Trinity by saying that in their quest to standardise the belief system of their 'forged religion' (*dīn-i ikhtirāʿ-ī*), Constantine the Great (d. 337 CE) and his successors persecuted Jews and Christians who had access to the untampered books. He describes the process of persecution as follows:

> Whoever entered any of their cities [that is, those under the rule of these kings] with a book on his possession had to take it to one of the religious overseers (*dārūghih-i dīn*) that were appointed (*taʿyīn namūdih*) for this purpose or had to show it to a person appointed by one of them. And either the overseer or the appointee would then have to examine the book to see whether it contained anything opposed (*mukhālifatī dārad*) to the foundations and ramification (*uṣūl va furūʿ*) of their false religion (*dīn-i bāṭil*) or

> against the book which Jerome had forged for them (*az barā-yi īshān sākhtih ast*), and they would then either burn the book or give it back to its owner.[86]

He then mentions that this process eventually led to the institutionalisation of the Inquisition and that every few years these inquisitors (*ingīzītūr*) would gather the books of each city for a similar process of examination, imposing punishments against repeated offenders that ranged from flogging to burning at the stake. The idea of persecuting noncompliance to a fledging orthodoxy and of the fixing of the biblical canon under Constantine is a somehow loose evocation of the First Council of Nicea of 325 CE. Further, the notion that a group of Jews and Christians had access to the true scriptures before the standardisation of a forged canon invites comparisons with the previously mentioned genealogy of *taḥrīf* in the work of ʿAbd al-Jabbar, according to which the Jews who rejected Roman ways went on to receive the Islamic revelation, while those who accepted Roman ways became the later Christians.[87]

In addition, this account also reads as a subtle nod to the history of a different kind of *taḥrīf*, namely that of the falsification of the canonical ʿUthmanic codex of the Qurʾan. According to some Shiʿa, particularly from the pre-Buyid period, the original Qurʾan was transmitted to ʿAli. This version of the book was supposed to be much lengthier, and it contained an explicit condemnation of the first three caliphs as well as praise for ʿAli and his descendants. After ʿAli's adversaries dismissed the integral version of the Qurʾan, he concealed it and transmitted it secretly to the Imams of his lineage.[88] The idea of the *taḥrīf* of Qurʾan is by no means accepted by a majority of Shiʿa, and was indeed opposed by major Shiʿi scholars in the second century AH.[89] However, this notion has been sufficiently widespread in the Shiʿi tradition to be easily recongisable in subtle references, such as in this passage of the *Sayf al-muʾminin*.

Until this point, this section draws exclusively from Christian sources. However, to make a final point about how the true revelation was kept inaccessible until the coming of Islam, Jadid al-Islam closes this passage with an account featuring Salman al-Farisi, which can be found with similar wording in Ibn Saʿd's *Tabaqat al-kubra* (*The Book of Major Classes*) and in Ibn Hisham's rendition of the *Sira*.[90] Although these sources are of course not Shiʿi per se, what matters is that they are brought about in reference to

Salman al-Farisi, who enjoys a special status in Shiʿism. In this well-known passage, Salman travels through the Levant meeting with priests and bishops from various different churches, but all of them pass away shortly after due to old age. The last bishop Salman meets with urges him to be patient, telling him that no other bishops had access to the Truth, which was soon to be revealed to him by the Seal of the Prophets:

> In this day and age I do not believe in anyone who comes along my way, but it is evident that the Messenger of the End of Times (*payghambar-i ākhar-i zaman*) is near, and he will revive (*iḥyāʾ kardan*) the people (*millat*) of Abraham, he will emerge from within the Arab realm and will be exiled from his land towards a palm-filled terrain (*nakhlistān*) between two stony fields (*sangistān*). Go and offer him your service and send him my regards.[91]

In this passage, we see once again how the Muslim source is quoted accurately even if it is not explicitly revealed, while the Christian references are loosely paraphrased or adapted, even when the source is mentioned. As a whole, however, what both this and the rest of the passages referred to in this chapter show is the cross-fertilisation of traditions, which mixes both historical and theological components. On a deeper level, we see how the process of confessionalisation of the Christian West finds its way into the text through subtle references to Protestant arguments against papal authority. Through this, and through the equally subtle importation of intra-Catholic debates on the popes and on the Vulgata, Jadid al-Islam *Catholicises* his theological adversary in the same way that he *Shiʿitisises* his idea of a rightful community of believers through his hadith citations. Thus, as already suggested in Chapter three, Jadid al-Islam adds a sectarian layer to the standard dimension of interreligious polemics. This makes his text a true intellectual production of its time, dispelling any doubts we may have harboured regarding the malleability and the capacity for renewal within the *dalāʾil* tradition.

Notes

1. David Thomas, 'Ali l-Ṭabarī', p. 671
2. Monferrer Sala, 'Fray Anselmo Turmeda', p. 328.
3. For the most detailed philological investigation on this regard, see Robert Beier,

'Una coincidència textual entre la Tuḥfa d'Anselm Turmeda', pp. 83–8. For the foundations of the discussion, see Asín Palacios, 'El original árabe de Disputa del Asno', pp. 1–51; See also Beier, 'Introduction' to *Anselm Turmeda,* pp. 9–10.

4. Koertner, 'We Have Made Clear the Signs', p. 3.
5. Ibid. p. 68–70.
6. Ibid. p. 120.
7. Ibid. pp. 205–6.
8. Ibid. p. 216.
9. Melchert, 'Khargūshī, *Tahdhīb al-Asrār*', p. 31.
10. Koertner, 'We Have Made Clear the Signs', pp. 124–5.
11. Ibid. p. 61.
12. Al-Tabari, *Dalaʾil al-imama.* See also Tihrani, *al-Dhariʿa*, vol. 8, pp. 241–7.
13. Tihrani, *al-Dhariʿa*, vol. 8, pp. 239, 248–9, 253. Many more works of this kind were written from the nineteenth century onwards. Notable examples include Muhammad Mahdi b. Muhammad Jaʿfar al-Musawi (d. late nineteenth or early twentieth century) and ʿAbbas b. Hasan b. Jaʿfar Kashif al-Ghitaʾ (d. 1905). See *al-Dhariʿa*, vol. 8, pp. 241, 247.
14. For a comprehensive introduction to the nature of this debate, see Cole, *Sacred Space and Holy War*, pp. 58–77; see Cole, 'Shi'i Clerics in Iraq and Iran, 1722–1780'; Modarressi, 'Rationalism and Traditionalism in Shīʿī Jurisprudence'. For a more detailed study on the general characteristics of these two schools, seen through a contemporary source, see Newman, 'The Nature of the Akhbari/Usuli Dispute in Late-Safawid Iran', pp. 22–51. For a more detailed comparison of two pillars of the schools in question, see Gleave, *Inevitable Doubt*, particularly pp. 29–84.
15. SM, p. 67. For the hadith version, see Ibn Babawayh, *ʿUyun akhbar al-Rida*, vol. 2, pp. 142–6.
16. SM, pp. 67–8.
17. Kohlberg, 'Beḥār al-Alnwār'. For information on who assisted Majlisi in the compilation of the *Bihar al-anwar*, see Mahdavi, *Zindiginamih-i ʿAllamih-i Majlisi*, vol. 2, p. 226. For biographical sketches of these figures, see Stewart, 'The Autobiography of Yūsuf al-Baḥrānī', pp. 217–23. See also Cole, *Sacred Space and Holy War*, pp. 49–52. For al-Hurr al-ʿAmili, see Bar Asher, 'Ḥorr-e ʿĀmeli'; Scarcia, 'al-Ḥurr al-ʿĀmilī'. See also Abisaab, *Converting Persia*, pp. 95–6.
18. Al-Radi, *Nahj al-balagha*, pp. 40–4.
19. SM, p. 76; Majlisi, *Bihar al-anwar*, vol. 54, pp. 198–9

20. SM, p. 76; Majlisi, *Bihar al-anwar*, vol. 54, pp. 199–200. (for the terms, in the cases in which the Persian version corresponds to the Persianised version of the Arabic sources, I give only the Arabic transliteration).
21. SM, pp. 76–7; Majlisi, *Bihar al-anwar*, vol. 54, p. 200.
22. SM, p. 77; Majlisi, *Bihar al-anwar*, vol. 54, p. 201.
23. SM, p. 79; Majlisi, *Bihar al-anwar*, vol. 54, pp. 201–2.
24. SM, p. 81.
25. Consider, for example, the opinions of Ibn Taymiyya and al-Ghazali (d. 1111), see Uri Rubin, 'Nūr Muhammadī'.
26. 'La transmission de la lumière constitue peut-être l'élément le plus important de la notion capitale de waṣiyya', see Amir-Moezzi, *La religion discrète*, p. 131, 126–33. See also Uri Rubin, 'Pre-existence and light', pp. 65–7.
27. See for example the prevalence of Ibn Shahrashub, Ibn Sa'd and al-Suyuti (d. 1505) and the absence of references to al-Bakri in the examples cited by Rubin, 'Pre-existence and light', pp. 65–70; notice also the absence of references to al-Bakri in Amir-Moezzi, *La religion discrète*, pp. 126–33, 205–7, 237.
28. SM, p. 390; Calepino, *Dictioranium Latinum*, n. p.
29. SM, pp. 390–2.
30. Ibid. pp. 405–6.
31. al-Tabrisi, *al-Ihtijaj*, vol. 2, pp. 232–3.
32. Majlisi, *Bihar al-anwar*, vol. 14, p. 178; also vol. 44, p. 223.
33. SM, p. 406. The versions of Ibn Babawayh and Majlisi are too similar to allow us to identify Jadid al-Islam's source with precision. See Ibn Babawayh, *al-Amali*, p. 427; Majlisi, *Bihar al-anwar*, vol. 44, p. 253.
34. Ayoub, *Redemptive Suffering in Islām*, pp. 35–6. For a good compilation of examples of parallelisms between Jesus and Husayn, see Sindawi, 'Jesus and Ḥusayn Ibn 'Alī'. For examples of different portrayals of Husayn's martyrdom in literature, see Sindawi, 'The Image of Ḥusayn Ibn 'Alī in "Maqātil" Literature'.
35. Amir-Moezzi, 'Remarques sur les critères d'authenticité du hadith', p. 26.
36. Pfeiffer, 'Conversion Versions'. See also Pfeiffer, 'Confessional Ambiguity vs Confessional Polarization', p. 139; Laoust, *Les schismes dans l'Islam*, p. 32.
37. Laoust, 'Les fondements de l'imamat dans le Minhâğ d'al-Ḥillī', pp. 3–55; see also Laoust, *Les schismes dans l'Islam*, pp. 301–4.
38. For the context of the elaboration of the *Nahj al-haqq*, see Pfeiffer, 'Confessional Ambiguity vs Confessional Polarization', pp.142–3; Pfeiffer, 'Conversion Versions'. For the cycles of refutations between al-Hilli and Ruzbahan Khunji,

see Hartmann, 'Staat und Religion in Transoxanien im frühen 16. Jahrhundert', pp. 347–50; see also Rizvi, 'Shīʿī Polemics at the Mughal Court', p. 57.

39. Amir-Moezzi, 'Remarques sur les critères d'authenticité du hadith', pp. 26–8.
40. Abisaab, 'Shiʿi Jurisprudence, Sunnism', pp. 9–10. For a comprehensive work on Astarabadi, see also Gleave, *Scripturalist Islam.*
41. Abisaab, 'al-Fāḍil al-Hindī'.
42. For a translation of the *Bab* with a short introduction, see al-Hilli, *Al-Babuʾl-Hadi ʿAshar.*
43. Schmidtke, *The Theology of al-ʿAllāma al-Ḥillī (d. 726/1325)*, p. 55; for a list of manuscripts and commentaries of the *Bab*, see the appendix, pp. 80–1.
44. SM, p. 407, al-Hilli, *Minhaj al-salah*, pp. 445–6.
45. SM, pp. 407–8. For the hadith versions, see al-Kulayni, *al-Kafi*, vol. 1, p. 295; Ibn Qawlawayh, *Kamil al-ziyarat*, pp. 123–4. See also the reference to this tradition in Ayoub, *Redemptive Suffering*, pp. 70–1. For a broader overview of the uses of al-Kulayni in the Shiʿi tradition, see Amir-Moezzi, *La preuve de Dieu.*
46. SM, p. 409; al-Qummi, *al-Fadaʾil*, p. 113. A similar version, although without the same wording (*li-yubashiranī bi-dhalika*) can be found in al-Tabari, *Bisharat al-mustafa*, pp. 283–4. Other versions also refer to the tablet, but without the same amount of details, and with different wordings. See, for instance Ibn Babawayh, *Kamal al-din*, pp. 305–7; Ibn Babawayh, *ʿUyun akhbar al-rida*, vol. 1, p. 409. See also Ayoub, *Redemptive Suffering*, p. 63; Jones, *The Power of Oratory*, p. 237, Amir-Moezzi, *La guide divin dans le shiʾisme original*, p. 188.
47. SM, pp. 409–10.
48. SM, p. 411; Ibn Babawayh, *al-Amali*, p. 109. A different version of the hadith can be found in Ibn Qawlawayh, *Kamil al-ziyarat*, p. 129.
49. Ibn Qawlawayh, *Kamil al-ziyarat*, pp. 140–1.
50. Nisaburi, *Rawdat al-waʿizin*, p. 155.
51. SM, pp. 411–12.
52. SM, p. 419. The *Kitab Sulaym b. Qays* does not contain this hadith; see Sulaym b. Qays, *Kitab Sulaym al-Qays.* Hossein Modarressi believes Sulaym b. Qays was a historic fabrication to legitimise Anti-Umayyad positions by the Shiʿa of Kufa. He does however believe that the book itself is from the period it is presumed to be and that its original version can be reconstructed. Maria Dakake has sided with him, while Mohammad Ali Amir-Moezzi has not completely dismissed the possibility of Sulaym b. Qays's historical existence. For a good summary of the different positions, see Gleave, 'Early Shhite Hermeneutics', pp. 85–6. For each individual position, see Modarressi, *Tradition and Survival,*

pp. 82–6; Amir-Moezzi, 'Note bibliografique sur le *Kitâb Sulaym b. Qays*', pp. 33–48; Dakake, 'Love, Loyalty and Faith', 346–56. For a more recent study, see Bayhom-Daou, '*Kitāb Sulaym ibn Qays* Revisited'.

53. SM, p. 419; for the hadith versions see Ibn Babawayh, *al-Amali*, p. 106; Nisaburi, *Rawdat al-wa'izin*, p. 155; Majlisi, *Bihar al-anwar*, vol. 43, p. 243. See also Ayoub, *Redemptive Suffering*, p. 75.
54. Ayoub, *Redemptive Suffering*, p. 75; for the hadith, see Ibn Shahrashub, *Manaqib al Abi Talib*, vol. 3, pp. 209–10.
55. Carnoy-Torabi, 'A biblioteca esquecida dos missionários do Ispaão', pp. 97–102.
56. Ibid. pp. 103–4.
57. De Dieu, *Historia Christi Persice*. See also De Bruijn, 'Dieu, Louis (Ludovicus) de'. For other details about his career, see Loop, 'Johann Heinrich Hottinger', p. 78.
58. SM, pp. 605–6.
59. Tertullian, *Adversus Marcionem*; Pseudo-Tertullian, *Adversus Omnes Haereses*. See also Arendzen, 'Marcionites'.
60. Optatus of Milevis, *De Schismate Donatistarum*, p. 8.
61. SM, p. 606; Jerome, *Chronicle*, p. 319.
62. Eusebius, *The Ecclesiastical History*, p. 310.
63 *The Book of the Popes*, pp. 36–7; *Le Liber pontificalis*, vol. 1, pp. 161–2.
64. For notes on the history of the assembly of the *Liber Pontificalis*, see Loomis, 'Introduction' to *The Book of the Popes*, pp. ix–xi; see also Duchesne, 'Introduction' to *Le Liber Pontificalis*, vol. 1, pp. i–xxxii.
65. For information on the manuscript that mentions the apostasy of Pope Marcellinus and the Council of Sinuessa and for the quotation in question, see *The Book of the Popes*, p. 36 fn. 2; Duchesne, 'Introduction' to *Le Liber Pontificalis*, vol. 1, p. lxxiv; see also Giorgi, 'Appunti intorno ad alcuni manoscritti', pp. 247–312.
66. Castro Romano, *Difesa della causa di S. Marcellino*, pp. 44–6; Langen, *Geschichte der römischen Kirche*, vol. 1, pp. 370–2; Allard, *Histoire des persecutions*, vol. 4, pp. 376–9; Duchesne, *Histoire ancienne de l'Eglise*, vol. 2, p. 92.
67. Opava, *Chronicon Pontificum et Imperatorum*, fols. 6v–7r.
68. SM, p. 606.
69. Opava, *Chronicon Pontificum et Imperatorum*, fols. 20v–21r. For notes on the importance of Opava and the circulation of his work see Ikas, 'Martinus Polonus', p. 327.

70. Peters, *The Magician, the Witch, and the Law*, p. 28.
71. Thomson, 'William of Malmesbury's Edition of the "Liber Pontificalis"', pp. 93–112.
72. *Le Liber Pontificalis*, vol 2. Notice 143, pp. 263–4, n. 143; Opava, *Chronicon Pontificum et Imperatorum*, fols. 20v–21r; Bourgain, 'Silvestre dans le Liber Pontificalis', pp. 355–7; Oldoni, 'Gerberto e la sua storia, I', pp. 655–9.
73. SM, p. 606; Platina, *The Lives of the Popes*, vol. 2, p. 171.
74. SM, p. 606; Platina, *The Lives of the Popes*, vol. 2, pp. 235–7.
75. SM, p. 606; Baronius, *Annales Ecclesiastici*, vol. 17, pp. 332–538; Rinaldi, *Annales Ecclesiastici*, vol. 22 pp. 384–405.
76. Kirsch, 'Pope John XXI'.
77. Kirsch, 'Pope John XXI'; Oestereich, 'Pope St. Gregory VII'. For the accusations of necromancy against John XXI, see Rinaldi *Annales Ecclesiastici*, vol. 22 pp. 390–1; for accusations against Gregory VII, see Foxe, *The Actes and Monuments of John Foxe*, vol. 2, p. 121.
78. Foxe, *The Actes and Monuments of John Foxe*, vol. 2, p. 121.
79. SM, p. 606; Cano, *Melchioris Cani Episcopi*, pp. 224, 402–3.
80. Horst, *Päpstlich Unfehlbarkeit wider konziliare Superiorität?*, pp. 190–1, 282–7; see also Walter, '"Quelle" oder "Steinbruch"?', pp. 88–91. For a more synthesised account of Cano's position on the Vulgata, see Walter, 'Melchor Cano. *De Logis Theologicis* (1563)', pp. 512–14. For another schematic overview of Spanish Neo-Scholasticism more in general, see Decock, 'Law and the Bible in Spanish Neo-Scholasticism', pp. 325–31.
81. Volz, 'Melchior Cano'.
82. SM, p. 607; Carnoy-Torabi, 'A biblioteca esquecida dos missionários do Ispaão', pp. 103–4.
83. Krstić, *Contested Conversions to Islam*, p. 85.
84. For the contents of the letter, see Jerome, 'Letter of Jerome to Pope Damasus'.
85. SM, p. 646.
86. Ibid. pp. 646–7.
87. Said Reynolds, *A Muslim Theologian*, pp. 86–8.
88. Kohlberg and Amir-Moezzi, *Revelation and Falsification*, p. 24. For a detailed study on the matter, including different nuances and versions of this account, see Kara, *In Search of ʿAlī Ibn Abī Ṭālib's Codex*, pp. 65–74; Brunner, *Die Schia und die Koranfälschung*.
89. Modarressi, 'Early Debates on the Integrity of the Qur'ān', pp. 26–32; Kara, *In Search of ʿAlī Ibn Abī Ṭālib's Codex*, pp. 66–7.

90. In the versions of Ibn Sa'd and Ibn Hisham, rather than rejuvenating or renewing the nation of Abraham, the wording points more towards being an envoy for his religion: '*yab'ath bi-dīn Ibrāhīm* (Ibn Sa'd)/ *mab'ūth bi-dīn* Ibrāhīm (Ibn Hisham)'. See Ibn Sa'd, *al-Tabaqat al-kubra*, vol. 4, p. 71; Ibn Hisham, *al-Sira al-nabawiyya*, vol. 1, p. 142. Mareike Koertner has identified a similar version in the *Musnad* of Ibn Hanbal (d. 855). See Koertner, 'We Have Made Clear the Signs', p. 61.
91. SM, p. 649.

5

Defending the Prophet and Condemning Christian Morality

While the *Sayf al-mu ʾminin* is mostly concerned with matters of scriptural interpretation as they pertain to theological dogma, and while the use of biblical signs dominates the argumentative embroidery of the text, with occasional complementary recourse to sources like the hadith, some sections of the book stand apart both structurally and thematically. For the purpose of their study, these can be grouped within two blocks: one concerned with Jadid al-Islam's direct responses to the challenges posed by Guadagnoli in his *Apologia*, and the other with matters of morality and ritual practices of Christians.

Response to Guadagnoli

The most obvious question to ask when examining Jadid al-Islam's responses to Guadagnoli is whether he worked exclusively with the 1631 Latin *Apologia* (that is, the *Apologia* properly speaking) or whether he also had access to the 1637 *Ijaba* and the 1649 *Considerationes ad Mahomettanos*. Another tempting line of inquiry would be to determine whether he also read Aimé Chézaud's *Mash-i misqal-i safa-yi A ʾinih-i haqq-numa*, which as we have seen in Chapter two was essentially an abridged Persian version of the *Apologia*. Answering these questions requires a certain amount of educated speculation, given the documentary gaps we face. To my knowledge, we do not have enough information to know whether our author was acquainted with Chézaud's text. As for his reading of Guadagnoli, however, it is possible to advance an approximate identification of the parts of the *Apologia* he chose to target. This does not necessarily resolve all the questions regarding the editions he could have used. However, while answering them would no doubt shed light on the history of the circulation of these texts, the importance of doing so is secondary to that of understanding the ways in which our author integrated Guadagnoli's objections into the broader thematic composition of his own work.

Some general thematic considerations are now pertinent. Although Guadagnoli's *Apologia* deals with many matters that are also implicitly addressed in the *Sayf al-muʾminin* as a whole, such as the discussion on the divine nature of the Gospels and the dogma of the Trinity, the passages in which Jadid al-Islam rebukes Guadagnoli more directly deal with debates on the character of Muhammad and on the sanctity of the Qurʾanic Scripture. Thus, even though the overall aim of the *Sayf al-muʾminin* is to make a case for Islam through the reinterpretation and correction of the Bible, the sections we will now analyse point instead towards a defense of Islam through an apology for its Prophet and its Holy Book. The *Apologia* and the *Sayf al-muʾminin* can be thus thought of as negative mirror images of each other, albeit with a nuance: while the *Apologia* is a defense of Christianity's Scriptures and Messiah complemented with an attack on Islam's Scripture and Prophet, the *Sayf al-muʾminin* can only be said to be the exact opposite to the extent to which its attack on Christian Scriptures is based on the accusation of *taḥrīf*. In other words, the acknowledgement in the Islamic tradition of a certain degree of prophetic value in Christian Scriptures, at least in their supposedly primordial and uncorrupted form, limits the scope of – or at least serves to qualify – their condemnation by Muslim polemicists like Jadid al-Islam.

In contrast, Christian polemicists did not need, in theory, to exercise the same degree of constraint vis-à-vis the Qurʾan. By and large, medieval Christian authors saw Islam as a variation of pagan heresy. Before the twelfth century, most of them knew less about Islam and its Scripture than their Muslims counterparts knew about Christianity. As such, common tropes of anti-Islamic polemics consisted merely of ad hominem attacks on the Prophet and of mischaracterisations of Muslim rituals: accusations of Muhammad as lustful and licentious were common currency in this kind of literature until well into the early modern period.[1] From the twelfth century onwards, European Christians began to study Islam more keenly given its cultural influence in Latin Europe.[2] As such, early Latin translations of the Qurʾan were conceived exclusively as tools for polemics. The earliest of these was commissioned by Peter the Venerable, abbot of Cluny (d. 1156), and undertaken by Robert of Ketton (d. 1157). After its completion, Peter the Venerable used this translation to write anti-Islamic treatises.[3] Similarly, in his Qur'anic translation, commissioned by the Archbishop of Toledo Rodrigo Jiménez de Rada (d. 1247), Mark of Toledo (d. 1216) included a preface presenting Muhammad as a pseudoprophet. The archbishop would then reproduce a similar biographic sketch of Muhammad in his own writings.[4]

This does not mean that the Qur'an was only ever approached by Christian polemicists in a dismissive fashion. For example, one of the classic Christian anti-Muslim polemics, the *Risala ila ahad al-muslimin* (*Treatise against a Muslim*) of Paul of Antioch, quotes verses from *Surat al-Ma'ida* (5:48) and *Sura Yunus* (10:94) as proofs of the divine origin of the books that preceded the Qur'anic revelation.[5] Likewise, Dominican friars of the thirteenth century pursued mildly conciliatory strategies. One of them, the Catalan Ramón Martí (d. 1285), included in his work a list of Qur'anic precepts that he deemed correct, and when defending Christians against the accusation of *taḥrīf*, he sometimes used the Qur'an in two rather contradictory ways: sometimes in support of Christian doctrine and sometimes as part of its refutation.[6] Similar contrasting treatments of the Qur'an and Islam will continue to inform Christian discourse in the early modern period. The question of context and intended audience will of course determine the tone of the arguments. Thus for instance, Jan Amos Comenius (d. 1670), who collaborated in an Anglo-Dutch project to produce a Turkish Bible for Mehmed IV (r. 1648–87), used conciliatory language to refer to the Prophet in a dedicatory note to the Sultan, despite having used many common tropes attacking the Prophet in another of his works.[7]

In Guadagnoli's case, he also had an ambiguous approach in his treatment of Islam. On the one hand, the motivation behind the writing of the *Apologia*, with its decidedly polemical nature, required him to address the question of the *taḥrīf* of the Bible and the legitimacy of the Muslim prophet in a militant fashion. In this sense, he was in tune with probably most European scholars of his time: for instance, the Dutch Calvinist theologian Johannes Hoornbeeck (d. 1666) rejected the idea of there being any prophetical signs in the Bible regarding the coming of Islam and reverted the accusation of *taḥrīf* against Muslims. Similarly, Jan Comenius argued that there were no contradictions between the different vernacular translations.[8] On the other hand, given the missionary goal of Guadagnoli's Arabic editions in particular, the recognition of a certain degree of moral authority in Islamic Scripture served him as a strategy of persuasion.[9] This explains to a certain extent the inclusion of Qur'anic citations in the *Apologia*, but even more importantly, this accounts for the differences between the Latin and the Arabic editions. For example, the *Apologia* properly speaking is divided into four *treatises* (*tractatus*): I. *De Sanctis Scripturis* (*On the Holy Scriptures*) II. *De Alchorano eiusque authore Mohammede* (*On the Qur'an and its author Muhammad*) III. *De Sacrosancto Trinitatis Mysterio* (*On the Sacrosanct Mystery of the Trinity*) and IV. *De Christi Divinitate* (*On the Divinity of Christ*).[10] This structure is also preserved in the first Arabic edition, the *Ijaba*. However, in the second one – that is, the *Considerationes* – the second *tractatus*, which includes most of the ad hominem attacks on Muhammad, is instead replaced by a section at the end of the text entitled *Inna al-Qur'an la yadaddad al-Injil fi-ma qala al-haqq* (*The Qur'an does not Contradict the Gospel in Asserting the Truth*), which is written in a more conciliatory tone.[11]

When examining the relevant sections in the *Sayf al-mu'minin*, it is clear that Jadid al-Islam's discussion revolves around themes that appear in the second *tractatus*. This implies that he used either the Latin edition or the first Arabic one (or both), but not the second Arabic edition (or at least not for the elaboration of this work). He starts by paraphrasing what roughly corresponds to a sub-section of the *tractatus* in question entitled *Mahometis calliditas magis aperitur* (*More Evidence of Muhammad's Cunning*),[12] in which Guadagnoli equates Muslim ritual practices with idolatry:

> The Muhammad of the Arabs invented a religion that bans idol worship and orders that only God be worshipped; yet at the same time he teaches idol worship. And he also issued an order (*farmān*) – although the accursed father [i.e. Guadagnoli] does not say in which book[13] – saying that on Friday, they [Muslims] should glorify [Him], and he ordered that on that day, just like in ancient idolatry (*bih dastūr-i but-parastī-yi qadīm*), everyone, male or female, should strip off their clothes and dance together.[14]

After refuting the idea that Islam encouraged naked ritual dancing, Jadid al-Islam moves on to rebuke Guadagnoli's understanding of the Muslim proclamation of faith – the *shahāda* – as a manifestation of *shirk* for acknowledging Muhammad as the Messenger of God.[15] To support his argument, he resorts to a parable: in it, a woman seeks Satan's advice after her husband tells her that he is considering joining the army in the wake of a foreign invasion. When she asks Satan whether her husband would be likely to be killed in combat if he enlisted, Satan hands her a letter, the meaning of which she interprets as a guarantee of his safety. But after her husband perishes in the battlefield, she goes back to Satan and confronts him for his deceitful message. In response, he bluntly says that it was she who had misinterpreted the letter. She had read it thus: 'You will go and come back, you will not die at the battle (*mī-ravī mī-āyī, namī-mīrī dar jang*)', whereas the correct reading should have been: 'You will go and not come back, you will die in the battle (*mī-ravī mī-āyī nah, mī-mīrī dar jang*)'.[16] Jadid al-Islam then compares Guadagnoli's defective reading of the *shahāda* as *shirk* to the woman's misreading of Satan's text.[17]

A similar critique is then directed against Guadagnoli's claim that the Qur'an itself proscribed the possibility of its interpretation. This appears in a sub-section of the same *tractatus* called *Sapientiam praestans paruulis* (*[The Lord] Granting his Little Ones Wisdom*)[18], in which Guadagnoli relies on a quote from *Sura Al 'Imran* (Qur'an 3:7): 'Only God knows the true meaning [of these verses] (*mā ya'lamu ta'wīlahu illā Allāh*)'.[19] In response, Jadid al-Islam notes that Guadagnoli had omitted the next part of the verse, which says: 'Those firmly grounded in knowledge (*wa-l-rāsikhūn fi-l-'ilm*)'.[20] Our author then needs to provide an explanation for who those 'firmly grounded in knowledge' were; and this he does by advancing a sectarian claim, comparing Guadagnoli's omission of the end of the quotation to the Sunnis' refusal to accept the Imams, who according to the interpretation he subscribes to, were the true '*rāsikhūn fi-l-'ilm*'.[21] This blending of Sunni and Christian interpretations of the scriptures is anything but banal. It highlights the sectarian political dynamic of the late seventeenth and early eighteenth centuries, when Safavid rule faced major internal and external challenges. During this time, Sunnis and even Shi'i-leaning Sufi groups were viewed by some influential ulama as a menace to a certain understanding of proper Shi'i doctrine, as we will see in more detail throughout the next chapter.

Another common trope of Christian anti-Islamic polemics reproduced by Guadagnoli and rebutted by Jadid al-Islam is that of the Prophet engaging in adultery (*zinā*). This is debated in the section *Qissih-i Rasul-i Khuda ba Mariyyih va Ayat-i Surih-i Tahrim* (*Story of the Messenger of God with Maryam and the Verse of Sura Tahrim*). Here, our author targets parts of the sub-section *De Mohammede, seu Mohammede, Alchoranicae sectae Auctore* (*On Muhammad, the Author of the Qur'anic Sect*).[22] According to Guadagnoli, Muhammad had committed adultery with his slave Maria (a clear reference to Maria the Copt, d. 637), and had upset Khadija as a result.[23] Jadid al-Islam chastises Guadagnoli for not revealing what sources he used to claim that Muhammad and Khadija ever had an altercation on the matter. He adds that if any such document existed, if would surely be a Sunni fabrication. He explains that Muhammad never took another wife during Khadija's lifetime nor before Aisha's coming of age and that Muhammad had been authorised by God to take the slave girl as an act of compassion so that she would not be abandoned.[24] More importantly, he argues that by accusing Muhammad of adultery for taking a slave girl as his concubine, Guadagnoli had revealed his of lack of familiarity with the overall tradition of the People of the Book, given that the Old Testament contained many precedents of prophets engaging in similar practices.[25] He then draws from the *Book of Deuteronomy* to show that the Israelites were legally allowed to keep female captives as concubines when engaging in war, provided that they abided by certain rules in their treatment of the captives. He complements this by returning to *Matthew* 5 to show that Jesus had not come to abrogate Mosaic Law, which leads him to conclude that, even within the internal logic of Christianity, there were no legal grounds to forbid such relations between masters and slaves.[26] Here we can begin to see what will be a constant throughout these sections, that is, the disputation of Christian practice through the disarticulation of their legitimising discourses *on their own terms*.

As we have begun to see already, a recurrent motif within the sections debating the *Apologia* is the idea that Muhammad promoted the practice of pagan rituals. We have already seen this in relation to the ritual surrounding the Ka'ba in Guadagnoli's interpretation, but there is another, perhaps more delicate matter, on this regard, namely the idea that the Prophet engaged in idol worship before being entrusted with the revelation. This idea transcends the realm of traditional Muslim–Christian polemics, as some ramifications of it have also been the subject of debate among the ulama. There is, for example, a discussion surrounding the validity and the implications of a hadith in which the Prophet is said to have offered Zayd b. ʿAmr b. Nufayl, a pre-Islamic monotheist (*ḥanīf*) from Mecca, a bag of meat offered to the idols. Zayd refuses and reprimands the Prophet. Muslim scholars have long debated the implications of this tradition. Some have focused on the fact that in none of its different versions does it say that Muhammad ate the meat after been cautioned against it. Shiʿi scholars have however rejected its validity altogether.[27]

The section called *Afkar-i Filip-i Padiri dar barih-i baʿsat va daʿvat-i Muhammad* (*Filippo's Thoughts on Muhammad's Prophetic Mission and Preaching*) is also concerned with similar issues. In it, our author responds to Guadagnoli's scepticism regarding certain passages of the biography of the Prophet and to the common Christian polemical trope of Muhammad's alleged madness.[28] Jadid al-Islam once again questions Guadagnoli's Arabic skills, disqualifying his philological training in Rome and condemning him as a mouthpiece for the devil, who had taken the message of Satan wherever he had preached: from Rome to India, to Transoxiana, to the Maghreb.[29] Our author then corrects some of Guadagnoli's inaccuracies regarding the age until which the Prophet had been raised by his wet-nurse and regarding the age until which he had allegedly engaged in pagan rituals before receiving the divine message.[30] Jadid al-Islam then dismisses Guadagnoli's attack and deflects the accusation of idolatry against the dogma of the Trinity, thus refuting Guadagnoli's disapproval of Islamic monotheism as one based on 'a single false God' (*yik Khudā-yi durūgh*).[31]

Another section that touches upon the question of idol worship, albeit from a different angle, is the one under the rubric of *Khabar-i gharaniq va ishkal-i Filip-i Padiri va naqd-i muʾallif* (*The Story of the Crain [or Maidens], the Doubts of Filippo and the Authors' Critique*). In it, our author starts by discussing the ritual prostrations that according to Saint Jerome – says our author – Abraham, Lot and Jacob practised as part of their religious worship. Jadid al-Islam confronts Guadagnoli for not recognising the prophethood of Muhammad, once again, on the basis of his having allegedly worshipped idols until the age of forty. He points out that, coming from a Christian, this argument was inconsistent, given that Christians recognise the Old Testament prophets as such, while continuing to believe that they also engaged in such rituals. It is in the context of this discussion that the famous episode of the Satanic Verses comes into question.[32]

As it is well known, this episode is part of the *Story of the Crains [or Maidens]* (*qiṣṣat al-gharānīq*), which appears in the histories of al-Waqidi (d. 823) and al-Tabari (d. 923). According to this account, Muhammad would have confused false revelations dictated by Satan with legitimate Qur'anic verses.[33] The incident of the Satanic Verses is linked to the verses from Surat Najm (53:19–20), which mentions three Goddesses worshipped by the tribe of Quraysh: '[Disbelievers], consider al-Lat and al-ʿUzza, and the third one, Manat (*A fa-ra'aytumu al-Lata wa al-'Uzzā/ wa Manata al-thālithata al-ukhrā*)'.[34] These in turned have been explained through certain interpretations of a verse from *Surat al-Hajj* (22:52):

> We have never sent any messenger or prophet before you [Muhammad] into whose wishes Satan did not insinuate something, but God removes what Satan insinuates and then God affirms His message. God is all knowing and wise
> *(Wa mā arsalnā min qablika min rasulin wa lā nabiyyin illā idhā tamannā alqā' al-Shayṭānu fī umniyyatihi fa-yansakhu Allāhu mā yulqī al-Shayṭānu thumma yuḥkimu Allāhu āyātihi wa Allāhu ʿalīmun ḥakīmun)*.[35]

The interpretation of this verse as an allusion to the Satanic Verses has largely been refuted by Muslims, including of course Shiʿi *mufassirūn*. For example, the *tafsīr* attributed to ʿAli Ibrahim al-Qummi (d. early tenth century) dismisses the story of the Satanic Verses as a Sunni fabrication. It offers instead an interpretation of the verse from Imam Jaʿfar al-Sadiq (d. 765), whereby Abu Bakr and ʿUmar are understood to be the 'insinuations' of Satan, which are removed by Imam ʿAli. Other Shiʿi scholars and exegetes would concentrate more on the interpretation of the meanings of certain words, with the Zaydi Imam al-Qassim b. Ibrahim al-Rassi (d. 860) arguing that the *umniyya* of Satan does not refer to his 'wishes or desires', but to his 'recitation', making it an allusion to incorrect or truncated recitations of the Qur'an.[36]

In his indictement of Muhammad as an idolator, Guadagnoli brings about the two abovementioned *Suras*.[37] In his rebuttal, Jadid al-Islam sides with the interpretation of the *Tafsir* of al-Qummi, dismissing the whole episode as a Sunni forgery. But more importantly, he argues that no Qur'anic

Sura shows the Old Testament Prophets engaging in practices of idol worship, in contrast to what the – allegedly fabricated – Christian Scriptures claimed.[38]

The remaining section on Guadagnoli deals with matters pertaining the relations between Muslims and the People of the Book. This passage, entitled *Ishkal-i digar-i Filip bih Musalmanan va pasukh-i an* (*Other Objections of Filippo and the Responses to These*), begins by addressing the question of the internal conflicts within the Muslim community and its relations vis-à-vis Christians. As would be expected from a Shiʿi text, it describes the struggles against the first three *Rashīdūn* Caliphs in laudatory terms. This topic leads the author to compare the cohesion of the Umma favourably to the divisions among Christians, citing the early schisms within the Church, the Reformation and the existence of local Churches like the Armenian Orthodox.[39]

Finally, while not immediately linked to the refutation of Guadagnoli, another section is worth mentioning here given the way in which it takes the arguments of the former passages to their most radical conclusion. This excerpt appears under the rubric *Luzum-i dushmani-yi Musalmanan ba Yahud va Nasara* (*The Necessity of Muslim Enmity Against Jews and Christians*), which is to say that it is written in the opposite spirit to the conciliatory addendum of Guadagnoli's *Considerationes* we mentioned earlier. It begins with the infamous motif of the blood-libel, according to which Jews drank Christian blood on Passover. In this rendition, however, the Christian blood is substituted by Muslim blood.[40] Jadid al-Islam then provides his translation of *Ecclesiasticus* 44 to further legitimise the need for this enmity:

> Let us praise these glorious men and the sons of their kin, for it is upon [this kin] that God Almighty has bestowed his glory and his greatness, for since the beginning of times He created them to be rulers, so that they would bring His message [to humanity]. Having honoured them with the robe of prophethood, He gave this Truth-bearing nation – that is, the Bani Israel – the power to rule. He gave them understanding and power, and through [the prophets] He delivered many of His Holy words – that is, His books. They are the ones who have inquired (*taftīsh namūdan*) into the sciences (*ʿulūm*) through knowledge (*ʿilm*) and through their own experience. They are the ones who have interpreted the Holy verses for the people. Thus, they

> are the people who have all the good qualities of rulership, and all good endeavours are with them. They rule with justice in their houses and the glory befalls upon their dynasty. For this, they were praised in their time and whoever was born from them was given their good name so that others would praise them.[41]

Jadid al-Islam reads this as a falsification intended to justify Christian (or Jewish) claims to political authority, at the expense of other groups, with Muslims included among them.[42]

Condemning Christian Morality and Ritual Practices

In addition to the above responses to Guadagnoli, some of which already address questions of marital relations and morality as they pertain to the integrity of the Prophet, other sections of the *Sayf al-mu'minin* expand on these issues more broadly. One that covers enough space in the book to be noticeable to the inquisitive eye, although without being central to it as a whole, is that of marriage vis-à-vis the practice of clerical celibacy in the context of the Catholic Church. As we noted briefly in the first chapter, marriage is the subject of one of Jadid al-Islam's minor works, the *Fava'id-i izdivaj* (*The Benefits of Marriage*). As we will see in more detail in the next chapter, there is evidence that our author wrote another one of his short treatises in preparation for his book-length works, which suggests that the same could have been the case with this latter piece. The themes of marriage, adultery and sexual morality were also common tropes in polemics. While it is problematic to establish causal relations between an author's biography and his production, it is nonetheless tempting to see in this theme a self-justification of Jadid al-Islam's own marriage and of his abandonment of priestly abstinence. Another hypothesis, which does not necessarily exclude the latter, is that during his first years as a missionary in Isfahan Jadid al-Islam could have had access to the *Disputationes de Sancti Matrimoni Sacramento* (*Disputations on the Holy Sacrament of Marriage*), a piece by the Jesuit Tomás Sánchez, whose work was available at the missionary library.[43] Despite the high reputation of its author and its moralistic intention, Sánchez's book had been at the centre of controversy for its explicit descriptions of sexual life, resulting in its inclusion in the Index of Forbidden Books.[44] Could Jadid al-Islam's defense of marriage have been also partially influenced by this work? Could its reading have guided our author to the conclusion that marriage should be permissible and desirable for people bestowed with religious authority? We can only speculate in this regard.

Let us now briefly consider the contents of the *Fava'id-i izdivāj*. Jadid al-Islam begins this *risāla* quoting the command from *Genesis* 2 to be fruitful and multiply. He then quotes from *Surat al-Dhariyat* (51:56): 'I created jinn and mankind except to worship Me (*wa mā khalaqtu al-jinna wa-l-insān illā li-ya'budūn*)', and from the famous sacred (*qudsī*) hadith 'I was a hidden treasure and I wanted to be known, so I created a creature who would know Me (*kuntu kanzan makhfiyyan fa-aḥbabtu an u'rafa fa-khalaqtu al-khalq li-kay u'raf*)'.[45] These quotes serve to prove that reproduction was a divine duty for humanity. Jadid al-Islam then rejects priestly celibacy as one of Saint Paul's innovations, who he disqualifies resorting to arguments similar to those used in the traditional discipline of critical examination of hadith transmitters, the *'ilm-al rijāl* (*the study of men*). The dismissal of Paul is based on two criteria: the first one is the fact that he did not chronologically coincide with Christ, and that therefore the chain of transmission (*isnād*) that would have linked them together was broken. This argument also appears in older examples of the genre. For instance, 'Abd al-Jabbar included a similar version of it in his *Tathbit dala'il al-nubuwwa*, most likely drawing from an account from Ibn Ishaq according to which the disciples of Christ refused to preach in remote lands, thus breaking the chains of transmission.[46] Jadid al-Islam's second argument against Paul consists of discrediting his moral character for having persecuted Christians before his conversion:

> None of this was mentioned by any of the twelve disciples, but rather by Paul, who led the nation of Jesus (pbuh) to perdition (*gumrāh kunandih-i ummat-i 'Īsā*). This guide of perdition (*ān żāll-i mużall*) introduced and promoted this innovation (*bid'at*) among the [God]-fearing (*tarsāyān*). This accursed [person] was not one of the disciples of Jesus. He was rather an enemy of him and of his followers, and caused them great trouble and brought them to the tribunal of the Jews to be punished. But even though Christians may argue that he repented from these kinds of acts and that even if their books contain evidence of his obscene disbelief-fostering

actions (*aʿmāl-i shanīʿih-i kufr-amīz-i ū*), he then uttered his repentance; [even then] it is also the case that this accursed [person] [Paul] did not even live at the time of Jesus.[47]

Jadid al-Islam then contends that if celibacy had indeed been desirable for monastic life, the founding of the Church of Rome would not have been entrusted to Saint Peter, a married man, and that Jesus would not have healed Peter's mother-in-law in Capernaum.[48] As for the argument that celibacy could be considered a practice of pious imitation of Christ, our author responds that each prophet had been blessed with different attributes and had adhered to different practices: '[The fact that] Jesus (pbuh) did not take a wife does not make this [celibacy] a necessary command (*īn amr lāzim nayāyad*)'.[49] As such, he sees no reason to hold Jesus's celibacy in a higher esteem than that of the customs and practices of other prophets:

> Not everything that was better for [the prophets] should necessarily be better for their nation[s] (*ummat*) [as a whole]. Otherwise, it would be necessary [to accept] that whatever was forbidden to a nation, could have been rendered permissible (*mubāḥ*) for them through the particular attributes (*khaṣāʾiṣ*) [of a given prophet]. For example: Jacob (pbuh) married two sisters, [thus] it would be [permissible] for the people of this noble man's nation to take two sisters in marriage if both of them were alive. Likewise, to the nation of David [it would correspond] a hundred wives, wanting a thousand would be better for the nation of Solomon (pbuh), and by the same token, for the nation of the Messenger of the End of Times, Muhammad Mustafa (pbuh), it would be allowed (*mubāḥ*) to want nine wives and to marry every woman upon whom their eyes fall and whoever they may like after divorcing. Therefore, anything other than what is explicitly mentioned as being particular to a given nation would be forbidden.[50]

Further, because of their exceptional mission, each prophet had been entrusted with special attributes that were not required from the rest of the people:

> Should [anyone] ask the reason (*chih ʿillat dārad*) why not having a wife was one of Jesus's particularities (*khaṣāʾiṣ-i ʿĪsā (as) būdih*), even though having a wife is better and whatever is better is worthy of prophets; the answer would be that it was in the public interest (*maṣlaḥat*)[51] to cast away (*dafʿ va*

> *raf*) any doubt among the Umma [regarding] the completion of the proof (*ḥujjat*) [of his prophecy].[52]

Jadid al-Islam sees in this fixation with the particularities of Jesus another faulty attempt to dismiss the prophethood of Muhammad. To elaborate on this point, he needed to provide an explanation for the celibacy of Jesus, which should not revolve around the assumption of his divine nature. For this, he first draws from *Micah* 7, which he translates as follows:

> Do not trust your friends and do not believe them, and do not have any hope on your leader and hide your head from the woman that sleeps by your side, for your enemies can be [among] your family.[53]

In interpreting this passage, Jadid al-Islam concludes that celibacy was the attribute through which Jesus could be known *not* to be the Seal of the Prophets, given that the latter should have descendants invested with charismatic authority:

> Had [Jesus] taken a woman [in marriage] and had he had children [with her], [this] could have cast doubts (*mushtabih mī shud*) on the Seal of the Prophets (peace and blessings upon him and his family), and it could have been said that the proof (*ḥujjat*) [of prophecy] would not have been clear to Christians. If one were to ask a Christian why he recognises Jesus (pbuh) as the Seal of the Prophets, but does not have faith in the Truth (*īmān bih ḥaqq nayāvardī*) and does not acknowledge the Messenger of the End of Times as the Seal of the Messengers, his answer would be: 'the Lord of Lords said in chapter 7 of the *Book of Micah* – who is one of our prophets – that the woman of the Seal of the Prophets will nourish (*infāq kardan*) him. This woman was not Jesus's [wife], and this friend that provided for the Seal of the Prophets was not ʿUmar, but rather the son of Jesus's wife. [Likewise], the insubordinate leader of the Seal of the Prophets was not Abu Bakr but Jesus himself. Almighty God said in the *Book of Isaiah* that the Holy Spirit would not be separated from the Seal of Prophets until the Day of Judgement nor [would it be separated] from his sons nor from the sons of his sons and so forth until the Day of Judgement. And this Holy Spirit was inside Jesus and it will then be transferred to his sons and it will not be separated from the sons of his sons until the Day of

> Judgement. Thus, we are right in not having faith in prophets [that came] after Jesus (pbuh). For if the Holy Spirit had been transferred from him to his sons, not to be withdrawn from them until the Day of Judgement, it would necessarily [follow] that the Seal of the Prophets will not be the Messenger you talk about [Muhammad], but rather Jesus. Therefore, the sons of Muhammad (pbuh) are not the proof [of prophecy] to the creation until the Day of Judgement; instead, the sons of Jesus are that proof, and they are the leaders (*Imams*), and the Holy Spirit will be with them until the Day of Judgement'.[54]

Jadid al-Islam concludes that if Jesus had been married, Christians could have made the case that he was the last prophet and that his descendants would have been the guardians of his message until the end of times.

Finally, our author addresses another common apology for celibacy, although this time from the Qur᾽an. He notes that in the past, scholars who defended the practice of celibacy had cited the case of Yahya (John the Baptist) as an authoritative example. Those who adhered to this thesis relied on the verse from Surat Al ῾Imran (3:39) in which Yahya's birth is announced: 'God gives you news of John, confirming a Word from God. He will be noble and chaste, a prophet, one of the righteous (*anna Allaha yubashshiruka bi-Yaḥyā muṣaddiqan bi-kalimatin min Allahi wa sayyidan wa ḥaṣūran*)'.[55] Jadid al-Islam suggests that the term *ḥaṣūr* (chaste) here was not meant to be taken literally, but rather as a description of someone who abstained from frivolous pleasures (*lahū va la῾b*). To justify his interpretation, Jadid al-Islam reproduces a story from Yahya's childhood in which he refuses to play with other children saying: 'God has not created us to play (*mā rā az barā-yi bāzī khalaq nakardih-and*)'.[56]

Unfortunately, the *risāla* is truncated. However, similar and related arguments appear in different sections of the *Sayf al-mu᾽minin*. For example, in the section entitled *Izdivaj va mamnu῾yat-i an bara-yi padiriyan va dukhtaran-i kilisa* (*Marriage and its Forbiddance for Priests and for the Daughters of the Church*), our author dismisses the account of the creation of Eve from Adam's rib as a Christian fabrication that permeated into Sunni sources.[57]

Another critique of celibacy and monastic life appears in the context of the section *Dar kilisa-ha chih mi guzarad* (*What Happens at Church?*). Here, the point of contention is the confinement of girls into monasteries, where according to our author they were subjected to indoctrination. A disapproving description of liturgical rituals then follows, with the harshest comments directed against the Eucharist:

> After they perform this libertine prayer (*namāz-i fārigh*), they bring a box full of [slices of] a paper-thin round bread, each of which measures five *shāhīs*, and in each of these there is an image that they identify as Jesus. Then, they take the box to a place where the girls kneel down and place it over a shrine built for this purpose. On it, they place many candles of camphorated wax on gold and silver chandeliers, and around it, they disperse flowers of different kinds. Since it is an obligation for each girl to be in a state of purity that day, each of them tells her sins of the [previous] week to priests who are appointed to hear people's sins. Having told their sins to the priests, each group of girls is then arranged by pairs and, with impeccable demeanour, they go towards [another] priest and bow to the bread, which they believe to be the son of God. After this, they come near the priest and kneel while the priest gives them one of the breads and says: 'this is the body and the blood of Jesus, [who is] both God and a real man'. After this, they teach the girls that when they are shown the bread they should say: 'we are not worthy of having you enter the dwelling of our hearts, but a word of yours suffices to intercede for our souls'. After this, the girls open their mouths and the priest throws a bread into their pharynx, and it is forbidden for them to touch the bread with their teeth, because the priests teach them that biting and chewing God would be unmannerly, and that if they bite [the bread], blood will spill [from it].[58]

The author then targets the sacrament of confession, describing how the girls were forced to tell their sins every time they became ill. He also describes how each monastic order or lineage (*silsilih*) adhered to a different set of customary manners (*adāb*) and the dress code prescribed by its founders, which allows him to draw parallels with the practices of Sufi orders. The section ends denouncing the ritual in which the girls were made to symbolically marry 'an idol they have carved and named after Jesus (*butī kih bih ism-i Ḥażrat-i ʿĪsā tarāshīdih-and*)'.[59]

Another section which raises similar points is the one devoted to the question of women's modesty (or lack thereof) in Christianity, which appears under the rubric of *Zan va hijab dar Masihiyyat* (*Women and Veiling in Christianity*). The core of the discussion revolves around the lack of veiling and the interaction between women and unrelated men. The author condemns the custom of men and women kissing each other as a form of greeting, as well as the debauchery and alcohol consumption in Christian engagement receptions, which he contrasts with the modesty and refinement of Arab and Persian weddings.[60] The section becomes more complex as it incorporates a critique of Pauline passages associated with marital relations, in the same vein as in the previous examples from the *Fava᾿id-i izdivaj*. Among the excerpts discussed is one from *Galatians* 4 in reference to the possibility of uniting oneself with Christ by believing in his message. Jadid al-Islam sees this as a step towards erasing distinctions between Greeks and Jews, men and women, masters and slaves. For him the ultimate logical consequence of this would be to justify promiscuity through the assumption that, at the end, all the believers would be united in Christ.[61] This interpretation seems to be confirmed by another passage from *Ephesians* 4 in which celibacy is portrayed as a key for harmony among the believers. He translates the passage thus:

> I implore you to accept this path and follow me on this path of humbleness, forbearance (*maẓlūmī*), and absolute patience. You should all care for each other, for if all of you became single, you will be together in peace, and it is this belief that I want you [to accept] and one to which you shall adhere: you have become one body and one soul.[62]

Finally, our author quotes his rendition of an excerpt from *1 Corinthians* 9, where Paul asks: 'Are Barnabas and I the only ones who cannot work for a living and who cannot marry a believing wife?'[63] This apparent lamentation appears in the context of the statement of Paul's rights as an apostle. In discussing it, our author sees in it a hypocritical excuse through which priests could justify their detachment from the responsibilities of marriage in order to indulge in promiscuity.

Dietary Restrictions and Legal Matters

Another set of passages dealing with Christian norms is devoted to the discussion of dietary customs and restrictions. This was also a common theme throughout the history of Muslim–Christian polemics, as different treatments of it appear in the works of Ibn Hazm, Samaw'al al-Maghribi and al-Qarafi, among others.[64] We have talked earlier about the tradition according to which Muhammad offered Zayd b. 'Amr b. Nufayl meat sacrificed to idols, and how by being chastised for it he was introduced to the notion of ritual purity in the slaughter of animals. This story exemplifies the centrality of dietary regulations to notions of orthopraxis. But beyond this trope, the recurrence of this theme in interreligious polemics can also be explained by the sheer tangibility of the ramifications of adhering to dietary norms, and their consequences in shaping Muslim–Christian interactions on the ground. European accounts of Iran – and of other Middle Eastern realms for that matter – abound in references to the dietary customs of Muslims. Jean Chardin, for example, revealed a certain degree of awareness of Islamic legal norms when explaining the reasons behind the prohibition of alcohol and pork and other impure (*najis*) animals.[65] Nicolas Sanson, on the other hand, emphasised the Persians' refusal to eat anything that had been torn apart by beasts, or even to eat from the same plate as Jews, Christians, Hindus or even Sunnis, let alone the meat of an animal that had not been properly slaughtered according to Islamic norms.[66] Further, questions of ritual slaughter and wine consumption were so recurrent in Iranian legal manuals from the mid-seventeenth century, that Rula Abisaab has suggested that they could have been written in response to the increasing visibility of non-Muslim subjects in the empire, and in response to questions brought to the ulama by Muslims living side-by-side with non-Muslims. For example, during his tenure as Shaykh al-Islam, Shaykh Baha'i identified a series of food items consumed by Georgians and allowed Muslims living among Christians to eat them. He also forbade Muslims from preventing Georgians from eating pork or drinking wine, and he even authorised Muslims to pretend to eat and drink these items for the purpose of pious dissimulation (*taqiyya*).[67] This is all the more notable given that, as a general rule, Shi'i jurists tend to hold stricter views on ritually-slaughtered meat (*dhabīḥa*) than most Sunnis – particularly Hanafis – which often leads them to forbid the consumption of meat slaughtered by Christians and Jews.[68] Abisaab has suggested, however, that the reinforcement of the stricter approach in this period was often politically motivated, noting how in other instances Shaykh Baha'i himself forbade Muslims from eating meat slaughtered by

Armenians, to dissipate Ottoman criticism against the Shah's alliance with the Julfan merchants.[69]

In addition to this context, and closer to the genesis of the cycle we are concerned with, depiction of the assemblies (*majlis*) from Akbar's court by ʿAbd al-Sattar Lahuri portray Jerome Xavier discussing dietary matters with Muslim scholars.[70] This of course became part of the rest of the chain of refutations and counter refutations of which the *Sayf al-muʾminin* constituted the last link. The first relevant section here is called *Ahkam-i gusht-i hayvanat dar Turat va bavar-i Nasara dar in barih* (*Rulings on Animal Meat in the Torah and Christian Beliefs in this Regard*). The discussion here revolves around the interpretation of *Genesis* 9:3, which states that Noah is allowed to eat all terrestrial animals. Our author introduces the discussion saying that it was suitable (*munāsib*) to write it 'so that these infidels [Christians] will not have any excuse [to justify their dietary practices] (*barā-yi ānkih īn kuffār hīch ʿaẕarī nadāshtih bāshand*)'.[71] To prove that this line must have been falsified, our author makes reference to *Deuteronomy* 14, of which he offers his own rendition:

> Do not eat impure (*najis*) animals. Instead, the [kinds of] animals that you should eat are the ox, the sheep, the deer, the goat, the ibex, the ewe, the gazelle, the bull – which is the male of the cow – the *mūr* – which is a male camel – the *s̱aybil* – which is a kind of mountain cow – and any animal with cloven hooves and which chews the cud. But among those with a cloven hoof and which chew the cud, do not eat those from the family of the camel, the rabbit, or hyrax.[72]

He accuses Saint Jerome of having added the camel to the list of forbidden animals:

> Jerome was a liar and was not protected from lying (*dar durūgh-gū rā ḥāfiẓ namī bāshad*). As such, he wanted to forbid what was allowed (*ḥalāl rā ḥarām kunad*), and since the general rule [for prohibition] was forgotten [that is, the rule of the cloven hoof], he introduced the camel, through his pen, into the category of forbidden meat.[73]

He then explains that Moses had added pork to the list following the criteria of the cloven hoof, and had also barred his community from eating aquatic animals without fins and scales.[74] According to this thesis, then, Saint Jerome would have made it permissible (*ḥalāl*) to eat all animals for which the restriction of the fins and scales did not apply, that is, all terrestrial animals. Further, since in *Deuteronomy* 14 the word 'impure' (*najis* [Jadid al-Islam]/ *immunda* [Saint Jerome]) was used instead of the word 'forbidden' (*ḥarām*), Saint Jerome (and Saint Paul before him) – Jadid al-Islam argues – had taken advantage of this terminological distinction to render *ḥalāl* certain *ḥarām* animals.[75] Our author feels the need to refute this logic:

> A way to resolve this contradiction [regarding the permissibility of eating certain animals] [is to say] that [some animals] are impure (*najis*) instead of forbidden (*ḥarām*). But he [Jerome] did not know that this way of reasoning would disgrace him further, because every time that Moses says in this passage [*Deuteronomy* 14] that one should refrain from eating any given animal because it is *ḥarām*, it proves a fortiori (*bih ṭarīq-i awlā*) that animals that are *najis* are also *ḥarām*. Thus, whatever is *najis* is *ḥarām*. By repeatedly following this kind of reasoning, whereby [certain animals] would be only *najis*, Jerome sought to make *ḥalāl* every animal he added [to the list]. However, since this line of reasoning does not stand its ground, he bastardised it (*khudish nīz ḥarāmzādih bīrūn āmad*), because aside from this bastard (*bih ghayr az ḥarāmzādih*), nobody else has introduced so many alterations into the Holy Books and into the sayings of the prophets.[76]

Jadid al-Islam sees this as a case of *taḥrīf* intended to circumvent the law and endorse illegal dietary practices. However, the argument becomes even more complex, as our author engages in an elaborate discussion on the legal implications of terms like impure (*najis*) and forbidden (*ḥarām*):

> [Christians] [will] see that whatever God Almighty considered as impure (*najis*) and forbidden (*ḥarām*) in the Torah – which He brought through Moses – is also impure and forbidden in the book that the Paraclete brought on behalf of the Creator. And, if there are reports in the books of the prophets about the impurity (*najāsat*) and the prohibition (*ḥarāmat*) [of something], and if it is also considered forbidden and impure in the book of this Paraclete, it is therefore also considered as such in the Torah of Moses and in the books of the prophets. Even though the abrogation (*naskh kardan*)

> of divine rulings (*aḥkām-i ilāhī*) was permissible (*jāʾiz*) at certain times and for certain people; yet, when it comes to existing beings (*aʿyān-i mawjūdāt*), it cannot be that a given animal would be impure in essence (*najis al-ʿayn*) at one point and later become pure (*pāk*). Nor can it be that an animal be considered *ḥalāl* at one point and become *ḥarām* after, because if such were the case the truth would be contingent on capriciousness (*qalb-i ḥaqāʾiq mī shavad*) and every one could apply their own reasoning (*īn nazd-i har ʿaqlī maḥāl ast*).[77]

Jadid al-Islam's accusation against Saint Jerome thus transcends the question of the accuracy of the translation or the integrity of the original text, to also address the internal logic of how Christian norms could be extracted from the scriptures, as we have also seen in previous passages. The way our author approaches the topic evokes the argumentative structure used in Islamic legal rulings: by arguing that impurity (*najāsat*) was a sufficient condition to make an animal *ḥarām*, our author implicitly points towards the *ratio legis* – or in Islamic terms, the *ʿilla* – behind the prohibition of certain kinds of meat. Further, according to the text, Moses had applied the same logic in the prohibition of pork, by referring to the rule of the cloven hoof, thus resorting to analogical reasoning (*qiyās*). In this excerpt, Jadid al-Islam is of course not concerned with debates on the extent to which *ijtihād* could be used to derive legal rulings, nor on the permissibility of relying on *qiyās*, which was a discussion of utmost centrality among Shiʿi jurists.[78] However, his reasoning does reveal a relatively sophisticated degree of juridical literacy, which also appears, albeit in a simplified manner, in European descriptions of Muslim customs, as in the abovementioned cases of Chardin and Sanson. The latter cases show how legal principles were so central to social norms that even uninitiated observers could grasp their basics. However, Jadid al-Islam's more elaborate treatment of the matter reveals a more refined knowledge of the principles in question and serves as another layer of evidence about his integration into scholarly circles.

Finally, Jadid al-Islam closes the section with a note on the prohibition of blood consumption. After citing the explicit prohibition of blood from *Deuteronomy* 12, he discusses how Christians have become so incongruent as to transgress the internal logic derived from their own sources of authority:

> Christians from this age have disbelieved not only with respect to God and the prophets, but also with respect to Paul and Jerome. Because, although Paul and his disciple Jerome authorised [eating] certain animals – both pure and impure – that God had forbidden, they did not authorise their followers to consume the blood of such animals. This belief stems from what Jerome himself has written, as [being] the word of God saying: 'you can take as food any creature that is alive and moves except those which have blood'. Also pointing towards the prohibition of blood is [another passage] that Jerome interpreted for them [Christians][as coming] from the tongue of Moses, who in *Deuteronomy* 12 said: 'Do not eat the blood of any animal, because in them their blood substitutes their souls, and therefore you should not eat their flesh and their souls. You should instead spill the blood on the ground like water'.[79]

Here also Jadid al-Islam's refutation of Christian practices – or of his representation of them – consists of pointing out how they contradict the internal logic of their own norms. Thus, after establishing that even Saint Jerome's allegedly tampered text pointed towards the prohibition of blood consumption, he shows how Christian practice betrays this restriction:

> Christians make a snake's venom out of every animal they want [to eat] (*har ḥayvānī rā kih mī khvāhand zahr-i mār kunand*), since they never slaughter it properly and never spill its blood on the ground. Instead, they choke it and eat it with its blood. When hosting guests, they slaughter pigs, cows or sheep, by splitting the flank of their throats with a bloody knife the size of a lancet. They then collect the blood in a vessel and put salt and vinegar on it to prevent it from rotting, and then cook some of it with spices and eat it.[80]

Once the prohibition is made clear and irrefutable, Jadid al-Islam is able to use it to attack once again the sacrament of communion. So even if as a Muslim he could not accept the physical reality of the transubstantiation of wine into blood, the condemnation of the sacrament is not expressed merely in terms of its feasibility, but rather in legal terms as a transgression of the laws derived from Scripture.

In a similar vein, the section *Haramat-i sharab-khvari dar Turat va Injil* (*The Prohibition of Wine-Drinking in the Torah and the Gospels*) addresses the prohibition of wine.[81] Jadid al-Islam starts by providing his interpretation of *Leviticus* 10:

> When He ordered the Children of Israel to abstain from wine, he did not say that they should abstain from drinking in excess. He ruled unconditionally (*muṭlaq ḥukm kardih*) that Aaron and his sons should not drink wine or any intoxicating substances (*mast-kunandih*), and He said that this shall be an everlasting ruling (*ḥukm-i ābadī*), which means that it cannot be abrogated (*kih dar ān naskh nīst*).[82]

He complements this with other explicit proscriptions from *Deuteronomy* 6. The most elaborate argument, however, begins with a reference to *Luke* 1, in which the Angel Gabriel announces the birth of John the Baptist to Zacharias. As the latter abstains from drinking wine to celebrate the occasion, the Holy Spirit blesses him with of overwhelming joy. Jadid al-Islam uses this passage to demonstrate that the prohibition was absolute and not dependent on the quantity of the substance ingested:

> According to the terminology used in Christian books, whoever is assisted by the Holy Spirit (*mu'ayyad-i Rūḥ al-Quds*) – such as John [the Baptist], Aaron and those among his children who were leaders of the Tribe of Israel – or anyone who was assisted by the Spirit of Faith (*Rūḥ-i īmān*) – like the rest of Aaron's children – should not only abstain from becoming inebriated, but even from tasting [wine]. Had God Almighty not considered drinking wine without becoming inebriated as a reprehensible (*qabīḥ*) practice, on the basis that it could be beneficial for the body, he would have granted these benefits to His loved ones and would have [only] prevented them from becoming inebriated.[83]

Here the author also treats the biblical passage like a Muslim scholar extracting the *'illa* of a ruling (*ḥukm*) using hadith. In this case, the *ratio legis* of the prohibition is traced back to the nature of the substance itself and not to its potential abuse.

Jadid al-Islam then discusses an excerpt from *Genesis* 9:21 in which Noah becomes intoxicated to the point at which his son Ham finds him laying naked outside his tent. He dismisses this account as another case of falsification. More importantly, he notes that the veracity of this passage would have been inconsequential for Christians, given that – like Sunnis – they did not abide by the examples of the prophets and Imams as models of emulation. However, for the Shiʿis the implications of a drunken prophet would have been more serious, given their belief in the notion of the pious emulation of the Imams (*taqlīd*). In addition, the Shiʿa have traditionally held a stronger position than Sunnis on the notion of the infallibility of prophets, as an attribute that is not only circumscribed to the specificity of their mission, but is rather an integral part of their prophetic ontology.[84] Consequently, Jadid al-Islam feels the need to elaborate on the question of the moral authority and judgements of the prophets of the Old Testament, adding that the self-evident Truth of the Creator should suffice to guide the believer along the path of righteousness:

> Whoever possesses full discernment (*ʿaql-i kāmil*) knows that the Creator exists, and whoever knows that the Creator exists would obviously acknowledge that He is just (*ʿādil*), and anyone who believes in Divine Justice should recognise that He does not act upon tyranny (*ẓulm namī kunad*). Therefore, since Christians claim to believe in all these precepts, they should also believe that someone who was designated by God to deliver a proof to His creation should refrain from performing bad acts (*fiʿl-i qabīḥ*). [This is] because if that person which God Almighty had designated as a proof for His creation performed bad acts, then God Almighty's proof for His creation would not be fulfilled. Because if anyone saw a prophet or deputy (*vaṣī*) [of God] committing a sin, he will not trust his words.[85]

It is thus clear to our author that God would not have allowed a prophet of his to engage in reprehensible acts because that would have put into question His message and the moral authority of the prophets He had chosen. The reasoning here can be thought of as an inversion of the logic of the *ʿilm al-rijāl*: that is, instead of examining the background of a character to determine the validity of what he reports, it is through the certainty as to the righteousness of the character – Noah as a prophet – that damning reports about him can be dismissed as fabrications. Jadid al-Islam concludes by resorting to another terminological analysis, this time related to the epithet given to Noah, first in the Latin Vulgate and then in the *Biblia Sacra Arabica*. The object of discussion here is the way in which God describes Noah in Genesis 7:

> Go into the ark, you and your whole family, because I have found you righteous in this generation. (*dixitque Dominus ad eum ingredere tu et omnis domus tua arcam te enim vidi iustum coram me in generatione hac* [Latin Vulgate]/ *wa qāla lahu al-Rabb udkhul anta wa jamīʿ ahl baytika ilā al-fulk li-anī raʾituka bārran amāmī fī hadhā al-jīl* [*Biblia Sacra Arabica*]).[86]

Our author argues that the word for 'righteous' or 'just', which in the Vulgata appears as 'iustum' and in the Bibila Sacra Arabica as '*bārr*', both of which terms have the connotation of simply being a 'good-doer' (*nīkū-kār*), should have been rendered instead as 'immaculate' (*maʿṣūm*). This *taḥrīf* – our author argues – extirpates the epithet of its theological implications – given that this term is the one used to refer to Muhammad, Fatima and the twelve Imams: the fourteen immaculate ones (*maʿṣūmīn*)– and, in so doing, presents Noah as vulnerable to sin.[87]

On Image Crafting

A final thematic block to consider is that which corresponds to matters of worship. The sections in question elaborate on the topic of *shirk*, in a way reminiscent to what we saw in parts of Chapter three and in the responses to Guadagnoli. This too was a recurrent motif of polemical exchanges in general and in particular in the cycle we are concerned with. In the *Fuente de Vida* and later in the *Aʾinih-i haqq-numa*, Jerome Xavier presents a dialogue between a priest and a Muslim philosopher (*ḥakīm*) discussing the permissibility of using representations of saints and of holy figures as aids for prayer, as well as on the use of relics as amulets.[88] The sections on this matter in the *Sayf al-muʾminin* – called respectively *Muqayisih-i but-parasti-yi Masihiyan va Hindiyan* (*Comparing Idolatry in Hinduism and Christianity*) and *Surat-sazi dar Masihiyyat* (*Image-crafting in Christianity*) – are not exactly direct responses to the said excerpts from the *Fuente* and the *Aʾinih*. However, they certainly touch upon similar issues, which were otherwise common currency in Muslim–Christian disputations.

Jadid al-Islam begins the discussion condemning what he sees as a hypocritical stance from Christians for accusing Hindus of idolatry while espousing similar practices:

> How come [Christians] curse other idol worshipers like themselves, such as the Hindu tribes, while the Hindus curse them [in return]? And when a third [group], like the tribe of the Muslims, comes forward to curse these two tribes [Hindus and Christians], neither of them accepts the curse as being directed to them. Instead, they accuse each other of being cursed and deny having anything to do with it. This is equivalent to [an example in which] two dogs enter a house, and when the owner of the house notices them, in order to [prevent] them from polluting [*najis kardan*] anything in the house, he shouts at them 'chikh, chikh'. Then the dogs look at each other and say: 'Chikh is your name, I have nothing to do with this'. Each one replies to the other in the same way and they quarrel until the owner of the house explicitly says 'both of you are Chikh'. In the same way, every time that Muslims curse idolatry, Christians say that Hindus are the idolaters and Hindus say that Christians are the idolaters; but in reality the cursing that Muslims have pronounced – and continue to pronounce – against idolatry applies to both.[89]

And adds:

> [Christians] turn a blind eye [to the fact that] keeping idols in their churches for the purpose of worship (*dar bāb-i ʿibādāt*) is very similar to giving a good name to Hindu idolatry (*but-parastī-yi Hindū rā nīk-nām bikunand*).[90]

Having thus equated Hindu and Christian practices, Jadid al-Islam rejects the standard Christian justification for using such images, namely that these are only intended to serve as representations of God. In his mind, this argument is no better than what Hindus would claim for themselves. He sees image crafting – whether in paintings or in statues – as contravening God's mandate in *Exodus* 20:4: 'do not craft for yourselves anything that resembles something else, neither from heaven above, nor from below heaven and above earth, nor from below the ground nor in the sea'.[91]

He then moves on to examine some biblical passages commonly quoted by Christians to justify the use of such images. At the heart of these are the precedents of Moses and Solomon edifying statues. The first such passage is from *Exodus* 31, of which he offers his translation:

> I show you a character by the name of Bezalel son of Uri from the tribe of the Jews. And I have filled him with the Spirit of God and with knowledge

> and wisdom (*ʿilm va dānāyī*) in all the works so that it could pretend to possess everything that he wants to build out of gold, silver, copper, marble, gems or wood. I have given him a partner by the name of Aholiab son of Ahisamach from the tribe of the Dan, and I have bestowed knowledge in the hearts of all of those who have been instructed to build the Tent of the Covenant and the Ark of the Testimony so that the tent can cover the ark instead of a cloth.[92]

The second one is from *Exodus* 15:

> When you build the Ark of the Covenant, place it over a golden pedestal so that it would be its headpiece, and on the two sides of the pedestal put two [statues] of angels made of gold so that they can adorn the flanks of the pedestal with their poles.[93]

Once again, Jadid al-Islam makes recourse to the argument of *taḥrīf* to dismiss them. However, in this case he employs another concept with legal undertones, namely that of *contextual indication* (*qarīna*/ pl. *qarāʾin*). He introduces it in the context of the alleged contradiction between Saint Jerome's text in these passages and the commonly held knowledge that prophets had always rejected image crafting:

> So it has been demonstrated from the numerous examples that we have mentioned from the books that Jerome translated, that God Almighty has unequivocally ordered not to craft images and that all the prophets that came to this world avoided image crafting. [Thus] this is a contextual indication (*qarīnih*) that these [passages authorising image crafting] are forgeries of the accursed Jerome and the Pope of Rome.[94]

As Wael Hallaq notes, the term *qarīna* in its ordinary use simply means a 'verbal or non-verbal element clarifying a part of speech extraneous to itself'.[95] However, in legal theory it is a technical term that alludes to 'the linguistic interpretation of the texts, and the knowledge that these texts, especially prophetic traditions, impart'.[96] When used in the latter sense, the term used is *qarāʾin al-aḥwāl* (circumstantial indicants). A good example of this would be the sum of all the biographical data on a hadith transmitter that can help assess his reliability by the examination of his moral integrity, judgement and knowledge. The presence of strong *qarāʾin* of this kind is, for some jurists, a necessary condition for accepting solitary hadith reports (*khabar al-wāḥid*) as sound hadith.[97] In this case then, Jadid al-Islam relies on the sum of the contextual knowledge about the practices of the prophets in the tradition he adheres to as an indication of the presence of *taḥrīf* in the passages of the *Exodus* in the Vulgata.

Finally, and according to the same rhetorical strategies we have previously seen, Jadid al-Islam examines whether the hypothetical integrity of the above passages would have justified the use of images. Unsurprisingly, he rejects this possibility on the basis that in the passages in question God did not order Moses nor Solomon to place statues of angels on altars, but only to adorn the Ark of the Covenant with the kind of ornamentation that would later be used in mosques.[98] To counter the pro-image stance of the allegedly falsified quotations from *Exodus*, our author cites a passage from *2 Kings* 18 in which Hezekiah smashes the gold snakes that Moses had fabricated and removes the sacred poles and all other signs that could be used for idolatry.[99] By way of epilogue, Jadid al-Islam responds – as he had previously done in the Guadagnoli sections – to the potential comparisons between Muslim rituals around the Kaʿba and pagan idolatry or the use of images in Christianity. His refutation here is rather conventional insofar as it consists of distinguishing the anthropomorphism of Christian imagery from the amorphous Black Stone. The section closes by anticipating the also conventional argument that Christians did not pray to the images but to whom they represent, which our author dismisses as an ineffective apology and as an implicit admission of *shirk*.[100]

Thus, through passages like these, Jadid al-Islam is able to address the core themes of Guadagnoli's *Apologia* without always referring to it explicitly. More importantly, since the topics of debate in Muslim–Christian polemics transcend the cycle in question and persist throughout history, the merits of the arguments do not reside in their originality per se. What matters instead is the richness of the body of proofs that our author brings forward, as well as the intricate ways in which he intertwines them with each other.

Notes

1. Tolan, *Saracens*, pp. 165–6, 182–3. For an overview of the history of this trope, see Tolan, *Faces of Muhammad*, pp. 44–100.
2. Tolan, *Saracens*, pp. 165–7.
3. Tolan, *Saracens*, pp. 15–16. For a comprehensive overview on Peter the Venerable's polemics, see Tolan, *Sons of Ishmael*, pp. 46–63.
4. Tolan, *Saracens*, pp. 182–6. See also Tolan, *Sons of Ishmael*, pp. 158–60.
5. Michel, *A Muslim Theologian's Response to Christianity*, pp. 88–90.
6. Tolan, *Saracens*, p. 239. For an overview of the missionary strategy of thirteenth-century Dominican friars, see *Saracens*, pp. 233–55.
7. Malcolm, 'Comenius, the Conversion of the Turks', pp. 485–8.
8. Ibid. pp. 506–8.
9. Heyberger, 'Polemic Dialogues between Christians and Muslims', p. 507.
10. Guadagnoli, *Apologia pro Christiana Religione*. The pagination for the treatises are I: pp. 5–151, II: pp. 152–370, III: pp. 371–474, IV: pp. 475–557.
11. Trentini, 'Guadagnoli controversista e islamologo', p. 311.
12. Guadagnoli, *Apologia pro Christiana Religione*, pp. 327–8.
13. This is Jadid al-Islam's own ellipsis.
14. SM, p. 188.
15. SM, pp. 191–2; Guadagnoli, *Apologia pro Christiana Religione*, pp. 197, 328.
16. SM, pp. 191–2.
17. Ibid. p. 192.
18. I am translating this subtitle in accordance to Rosalind C. Love's rendition of this verse. See Love, *Three Elevenths Century Anglo-Latin Saints' Lives*, p. 59, fn. 6.
19. Guadagnoli, *Apologia pro Christiana Religione*, p. 213; Qur'an 3:7 (I use M. A. S. Abdel Haleem's translation here, to refer to a standard translation. *The Qur'an*, p. 34).
20. SM, p. 193; Qur'an 3:7, *The Qur'an*, p. 34.
21. SM, p. 193.
22. Guadagnoli, *Apologia pro Christiana Religione*, pp. 297–309.
23. Ibid. p. 304.
24. SM, pp. 562–3, 566–7.
25. SM, pp. 562–4.
26. Ibid. pp. 564–5.
27. For a detailed study of the different versions and interpretations of the hadith

referring to this story, see Kister, 'A Bag of Meat', pp. 267–71. For debates on its implications, see 'A Bag of Meat', pp. 271–4.

28. SM, p. 583.
29. Ibid. p. 586.
30. Ibid. pp. 587–8.
31. Ibid. p. 589.
32. Ibid. p. 621.
33. For a good overview on the debates and the tradition of the Satanic Verses, see Ahmed, *Before Orthodoxy*, pp. 1–10.
34. Abdel Haleem's translation, *The Qur'an*, p. 347. For more on these verses, on the Goddesses, and their link to the Satanic Verses, see Ahmed, *Before Orthodoxy*, pp. 56–9.
35. SM, p. 621. The Qur'anic translation is from Abdel Haleem. *The Qur'an*, pp. 212–13.
36. Anthony, 'The Satanic Verses in Early Shi'ite Literature', pp. 230–3. For the reference to al-Qummi, see al-Qummi, *Tafsir*, vol. 2, p. 85.
37. Guadagnoli, *Apologia pro Christiana Religione*, pp. 305–6.
38. SM, pp. 621–3.
39. Ibid. pp. 640–1.
40. Ibid. pp. 655–6.
41. Ibid. pp. 656–7.
42. Ibid. p. 657.
43. Carnoy-Torabi, 'A biblioteca esquecida dos missionários do Ispaão', pp. 103–4.
44. Ellis, Havelock and Addington Symonds, *Sexual Inversion*, p. 90.
45. Jadid al-Islam, 'Fava'id-i izdivaj', pp. 302–3. For the Qur'anic verse, I use M. A. S. Abdel Haleem's translation; see *The Qur'an*, p. 344.
46. Said Reynolds, *A Muslim Theologian in a Sectarian Milieu*, pp. 167–9.
47. Jadid al-Islam, 'Fava'id-i izdivaj', pp. 304–5.
48. Ibid. p. 305
49. Ibid. p. 305
50. Ibid. pp. 307–8
51. I translate the term *maṣlaḥa* as 'public interest', following Wael Hallaq. The term is used to refer to a form of legal reasoning that is not directly based on revealed texts. See Hallaq, *Sharīʿa Between Past and Present*, p. 109.
52. Jadid al-Islam, 'Fava'id-i izdivaj', p. 308.
53. Ibid. p. 308.
54. Ibid. p. 308.

55. Ibid. p. 309; Qur'an 3:39 (translation by M. A. S. Abdel Haleem. *The Qur'an*, p. 37).
56. Ibid. p. 310
57. SM, pp. 105–8.
58. Ibid. pp. 437–8.
59. Ibid. pp. 438–9.
60. Ibid. p. 478.
61. Ibid. p. 479.
62. Ibid. p. 479.
63. Ibid. p. 480.
64. Lazarus-Yafeh, *Intertwined Worlds*, p. 138; Sarrió Cucarella, *Muslim-Christian Polemics across the Mediterranean*, pp. 189–92.
65. Chardin, *Voyages du Chevalier en Perse*, vol. 6, pp. 318–19, 361.
66. Sanson, *Voyage*, pp. 93, 254.
67. Abisaab, *Converting Persia*, p. 67.
68. Ibid. pp. 64–5.
69. Ibid. pp. 65–6.
70. Alam and Subrahmanyam, 'Frank Disputations', p. 502.
71. SM, p. 173.
72. Ibid. p. 173.
73. Ibid. p. 173.
74. Ibid. p. 173.
75. SM, pp. 173–4. For the term in the Vulgata, see Jerome, *Vulgata* (online edition).
76. SM, p. 174.
77. Ibid. p. 175.
78. For an overview of Shi'i positions on *qiyās*, refer to Gleave, 'Imāmī Shī'ī Refutations of *qiyās*'.
79. SM, p. 175.
80. Ibid. pp. 175–6.
81. Ibid. p. 178.
82. Ibid. p. 178.
83. Ibid. p. 179.
84. Consider, for example, what al-'Allama al-Hilli says in his *Minhaj al-salah*. When listing the characteristics of the prophets he says: 'He [meaning, any prophet] is infallible (*ma'ṣūm*) from the beginning until the end of his life. For the absence of obedience in the hearts is the obedience of those who earlier

in life became acquainted with [different] kinds of disobedience, great sins, and [all of] that which is repulsive to the soul (*fī annahu maʿṣūm min awwal ʿumrihi ilā akhirihi, la-ʿadam inqiyād al-qulūb ilā ṭāʿat man ʿuhidu minhi fī sālif ʿumrihi anwāʿ al-maʿāṣī wa al-kabāʾir wa mā tunafir al-nafs minhī*)'. Al-Hilli, *Minhaj al-salah*, p. 527.

85. Ibid. p. 180.
86. SM, p. 182. The Bible translation here is from the New International Version. The quote from the *Biblia Sacra Arabica* appears in the *Sayf al-muʾminin*. See SM, p. 151. For the Quote from the Latin Vulgate see Jerome, *Vulgata* (online edition).
87. Ibid. p. 182.
88. Xavier, *Fuente de Vida*, pp. 326–36; see also Camps, *Jerome Xavier S.J. and the Muslims of the Mogul Empire*, pp. 95–6; Didier, 'Jerónimo Xavier, un Navarro en la India', p. 151.
89. SM, pp. 440–1.
90. Ibid. p. 441.
91. Ibid. p. 442.
92. Ibid. p. 443.
93. Ibid. pp. 443–4.
94. Ibid. p. 445.
95. Hallaq, 'Notes on the Term *qarīna* in Islamic Legal Discourse', p. 475.
96. Ibid. p. 475.
97. SM, pp. 178–9.
98. Ibid. p. 179.
99. Ibid. pp. 445–6.
100. Ibid. pp. 446–9.

6

Sufis as the Christians of the Umma

While the refutation of Christianity constituted the overarching thread of Jadid al-Islam's intellectual production, another major theme that is present throughout his work is his anti-Sufi position. Not only does this constitute the topic of one of his minor pieces, the *Risalih dar radd-i jamaʿat-i sufiyan*, but it also surfaces in many sections of the *Sayf al-muʾminin*. The sole surviving manuscript of this *risāla*, kept at the Sipahsalar Library, is undated.[1] However, explicit references to it in the *Sayf al-muʾminin* make it clear that its composition preceded that of his magnum opus and suggest that it was written in preparation for this work.[2] Moreover, Rasul Jaʿfariyan has identified certain phrases in the *risāla* that are identical to some of the *Hidayat al-zallin*.[3] This alone should justify taking a closer look at Jadid al-Islam's anti-Sufi passages and work. But there is a yet more important reason for examining this aspect of his intellectual output, namely that through it our author was able to position himself within the framework of other discussions, which for his scholarly coreligionists in Isfahan were more important than engaging in Muslim–Christian disputations for their own sake. It is not clear the extent to which his anti-Sufi *risāla* was read by subsequent scholars, let alone the relevant passages in the *Sayf al-muʾminin*. However, the thematic makeup of his work and the chronological context in which it was conceived suggest that his own views on the matter were informed by those of his more authoritative peers. What is also clear is that he tailored his work in such a way that it could appeal to an audience that could potentially discern in it contemporary debates on the legitimacy (or lack thereof) of mystical thought.

Sufis, the Ulama and the State in Safavid Iran

First, a short overview of the reception of Sufism in the Safavid period is in order. Throughout the Safavid Period the relationship between the ulama, the state and its institutions, and what can loosely be grouped under the umbrella-term of 'Sufism' was marred by contradictions and changing attitudes. The early history of the dynasty was closely linked to organised Sufism. As is well known, before becoming a political dynasty, the Safavids started as a Sunni Sufi order (*ṭarīqa*) when its founder, Shaykh Safi al-Din Ardabili (d. 1334), inherited Zahid-i Gilani's (d. 1301) Zahidiyya order. The latter order claimed to be connected to ʿAli and Muhammad, and was therefore inclined towards a certain kind of non-sectarian ʿAlid devotionalism, which characterised Sufism of this era in general.[4] Morimoto has now decisively shown how, even before becoming a ruling political dynasty, the Safavids claimed to have *sayyid* status.[5] However, as he has also demonstrated, at this time, and in the case of people claiming the status of *sayyids*/*sharīfs*, sectarian lines were rather blurred.[6] Under Shaykh Safi's descendants Junayd (d. 1460) and Haydar (d. 1488), the order began to be associated with Shiʿism, although still often infused with elements of the folk-religiosity practised by the Qizilbash tribes; and under Shah Ismaʿil, with the establishment of the Safavid political dynasty, Twelver Shiʿism finally became state religion.[7] During his tenure, Shah Ismaʿil started a campaign of persecution against Sunni Sufi orders, such as the Naqshbandis, the Khalvatis and the Kazarunis. In contrast, Shiʿi orders such as the Haidaris and the Niʿmatullahis were favoured by the state, and at times their adepts even intermarried with members of the Safavid house.[8]

Throughout the sixteenth century, legalistic Twelver Shiʿism became institutionalised slowly but steadily through the courtly patronage of émigré scholars from Ottoman Levant.[9] This did not immediately eradicate forms of popular piety practised by the Qizilbash or by the various Sufi orders themselves. However, the Safavids did enforce practices such as the ritual cursing (*tabarruʾ*) of the first three caliphs, which repelled adherents of orders like the Naqshbandiyya, since its chain of authority (*silsila*) connected them to the Caliph Abu Bakr (d. 634) and since they openly combated the ascendance of Shiʿism in fifteenth-century Herat.[10] In addition, partisan confrontations between the orders also affected the Shiʿi Niʿmatullahis and Haidaris, who managed nonetheless to establish strongholds in various cities.[11]

With the decline of the Qizilbash under Shah ʿAbbas I, other social actors – such as the Georgian slave-soldiers – acquired greater influence within the state. In terms of religious authority, this process led to the consolidation of high-ranking ulama in positions of power, constituting what Said Amir Arjomand has called the 'clerical hierocracy'.[12] The most powerful among the latter would go on to attain positions like Shaykh al-Islam or, in the later years of the dynasty, *mullā-bashī*. Throughout the first half of the seventeenth century, influential members of the clerical hierocracy adhered to the philosophical tradition of *ʿirfān*, which Arjomand has called 'high Sufism'.[13] Among the greatest exponents of this trend to enjoy a high status at the court were Mulla Muhsin Fayz-i Kashani (d. 1680) and Muhammad Taqi Majlisi (d. 1660), both of whom were patronised by Shah ʿAbbas II.[14] Other mystically inclined thinkers, who were not necessarily patronised by the court, like Mulla Sadra (d. 1636) or ʿAbd al-Razzaq Lahiji Gilani (d. 1662), contributed nevertheless to the intellectual renaissance of what would later be grouped under the umbrella-term of the 'School of Isfahan'.[15] Although *ṭarīqa* Sufism was already in decline at that time, many of these thinkers distanced themselves from practices of folk-devotionalism. For example, in his *Kasr asnam al-jahiliyya fi-l-radd ʿala al-mutasawwifa* (*Smashing the Idols of Ignorance* (*or paganism*) *through the Refutation of Pseudo-Sufis* (or *Sufi-Pretenders*)), Mulla Sadra draws a distinction between mystically inclined philosophers and practitioners of popular piety, whom he disqualifies as Sufi-pretenders (*mutaṣawwifa*).[16] A similar attitude can be observed in the writings of Fayz-i Kashani: in his *Sharh-i sadr* (*The Opening of the Heart*) he defends Sufis from 'worldly scholars' (*ʿulamāʾ-yi dunyā*), and in his *al-Muhakama* (*The Judgement*) he argues for the complementarity of the people of knowledge and wisdom (*ʿilm va maʿrifat*) – the ulama – and the people of asceticism and worship (*zuhd va ʿibādat*) – that is, Sufis.[17] However, in another short *risāla* he condemns chanting (*ghināʾ*) and ritual remembrance (*dhikr*), and in his *al-Insaf* (*Justice*) he chastises those who saw in the study of Sufi poets and philosophers a path into forms of knowledge otherwise inaccessible in the Qurʾan and the hadith.[18]

Anti-Sufi Literature in the Late Safavid Period

Towards the second half of the seventeenth century, organised Sufism experienced an inexorable decline. Earlier scholarship attributed this phenomenon to officially sanctioned suppression.[19] Andrew Newman, drawing on Kathryn Babayan's terminology, has explained this in terms of a factional conflict whereby the anti-mystical 'Rustam Beg cabal' gained ascendancy at the court at the expense of the pro-Sufi 'Shaykhavanid cabal', to which the likes of Mir Damad and Shaykh Baha'i belonged.[20] More recently, however, Ata Anzali has convincingly argued that the waning of the orders was a consequence of the conversion of the majority of the population to Twelver Shi'ism.[21] Whatever the case, what is clear is that this period witnessed an unprecedented proliferation of anti-Sufi refutations (*radd/rudūd*). Ata Anzali has identified close to twenty anti-Sufi *rudūd* from between the 1630s and the 1730s, with the largest number of treatises written between 1651 and 1666.[22] One of the major themes in these works was the condemnation of the *Abu Muslimnamihs*, a series of folk narratives celebrating the exploits of the hero of the Abbasid Revolution, Abu Muslim Khurasani (d. 754–5). The genre was associated with the messianism and heterodoxy of the early Safavids and of other *ghuluww* orders, and was thus deemed reprehensible by some legally minded scholars. Among the fiercest detractors of the genre was Mir Lawhi (d. 1672), who reproached the influential Muhammad Taqi Majlisi for its promotion.[23]

But the most important development of the second half of the seventeenth century was the emergence of a trend of anti-Sufism which was embedded within a broader attack on philosophy, both of the *'irfānī* kind and of Greek scholasticism more generally. Why this was the case has been a matter of some debate. Regarding the attack on *'irfān*, Arjomand has advanced the thesis that, despite been politically quietist, *'irfān* was seen as a threat because it 'undermine[d] hierocratic authority – lessening the importance of the hierocratic action and thereby strengthening the hand of the state – and consequently the preponderance of state-initiated acts in the overall pattern of societal action'.[24] The major representative of this trend was Muhammad Tahir-i Qummi (d. 1689), a mid-ranking scholar who rapidly ascended to various positions of power, being appointed Friday prayer leader in Qom paradoxically by the *ʿirfānī*-leaning Shah ʿAbbas II, and later promoted to Shaykh al-Islam in Qom under Shah Sulayman.[25]

Past scholarship had attributed to Qummi the *Hadiqat al-Shiʿa*, a text written in the Deccan in Southern India towards 1648 which then circulated widely in Iran.[26] This work condemns the doctrines of the divine incarnation (*ḥulūl*) and union with God (*ittiḥād*) in association with classical figures of the Sufi tradition such as Mansur al-Hallaj (d. 922) or Abu Yazid Bistami (d. *c.* 874), and directs other attacks against the philosopher Muhyi al-Din Ibn ʿArabi (d. 1240) and against the aforementioned *Abu Muslimnamih* tradition.[27] The targeting of Ibn ʿArabi would go on to become, by the mid to late seventeenth century, the major leitmotif of anti-Sufi treatises in Iran.[28] At the forefront of these attacks was Tahir-i Qummi, who authored various pieces with anti-Sufi content.[29] In his *Risalih-i radd-i sufiyyih* (*Treatise Refuting the Sufis*), written in response to Taqi Majlisi, Qummi rejects the existence of any historic links between Sufism and Shiʿism, noting that no Sufi lodges (*khānqāhs*) were ever established near any major Shiʿi centres like Qom, Astarabad, Sabzavar, Jabal ʿAmil or Hilla.[30] He also condemns Sufi practices such as abstaining from eating meat for forty days, which he associates with Sunnis, and goes to the extent of saying that the only truth to have ever been uttered by a Sufi was ʿAlaʾ al-Dawla al-Simnani's (d. 1336) admission that the devil had been whispering to him throughout his twenty-three years of practising Sufism.[31] In addition to this *risāla*, Qummi engaged in a full-scale attack on philosophy in his magnum opus, the *Hikmat al-ʿarifin* (*The Philosophy of the Gnostics*), in which he condemns Ibn ʿArabi's brand of philosophical mysticism, specifically targeting Mulla Sadra.[32]

A major Akhbari scholar who engaged in attacks on Sufism was the famous biographist, hadith scholar and jurist al-Hurr al-ʿAmili. He included several anti-Sufi traditions in his collections, and drew heavily on the *akhbār* (or hadith) of the Imams to refute many of the aforementioned Sufi concepts of *ḥulūl*, *ittiḥād* and *waḥdat al-wujūd* (unity of existence).[33] The powerful Muhammad Baqir Majlisi also contributed to the anti-Sufi environment, directing the bulk of his condemnation to the idea of *waḥdat al-wujūd*, through his treatise *ʿAqaʾid al-Islam* (*The Doctrines of Islam*).[34] Finally, anti-Sufism also crept into works that were not strictly speaking of a legal nor a theological nature. An example of this can be found in the *al-Anwar al-nuʿmaniyya* (*The Auspicious Lights*), a literary anthology written by the Akhbari scholar Niʿmat Allah al-Jazaʾiri (d. 1700–1). This work also reproduces arguments against Ibn ʿArabi and retells stories in which, at times al-ʿAllama al-Hilli and at times Imam Riza, chastise dervishes for their ritually unlawful practices such as neglecting prayer or hitting their heads and spilling blood on the tomb of Imam Riza.[35]

Anti-Sufi sentiment thus became a dominant trend among the most influential ulama of the time. Whether this was because of or despite the weakening of the moral and de facto authority of the state in the final decades of the dynasty is a matter of debate. On the one hand the patronage enjoyed by the clerical hierocracy hostile to Sufism and philosophy would suggest that there was indeed a concerted effort to scapegoat Muslim groups deemed as heterodox in the eyes of the new establishment, much in the way non-Muslim minorities were targeted around the same time. However, it could also be that it was precisely the fragility of the state that created a power vacuum that was filled by some ulama seeking to consolidate their influence above – rather than within – the structures of the waning political and institutional system. Whatever the case it seems clear that religious scholars seeking any sort of recognition in this milieu had at least to play lip service to these anti-Sufi anxieties. This is the context within which Jadid al-Islam's anti-Sufi stance must be understood.

Jadid al-Islam's *Risalih dar radd-i jamaʿat-i sufiyan*

Jadid al-Islam starts his *Radd* by comparing the charismatic authority of Christian priests to that of Sufi shaykhs (*pīrs*) and by establishing a genealogical link between Christianity and Sufism:

> So know dear [brothers] that your humble servant [has found] through the exploration of Christian books and of the discourse of the religious authorities (*pīrān*), and of the positions (*awżāʿ*) and methods (*aṭvār*) of this sect (*mazhab*), that this sect of Sufism (*mazhab-i taṣavvuf*) has been linked to Christianity since ancient times and that the two have continued to mix with each other until this day. Christians have supported [the idea] of the unity between their priests – through laborious study (*riyāżat*) and acquisition [of knowledge] (*kasb*) – with the Holy Spirit, who they consider as one

> of the persons of the Trinity. Likewise, Sufis now believe that anyone can be united with God by following the mystical path under the supervision of the major Sufi guide of the order (*pīr-i kāmil*).[36]

This comparison between Christian priesthood and Sufi *pīrhood* was of course no novelty at the time of Jadid al-Islam's writing. This idea had a long history, with one of the most important examples being that of Ibn Taymiyya's *Al-jawab al-sahih li-man baddala din al-Masih* (*The Correct Reply to the One that Altered the Religion of the Messiah*). As we will see Jadid al-Islam doing throughout this text, Ibn Taymiyya also traced the concept of *waḥdat al-wujūd* (unity of existence) back to what he considered Christian practices of idol worship and polytheism (*shirk*).[37] One key difference, however, lies within their respective sectarian undertones: Ibn Taymiyya included the Shiʿa in his condemnation of Sufis and Christians, arguing that they all ascribed the attribute of infallibility to people other than the prophets, to Imams, *pīrs* and priests respectively.[38] Jadid al-Islam, by contrast, seeks to rebuke the idea of the charismatic authority of the *pīrs* (and of the priests, by analogy), while retaining that of the Imams. The challenge this poses is not immediately resolved in the *Radd*, which then takes a different turn, much more in line with the attack on philosophy made by Qummi and other late Safavid ulama.

Jadid al-Islam moves on to propose a genealogy of the term 'Sufi' by resorting to the same kind of etymological arguments that we have seen in various sections of his *Sayf al-muʾminin*. Noting that European languages did not distinguish between 's' and 'ṣ', he turns to Calepino's lexicon, to the entry on the term 'Sophism' which, he argues, was at the origin of both *ṣūfī* and *sūfī*, the latter referring to the early Greek philosophers known as the Seven Sages of Greece.[39] Before elaborating on the philosophical connections between the Greeks and the Sufis, he condemns the ritual practices of the latter in a way reminiscent of the more mainstream Safavid philosophers, including those with *ʿirfānī* inclinations:

> So it thus happens that a group of Muslims, the majority of whom are poor and needy – for as Sufi *pīrs* show, men can reach a state in which the yoke of slavery has fallen from people's necks and yet be enslaved by others – have joined Sufi groups. And in order to prevent their many transient worldly

> duties from stopping them from learning about their religious obligations, and hoping to reach a state in which those obligations would be suspended, they gather in a place to chant and recite poetry, just as evil-doers like [Muhammad Shirin] Maghribi (d. *c.* 1407–8) and [Farid al-Din] Attar did. Thus, sometimes through ritual remembrance (*ẕikr*), sometimes through ecstasy (*wajd*) and sometimes in chanting (*samāʿ*), they deprive themselves from listening to lectures on the remembrance of the family of the Prophet (*manāqib- va fażāʾil-i ahl-i bayt-i Rasūl*). And in the same way that people of ancient evil sects would rejoice before their idols and recite poetry [for them], this other group [Sufis] plays melodious music for a beautiful boy who is present at such assemblies (*majlis*); and they consider this kind of movements as acts of worship (*ʿibādāt*). And thus, when Pythagoras appeared amongst the [old] philosophers (*ḥukamā*) and the people of the evil sect (*mardum-i bad-maẕhab*), for our benefit he called himself a philosopher (*filusūf*), meaning 'one who loves knowledge'.[40]

Having thus linked Sufis to paganism and pre-Pythagorian philosophy, Jadid al-Islam condemns them in the harshest of terms, arguing that, as self-proclaimed Muslims, they could not count on the excuse of their ignorance of revelation:

> But these Christians of today – that is, Sufis – are worse than those [other] Christians, because the divine grace (*luṭf-i ilāhī*) was infused into them and they were born into Islam and they knew of its existence. And yet, they have extended their hands [reaching out] to the robes of the speeches of the [old] philosophers (*ḥukamā*) and of the ignorant Sufi *pīrs*, and they have closed their eyes to the hadith of the Prophet's family. They have taken a newly lit path that is not indicated in any hadith, and have adopted ritual practices (*ʿibādāt*) like dancing, whirling, chanting, lovemaking and other customs in which they engage with each other.[41]

What is important to note here is that Jadid al-Islam does not draw a distinction between philosophical mysticism and practices of popular piety. Nor does he resolve the tension between rejecting Sufi gatherings and practices of charity like those which can be found in Twelver Shiʿism itself.[42] Following a more conventional practice, he reproaches Sufis for appropriating the term *awliyāʾ Allāh* (friends of God), saying that it should be reserved for the companions of the Prophet, but 'not [for] those ignorant *pīrs* which at the beginning of the path stepped away (*pā az dāʾirih-i bandigī bīrūn gashtih*) and went out saying "I am the Truth (*anā al-ḥaqq*)"', a clear reference to the Sufi poet al-Hallaj, who was famously martyred for this utterance.[43]

Jadid al-Islam then proceeds, like Qummi and his likes, to target Ibn ʿArabi, referencing a famous passage from the *Fusus al-hikam* (*The Bezels of Wisdom*) in which the latter claims that God did not reprimand Samarians from worshipping calves because He wanted to be worshipped in all forms.[44] This leads our author to elaborate on the Sufi connection to Greek Paganism and to the worship of images, as in the sections we explored in the previous chapter:

> [Pagans] build idol temples into which they carve faces of men and women, which they in turn worship, and to whom they vow and offer sacrifices. [They do so] believing that these gods will bring them whatever they need. And when the demons enter in the mouth cavities of these idols and speak to them, then they associate many beliefs with these faces. They believe that the people they have deified were brought into the world by women who had relations with deities. And [they believe] that these deities have often fought each other over women and their children or over government; and that they have dominated each other. And thus the victor and the defeated have been portrayed in whatever image they have chosen [for them], saying: 'these trees and stones and animals are all deities who other deities have carved'.[45]

Jadid al-Islam complements this by referring to Calepino's lexicon once again, citing the entry on Saturn, the father of Juno and Jupiter through his wife Opis.[46] Jadid al-Islam mentions this as an example of the pagan belief in mixed divine/human offspring, saying that in these societies people who excelled in a given skill were deemed to be 'sons of gods' and were worshipped after their deaths as fully-fledged deities. As a result, our author claims, 'new' deities were often associated with 'older' ones, which explains why Cicero, for example, spoke of three different gods, all of which were known by the name of Jupiter.[47] Our author sees in the Christian concept of the Trinity the continuation of this pagan trifurcation of Jupiter, and reproaches Sufis not only for failing to condemn such an idea, but for taking it to its most extreme conclusion, by declaring that 'everything is God (*hamih chīz Khudā-st*)'.[48] He observes that such doctrines often had implications at the level of orthopraxis and ritual observance, as in the many cases in which Sufi *pīrs* neglected their fast, claiming that their superior state of spiritual consciousness exempted them from the obligation to follow legal precepts.[49] As the previous examples from Qummi and Niʿmat Allah al-Jazaʾiri show, this retelling of stories about Sufis overlooking legal obligations on prayer was one of common recurrence in the anti-Sufi literature of the time.

At this point in his treatise Jadid al-Islam anticipates the question of how he could claim to know the content of Sufi doctrine and the relationship between the *pīrs* and their spiritual followers (*murīds*). He answers by assuming the role of the native informant who has inside knowledge of Church practices. He insists on the indistinguishable nature of priesthood (*pādirī-garī*) and *pīrhood* (*pīrī*), as well as on the similarities between convent and *ṭarīqa* life. He portrays himself as having attained a high enough rank within the Church, to have been in a position to influence young novices: 'I, who for a moment was myself a priest (*pādirī*) and a *pīr*, had spiritual followers (*murīdān*)'.[50] He closes the section with a statement similar to that of the introduction to his anti-Christian polemics, emphasising the redemptive aspect of his conversion and the expiatory nature of his writing:

> I thus now write a refutation of the Christian faith hoping that those who were at the time [my] spiritual followers (*murīdān*) will see it and read it. And [I hope] that upon seeing that I was disgusted by the religion I once followed, and that I have chosen the Truth [Islam], they too will follow my steps and turn into the Truth.[51]

Our author then moves on to challenge those (conceivably *ʿirfānī* philosophers) who saw no harm in the doctrine of *waḥdat al-wujūd*, claiming that this concept had to be understood at a symbolic level and that it had more to do with Hellenic philosophy than with the practices of *ṭarīqa* Sufism.[52]

As part of his argumentative methodology, and similar to what we have seen in his anti-Christian polemics, he resorts to hadith. This resource can also be found in the works of his predecessors in anti-Sufi or even in *ʿirfānī* anti-dervish works, as both Fayz-i Kashani and Niʿmat Allah al-Jazaʾiri recurred to hadith to prove the impermissibility of chanting.[53] Likewise, in his aforementioned rejection of Sufi abstention from meat, Qummi drew from al-Kulayni's *al-Kafi*;[54] while al-Hurr al-ʿAmili, true to his Akhbari convictions, based almost his entire anti-Sufi refutation on hadith-based arguments.[55] Following this practice, Jadid al-Islam also quotes from a series of hadith, including one which he interprets as censoring speculation on the nature of God: 'whoever thinks about the nature of God's substance becomes ruined (*har kas fikr dar ẕāt-i Khudā-yi taʿālā kunad kih chih gunāh ast, halāk mī shavad*)'.[56] He then censures Sufi philosophers for their disregard for hadith-based methodology:

> They [philosophers] will say: 'we are not concerned (*kār nadārīm*) with the hadith of the Prophet (saw) and we know everything that the philosophers (*ḥakīmān*) and our guides (*muqtadāyān*) in the art of philosophy (*ḥikmat*) – such as Socrates, Plato, Aristotle and the rest of them – have written for us in their books. And they have proven to us [the question of] *waḥdat al-wujūd* and other intellectual questions (*masāʾil-i ʿaqlī*), and therefore we follow them'.[57]

He disapproves of sympathisers of Greek philosophers for failing to condemn them as pagans under the excuse that they had lived before the time of the Qurʾanic revelation. For our author, this justification was not sufficient, given that, while God had provided every nation with prophets for their guidance – from the time of Adam to the time of Moses – Greek philosophers could not be counted among them. He emphasises the fact that philosophy was not taught during the time of the Prophet Muhammad, and that it only started to flourish in Baghdad after the arrival in the city of thousands of enemies of God (*mulḥids*). He compares this with the situation in Isfahan in his time, saying that unbelievers had come to the city and were being treated 'with great esteem (*bā iʿtibār-i ghalabih*)', and that 'many of them [were] ulama, jurists and followers of the family of the Prophet'.[58] He then dismisses some non-Shiʿi hadith that Sufis referred to when justifying the practice of ritual remembrance and – with it – the authority of their spiritual 'axis' (*quṭb*). In response, he quotes a story from al-ʿAllama al-Hilli's *Kashf al-haqq wa nahj al-sidq*, which portrays a group of Sufis, one of whom refuses to pray under the pretext that he was connected (*wāṣil*) to the divine, and that physical prayer was for him like a veil (*ḥijāb*) that obstructed his special relationship with God.[59]

In denouncing the financial support given to philosophy through pious endowments (*waqf/awqāf*), Jadid al-Islam recalls a conversation in which a religious scholar confessed to having studied philosophy out of financial pressure.[60] This leads our author to address some common arguments used by apologists of philosophy. He rejects the claim that the introduction of philosophy to the Dar al-Islam was inevitable given the historical contacts between Muslims and Christians. He claims that this could not have been the case, because the reclusive nature of Christian monastic life – which he describes in terms similar to those used in the *Sayf al-mu'minin* and the *Fava'id- Izdivaj* – was not conducive to such exchanges.[61] Moreover, he contrasts the dissemination of knowledge within the Christian monasteries with that of the madrasas, noting that teachers in the monasteries did not bring their books to their seminaries, instructing their students instead to spend two years reading philosophy on their own before attending classes.[62]

Our author then preempts the objection of why he had not discouraged people from the pursuit of reason (*ʿaql*) and philosophy (*ḥikmat*) in a more active fashion immediately after his conversion. He responds by acknowledging that reason and philosophical reflection were not necessarily harmful in and of themselves. But he qualifies this by saying: '*ʿaql* is that which leads to grace (*tawfiq*)', and by clarifying that he would encourage people to 'get acquainted with the [kind of] *ḥikmat* that God and his Prophet have given [to humanity]'.[63] To which he adds: 'the real *ḥikmat* is in the hadith and [therefore] following the hadith would lead [you] through the path to heaven. This makes the difference between the Shiʿi and the infidel (*kāfir*)'.[64] This is a subtle reference to a verse from *Surat al-Baqara* (2:269):

> He gives wisdom to whoever He will. Whoever is given wisdom has truly been given much good, but only those with insight bear this in mind (*Yu'tī-l-ḥikmata man yashā'u wa man yu'ta al-ḥikmata fa-qad utiya khayran kathīran wa mā yadhakkaru illā ulū alā-l-bābi*).[65]

Like many Qur'anic verses, the latter has long attracted scholarly attention among the *mufassirūn*. To give an example from the Safavid period, in his *Tafsir al-safi* (*The Pure Exegesis*), Fayz-i Kashani quotes, among other sources, from Imam Jaʿfar al-Sadiq in reference to this verse: 'nobody knows what I have deposited and prepared in wisdom, except those whom I have drawn close to myself and endowed with it (*lā yaʿlam mā aʾwdaʿtu wa hayāʾtu fi-l-ḥikma illā man istakhlaṣtuhu li-nafsī wa khaṣaṣtuhu bihā*)'.[66] While it would be perhaps tempting to see in this line of argumentation the influence of the ascendant Akhbarism of the time, we should be cautious in this regard. Recourse to hadith alone was not exclusive to Akhbaris, nor was it the rejection of certain schools of philosophy. Major mujtahids of the past, many of whom would be a posteriori associated with the Usuli line of this period, where critical, for example, of the dominance of *kalām* in certain scholarly circles.[67] We should rather read these lines as topoi intended to reflect the wider rejection of philosophical inquiry outlined earlier. The nature of this condemnation could of course draw from different kinds of argumentation, including Akhbari ones, without necessarily implying a full adherence to this latter trend.

Moving forward, our author closes this section by dismissing the idea that studying Greek philosophy could help Muslims refute it better. If this were the case – our author thinks – then Muslims would also have to devote time to the study of other problematic ideologies, leaving no time for the study of Scripture.[68] Finally, after expounding the alleged pagan (Hellenic) roots – or at the very least, the pagan connections – of Sufi doctrine, Jadid al-Islam moves on to explore the latter's ties to Christian scripturalism, using the same kind of argumentative resources we have seen in the *Sayf al-muʾminin*. He first quotes from Saint Paul's *Letter to Timothy* 3:

> All of you are sons of God with faith [in the fact] that Jesus is God [. . .] Jesus embodies God in himself and in [his] religion there is no more reason among you to differentiate each other and to say that 'I am Jewish and he is Greek, I am a slave and he is a master, I am a man and that one is a woman'; since all of you are made one in Jesus, who is God, and all of you embody Him (*ū rā dar khūd pūshānīdih-īd*).[69]

He then complements this with a fuller version of the same quote from *1 Corinthians* 8 which we have already encountered in the *Sayf al-muʾminin*, namely that in which Saint Paul was asked whether it was permissible to eat meat sacrificed to idols. Saint Paul's answer, which our author considers again as an apology of pantheism, reads:

> There are no idols in this world, and nothing is God but the one God. And no matter how many people on earth and in heaven are said to become gods, it is not true that there are many gods and lords. For me there is only one God [who] is [our] father, and everything comes from Him, and we are all in Him; and there is one Lord Jesus Christ [who is] God, and we are all united in Him. But not everybody knows this, and as a consequence, some people whose hearts have fallen ill to [Satan's] whispering (*vasvās*), have become impure (*najis*) because of this.[70]

The rest of the text incorporates other arguments and quotations also used in his anti-Christian work, from a detailed disarticulation of Saint Paul's logic and the denial of the double-substance (*dhāt*) of Jesus, to the use of other biblical quotations to condemn pantheism.[71] In the same way that in the *Sayf al-mu'minin* the author accuses Christians of hypocrisy for condemning Hindus while adhering to idolatrous practices, he condemns Sufis for following Christians while pretending to be Muslims.[72] And to refute the idea of the Qur'anic support for Sufi doctrines and to defend the authority of the Imams, he quotes the same verse we have seen before in his response to Guadagnoli: 'Only God Knows the true meaning/ Those firmly grounded in knowledge [. . .] (*wa mā ya'lamu tā'wīlahu illā Allahu wa-l-rāsikhūn fi-l-'ilm*)'.[73]

Anti-Sufism in the *Sayf al-mu'minin*

Although the aims and scope of the *Radd* differ from those of the *Sayf al-mu'minin*, there is a clear thematic overlap in some relevant sections. In accordance with the overall structure of the book, the passages on Sufism in the *Sayf al-mu'minin* are embedded within the author's commentary on the *Biblia Sacra Arabica* and are linked to his various accusations of *taḥrīf* against Saint Jerome. As is the case with the *Radd*, in the *Sayf al-mu'minin* the anti-Sufi passages also seek to expose the supposedly Pagan and Christian roots of Sufism, particularly with regards to issues like the dogmas of the Trinity and the incarnation of Christ, as well as the sacrament of communion as manifestations of *waḥdat al-wujūd*.

As we have seen in Chapter three, the notion of *waḥdat al-wujūd* is invoked in relation to the enigmatic figure of Melchizedek, who in the text of *Genesis* appears not to have had any progeny or ascendancy and is thus described in terms that should, in Jadid al-Islam's eyes, be reserved for God.[74] But there are yet other sub-sections in the book that present the motif of the Sufi/Christian connection from other angles. Many of these are found within the commentary on the *Book of Genesis*. In one of them, for example, our author expands on the faux etymological link between the Sufis and Sophists, but in a way that differs from the above examples from the *Radd*: here, Jadid al-Islam suggests that the idea of Adam and Eve being ashamed of their nakedness was also an instance of *taḥrīf* by Saint Jerome – who he accuses of being an intellectual heir of the Greek Sufi/Sophists (*Ṣūfiyān-i Yūnān*) – in this case intended to justify the wearing of woolen garments characteristic of Sufi attire (*libās-i ṣūfī*).[75] Jadid al-Islam then proceeds to refute Sufi claims to secret esoteric knowledge in a sub-section entitled *Sufiyan-i ma Nasara-yi Ummat-and* (*Our Sufis are the Christians of the Umma*). Here he dismisses the charismatic authority of the Sufi *pīrs*, noting that Sufi practitioners in the early stages of initiation would, in their quest for spiritual guidance, 'cling to the robes of the will of every ignorant *pīr* that they find (*har yik pīr-i jāhilī paydā kardih dast dar dāmān-i irādat-i ū mī zanand*)'.[76] He then adds a sectarian layer, as he seeks to refute the Sunni claim, reminiscent of the aforementioned thesis by Ibn Taymiyya, of the Shiʿi origins of Sufism. To make his case, he once again resorts to the motif of tracing the origin of Sufi practices back to Christianity through Saint Paul, who he once again accuses of transgressing Mosaic Law through his abrogation of circumcision in *Galatians* 5.[77]

A more novel example of Jadid al-Islam's treatment of the Sufi/Christian/Pagan connection comes from a passage from *Genesis* 6, which reads:

> When human beings began to increase in number on the earth and daughters were born to them, the sons of God (*Banū Allāh* in the *Biblia Sacra Arabica*/ *farzandān-i Khudā* in Jadid al-Islam's translation) saw that the daughters of humans were beautiful, and they married any of them they chose. Then the Lord said: 'My Spirit will not contend with humans forever, for they are mortal; their days will be a hundred and twenty years.' The Nephilim (*Gigantes* in the Latin Vulgate/ *jabābira* in the *Biblia Sacra Arabica*/ *jīkantas* in Jadid al-Islam's translation) were on the earth in those days – and also afterward – when the sons of God went to the daughters of humans and had children by them.[78]

The first point of contention here is how to interpret the meaning of 'sons of God' and 'giants' in the context of the text. In addition to the rather predictable denunciation of the term 'sons of God' as a pantheistic concept, our author sees an inconsistency between the Christian denial of the existence of the jinn and the acknowledgment of the existence of these giants, which again leads him to the suspicion of *taḥrīf*. Our author argues that if these giants and angels had indeed existed, they would have procreated with human females, resulting in hybrid creatures like the ones that appear in Hindu scriptures. He then goes on to consider another rather bogus etymological analysis: he claims that the term that Saint Jerome had chosen to translate as God, the Latin *Deus* – based on the cognate of the equivalent Greek term *Theos* – was in reality the word *dīv* in the Hebrew sources, which was more closely related to *daimon*, the Greek word for demon.[79] From this, he concludes that the notion of God's offspring originated in Geek pantheism and permeated into Christianity and Sufism, resulting in the Sufi idea of unity with God. He closes the section with an overarching condemnation of his ideological foes:

> I do not know which of these four groups, namely Greeks, Latins [Romans], Christians, or Sufis are more deserving of being cursed. It might ultimately be easier to curse Sufis in this case, since they took their sect from the Christians, and these took theirs from the Latins and the latter from the Greeks. Thus, whenever we curse the Sufis, we are also directing our curse against the other three groups.[80]

This section is thus thematically homologous with the passage of the *Radd* on the birth of Jupiter and the belief in demigods, both by its sheer denunciation of the alleged Greek origins of Christian and Sufi pantheism, and by its recourse to etymological analysis of key terms as an argumentative strategy.

Finally, the section *But-parasti dar Masihiyyat va mas'alih-i wahdat al-wujud* (*Idolatry in Christianity and the Problems of the 'Unity of Existence'*) ties together many of the thematic motifs of the text: the idolatrous nature of Christian rituals, the idea of Saint Paul as a spearhead of pantheism, and the connection of the latter creed to Christianity and Sufism. The condemnation of Paul here is at its severest tone:

> But ever since, this plague (*ṭāʿūn*) of idolatry and all other acts of disbelief have befallen the nation of Jesus by the offspring (*ṭufayl*) of the accursed Paul, who came from the dog-herding tribe (*qabīl-i sag-gar*) and infiltrated the [tribe of] the servants of God in order to putrefy their environment, to the extent that today no one among them [Christians] has had his soul spared by this plague. But the source of each plague is poisonousness and each poison is a treatment for another poison. Thus, having ingested a certain amount of the venom of this soul-murdering viper (*afʿā-yi qātil-i arvāḥ*) that is Paul, it is only suitable that I should offer a response to his speech, mixed with the fresh antidote of discernment (*tariyāk-i fārūq*)[81], in order to protect [the believers] from the poison of the plague of Christianity.[82]

To respond to Paul's 'venom', Jadid al-Islam quotes yet again the passage from *1 Corinthians* 8 in which Paul is asked about the permissibility of eating meat offered to idols. Jadid al-Islam provides his translation of Paul's response, which he interprets as another expression of pantheism: 'Know that in this world no one thing is either an idol or God, but rather everything is one God'.[83]

Our author then compares Paul's statement to a couplet from the Sufi poet Shaykh Mahmud Shabistari (d. 1340): '*Musalmān gar bidānastī kih but chī-st/ bidānastī kih dīn dar but-parastī-st* (If Muslims knew what an idol is/ they would know that there is religion in idol-worship)'.[84] In Jadid al-Islam's mind then, Saint Paul, Shabistari and – implicitly through *taḥrīf* – Saint Jerome are doctrinally undistinguishable. Thus, for him the refutation of one of them should be considered as the refutation of the three:

> Since every time that we refute the words of Paul, the accursed hypocrite, we refute the words of his disciple Jerome, who – based on the words of this accursed one [Paul] – introduced all this disbelief into the Holy Books and forged a book for the Christians based upon it; [thus], through the refutation of this deceiver who leads astray (*żāl-i mużall*) we can also indisputably refute the words of Shabistari and his followers.[85]

Jadid al-Islam closes the section seeking once again to refute Christians on their own terms, this time by proving that idol worship was forbidden even in the allegedly forged Scriptures of Saint Jerome. To make his point, he then refers to a passage from *Baruch* 6, in which God summons the Israelites and warns them that they will be vanished to the land of the disbelievers. The passage contains, however, the antidote against the idolaters:

> Oh Children of Israel! The time will come when you will be scattered among the disbelievers because of the sins that you committed against the Almighty, and as a punishment and in order to test you, the Praised One will mix you with them. Yet, out of kindness and goodwill, He will warn you [what to do] when you enter their land – since at that time they did not allow disbelievers to build their temples and worship their idols in the land of Islam –.[86] When you enter the land of the disbelievers, you will see what you never saw in your own land. They build gods out of gold, silver, stone and wood, which they carry on their shoulders, and they carry them so that the disbelievers would fear them. So be warned, less you fear the idols as those crowds do. Therefore, in order for you not to fear them when the time comes, I now teach you that as soon as you notice that a group of people either in front or behind them – that is, the idols –[87] is bowing to them and worshiping them, at that point you will implore the God of the Worlds (*Khudāvand-i ʿālamiyān*) from the bottom of your heart and say 'oh, Lord of the Worlds, only before you I bow and only you shall I worship'.[88]

In choosing this citation, Jadid al-Islam is able to demonstrate that the biblical text itself condemned the adoration of images, while also pointing towards the possibility of redemption for those who were exiled to the land of the idolaters. By showing that Israelites who were exposed to idolatry were nonetheless given the remedy against it, the choice of the passage harmonises with the language with which the author introduced the section, namely the simile of the venom and the antidote. More importantly, by alluding to the redemption of those who have witnessed idolatry, the passage is also in tune with the prevalent theme of the redemption of our author. By extension, this is also a subtle reminder that, having lived (and worshipped) in the land of the disbelievers himself, Jadid al-Islam has the intellectual and moral authority to warn Muslims against the tenets and practices of Christianity.

Concluding Remarks

As we have seen, Jadid al-Islam's anti-Sufi thought as attested both in his *Radd* and in the *Sayf al-muʾminin* is as much an anti-philosophical stance as it is a specifically anti-Sufi one. While few of his arguments or rhetorical figures could be considered innovative if taken in isolation, the value of this aspect of his work resides in its blending of the anti-Sufi and anti-philosophical arguments prevalent in the late Safavid period with the more common tropes of interreligious polemics. Through this cross-fertilisation of polemical traditions (that is, the anti-Sufi and the interreligious), Jadid al-Islam is able to simultaneously enrich both: on the one hand, his authoritative knowledge of Christianity allows him to add to the pool of anti-Sufi arguments of late Safavid *rudūd* that of the alleged Pagan and Christian origins of Sufism. And on the other hand, the incorporation of anti-Sufi sections and tropes into his wider anti-Christian treatise, while also not completely unprecedented within the larger history of Islamic critiques of Christianity, is nonetheless more significant in the context of the anti-mystical bent that characterised the milieu in question.

As for whether the nature of the arguments in Jadid al-Islam's anti-philosophical and anti-mystical work can help shed light on his position on broader discussions, such as legal or theological debates, I would advocate a certain degree of caution. Aside from the obvious historiographical fallacy of attributing to a thinker a fully-fledged doctrine on questions he did not engage in explicitly,[89] Jadid al-Islam's text itself and the meagre information we have on his post-conversion career do not render the challenge of speculation easy. As we have seen, Jadid al-Islam's critique of Greek philosophy is at times coupled with an endorsement of hadith-based argumentation and with a passionate defense of the study of Scripture as a unique source of guidance, as is evident in his statements on the *ḥikma* and the *ʿaql* of hadith. However, as I have noted earlier as well, this alone does not suffice to attribute Akhbari sentiments to Jadid al-Islam, beyond perhaps a façade topical influence. In a similar fashion, we should be careful not to see Fazil-i Hindi's previously mentioned encouragement of Jadid al-Islam as an indisputable evidence of our author's Usuli leanings only because of Fazil-i Hindi's Usuli background. To begin with, the fact that Fazil-i Hindi's approach to philosophy remains understudied makes it difficult to draw more conclusions about the implications of our author's engagement with him.[90] Further, it was common for this generation of scholars to exhibit both Usuli and Akhbari traces in their work, as both Abisaab and Newman have observed in the case of Muhammad

Baqir Majlisi.[91] But more importantly, as Gleave has showed in his analysis of al-Hurr al-ʿAmili's references to al-ʿAllama al-Hilli in his anti-Sufi works, scholars could approve of someone else's theological thought while rejecting their views on legal methodology.[92] If such methodological and doctrinal permissibility is present in legal texts and in anti-Sufi works from authors with a rigorous upbringing in Islamic theology, it is then hardly surprising to find it in Jadid al-Islam's refutation of Christian theology, which did not need to adhere to any specific legal trend.

Therefore, in the same way the examples from previous chapters show how our author brings together Christian and Muslim sources, here we can see him drawing from multiple argumentative methodologies and motifs used in the *rudūd* tradition, without having to take sides on disputations that were not instrumental to his objective.

In the end, at the heart of Jadid al-Islam's work is his quest to define his understanding of proper Shiʿi orthodoxy and orthopraxis. For our author, what matters the most is that through their doctrines and practices, Christians and Sufis – and by association, scholastic philosophers – are equally deserving of condemnation.

Notes

1. Jaʿfariyan, *Din va siyasat*, pp. 53–4. For the colophon of the work in the critical edition, see Jadid al-Islam, 'Risalih dar radd-i jamaʿat-i sufiyan', p. 929.
2. SM, p. 65.
3. For Jaʿfariyan's observation, see Jadid al-Islam, 'Risalih dar radd-i jamaʿat-i sufiyan', p. 916, fn. 2.
4. For a comprehensive narrative of the early developments of the order, see Mazzaoui, *The origins of the Safawids*, pp. 41–7. For the connection of the Zahidiyya to ʿAli and the Prophet, see p. 53.
5. The question of whether the Safavids claimed *sayyid* status before becoming a ruling dynasty has a long and convoluted history. For the most comprehensive summary of the debate and for what is perhaps the most uncontestable evidence to the fact that the order did claim such a status before Shah Ismaʿil, see Morimoto, 'The Earliest ʿAlid Genealogy of the Safavids'.
6. Morimoto, 'How to behave towards *sayyids* and *sharīfs*', p. 17.
7. For the developments under Shaykh Safi's descendants, see Mazzaoui, *The*

Origins of the Safawids, pp. 69, 71–2. For examples of heterodox practices, consider the cases of ritual cannibalism of the early Qizilbash; see Bashir, 'Shah Ismāʿīl and the Qizilbāsh', pp. 234–56. See also Calmard, 'Shiʾi Rituals and Power'.

8. Algar, 'Naqshbandīs and Safavids', p. 6; Lewisohn, 'Sufism and the School of Isfahān', pp. 76–7.
9. For a good overview of this process, see Abisaab, *Converting Persia*, pp. 15–20. Andrew Newman has, however, expressed scepticism about this thesis. See Newman, 'The Myth of the Clerical Migration'. See also al-Muhajir, *al-Hijra al-ʿamiliyya ila Iran.*
10. Anzali, *'Mysticism' in Iran*, pp. 27–8; Algar, 'Naqshbandīs and Safavids', pp. 26–8.
11. Calmard, 'Shi'i Rituals and Power II', pp. 144–5.
12. Arjomand, *The Shadow of God and the Hidden Imam*, p. 122. See also Anzali, 'Mysticism' in Iran, pp. 30–1.
13. Arjomand, *The Shadow of God and the Hidden Imam*, pp. 261–3, 269–70. For an overview of the adoption of *ʿirfān* as a specifically Shiʿi brand of mystical philosophy and its developments in the post-Shah ʿAbbas era, see Anzali, *'Mysticism' in Iran*, pp. 116–56.
14. Newman, 'Sufism and Anti-Sufism in Safavid Iran', p. 99.
15. For more on Lahiji, see Rizvi, 'A Sufi Theology', pp. 91–2; Lewisohn, 'Sufism and the School of Isfahān', pp. 103–12. For more on Mulla Sadra, see Rizvi, 'Mollā Ṣadrā Širāzi'. For a general overview on the School of Isfahan, see Bdaiwi, 'The Isfahan School of Philosophy'; Rizvi, 'Isfahan School of Philosophy'; Nasr, 'The School of Isfahan'. See also, Newman, 'Towards a Reconsideration'.
16. Zarrinkub, *Dunbalih-i justuju dar tasavvuf-i Iran*, p. 95–6; Rizvi, 'The *takfīr* of the Philosophers', pp. 252–3.
17. Zarrinkub, *Dunbalih-i justuju dar tasavvuf-i Iran*, pp. 117–20. See also Rizvi, 'The *takfīr* of the Philosophers', p. 253; Babayan, *Mystics, Monarchs, and Messiahs*, p. 417. For an overview on Kashani, see Algar, 'Fayż-e Kāšānī'.
18. Zarrinkub, *Dunbalih-i justuju dar tasavvuf-i Iran*, pp. 117–20. For his condemnation of *ghināʾ* and *dhikr*, see Fayz-i Kashani, *Dah risalih*, p. 104. For more on *al-Insaf*, see Lewisohn, 'Sufism and the School of Isfahān', p. 125; also Newman, 'Fayd al-Kashani and the Rejection of the Clergy/State Alliance', p. 44. For a general overview on Kashani's stance on the matter, see Newman, 'Clerical Perceptions of Sufi Practices'.
19. Ata Anzali calls this paradigm, the 'suppression model', see Anzali, 'Mysticism'

in Iran, p. 26. For examples of what he has identified as proponents of this model, see Arjomand, *The Shadow of God and the Hidden Imam*, pp. 112–19; Nasr, 'Religion in Safavid Persia', pp. 279–80.

20. Newman, 'Clerical Perceptions of Sufi Practices', p. 137; Babayan, 'The Waning of the Qizilbash', p. 202.
21. Anzali, *'Mysticism' in Iran*, pp. 25–6.
22. Ibid. pp. 39–41.
23. Babayan, *Mystics, Monarchs, and Messiahs*, p. 149. See also Abisaab, *Converting Persia*, p. 134; Rizvi, 'A Sufi Theology', p. 87; Newman, 'Fayd al-Kashani and the Rejection of the Clergy/State Alliance', p. 40.
24. Arjomand, *The Shadow of God and the Hidden Imam*, p. 174.
25. Newman, 'Sufism and Anti-Sufism in Safavid Iran', p. 102; Anzali, *Opposition to Philosophy*, p. 17.
26. For centuries, this work had been mistakenly attributed to Ahmad b. Muhammad al-Ardabili (d. 1583), but – as Muhammad Taqi Danish-pazhuh and Andrew Newman believe – it could very well have been written (at least partially) by Tahir-i Qummi. See Newman, 'Sufism and Anti-Sufism', pp. 99–102. See also Anzali, *Opposition to Philosophy*, pp. 23–4.
27. Rizvi, 'A Sufi Theology', p. 86; Newman, 'Sufism and Anti-Sufism', pp. 96–7; Babayan, *Mystics, Monarchs, and Messiahs*, p. 411.
28. Rizvi, 'The *takfir* of the Philosophers', pp. 249–50.
29. For more examples of Qummi's condemnation of Sufis in other works, see Rizvi, 'The *takfir* of the Philosophers', p. 257.
30. Qummi, 'Risalih-i radd-i sufiyyih', pp. 137–8. See also Rizvi, 'The *takfir* of the Philosophers', pp. 251, 256; Babayan, *Mystics, Monarchs, and Messiahs*, pp. 411, 451.
31. Qummi, 'Risalih-i radd-i sufiyyih', p. 141.
32. For a major study of the *Hikmat al-ʿarifin*, see Anzali, *Opposition to Philosophy*. See also on Anzali, *'Mysticism' in Iran*, pp. 33, 45–7.
33. Gleave, 'Scriptural Sufism and Scriptural Anti-Sufism', pp. 159–62.
34. Rizvi, 'The takfīr of the Philosophers', p. 252.
35. Al-Jazaʾiri, *al-Anwar al-nuʿmaniyya*, vol. 2, p. 282. For more on this work, see Rizvi, 'Sayyid Niʿmat Allāh al-Jazāʾirī and his Anthologies', pp. 237–8.
36. Jadid al-Islam, 'Risalih dar radd-i jamaʿat-i sufiyan', p. 896.
37. Michel, *A Muslim Theologian's Response to Christianity*, pp. 5–14.
38. Ibid. pp. 37–8.
39. Jadid al-Islam, 'Risalih dar radd-i jamaʿat-i sufiyan', pp. 897–8. Calepino indeed

has entries for Sophistas in both of his dictionaries. See Calepino, *Dictionarium Latinum* (no pagination); Calepino, *Dictionarium Linguarum Septem* (no pagination). The Seven Sages of Greece refers to Thales of Miletus (d. 546 BCE), Solon of Athens (d. 558 BCE), Chilon of Sparta (d. sixth century BCE), Pittacus of Mytilene (d. 568 BCE), Bias of Priene (d. sixth century BCE), Periander of Corinth (d. 627 BCE) and Cleobulus of Lindos (d. 600 BCE).

40. Jadid al-Islam, 'Risalih dar radd-i jamaʿat-i sufiyan', pp. 898–9.
41. Ibid. p. 899.
42. Ibid. p. 900.
43. Jadid al-Islam, 'Risalih dar radd-i jamaʿat-i sufiyan', p. 901. For al-Hallaj's utterance, see Sells, *Early Islamic Mysticism*, p. 270.
44. Jadid al-Islam, 'Risalih dar radd-i jamaʿat-i sufiyan', p. 901. For the passage from Ibn ʿArabi, see Ibn ʿArabi, *Fusus al-hikam*, p. 192
45. Ibid. p. 902.
46. Jadid al-Islam, 'Risalih dar radd-i jamaʿat-i sufiyan', p. 902; Calepino, *Dictionarium Latinum*, n.p. (The *Dictionarium Septem Linguarum* does not contain an entry on Jupiter).
47. Jadid al-Islam, 'Risalih dar radd-i jamaʿat-i sufiyan', pp. 902–4.
48. Ibid. p. 904.
49. Ibid. pp. 905–6.
50. Ibid. p. 906.
51. Ibid. p. 906.
52. Ibid. pp. 906–7.
53. Fayz-i Kashani, *Dah risalih*, p. 104; al-Jazaʾiri, *al-Anwar al-nuʿmaniyya*, vol. 2, p. 282.
54. Qummi, 'Risalih-i radd-i sufiyyih', p. 141.
55. Gleave, 'Scriptural Sufism and Scriptural Anti-Sufism', pp. 160–6; Rizvi, 'The *takfir* of the Philosophers', p. 247.
56. Jadid al-Islam, 'Risalih dar radd-i jamaʿat-i sufiyan', p. 907. There are some difficulties in the attribution of this hadith, as there are many similar versions of it. The wording of the *matn* is closer to the version that appears in Ibn Babawayh's *Kitab al-Tawhid*: 'Those who have thought about [the nature of] God have been ruined (*Man fakara fi Allāh kayfa kāna halak*)'. See Ibn Babawayh, *Kitab al-Tawhid*, p. 460. However, Jadid al-Islam claims to have taken it from al-Kulayni, who has indeed a version of it in *al-Kafi*: 'talk about anything, but do not talk about the substance of God (*takallamū fi kulli shayʾ wa lā tatakallamū fi dhāt Allāh*)'. See al-Kulayni, *Kitab al-Kafi*, vol. 1, p. 92.

57. Jadid al-Islam, 'Risalih dar radd-i jamaʿat-i sufiyan', p. 907.
58. Jadid al-Islam, 'Risalih dar radd-i jamaʿat-i sufiyan', pp. 908–9. See also Rizvi, 'The takfīr of the Philosophers', p. 256.
59. Jadid al-Islam, 'Risalih dar radd-i jamaʿat-i sufiyan', pp. 910–11. Al-Hilli, *Kashf al-haqq wa nahj al-sidq*, pp. 58–9.
60. Jadid al-Islam, 'Risalih dar radd-i jamaʿat-i sufiyan', pp. 912–13.
61. Ibid. pp. 912–13.
62. Ibid. p. 915.
63. Ibid. p. 916.
64. Ibid. pp. 916–17.
65. The Qurʾanic translation is from Abdel Haleem's version. *The Qurʾan*, p. 31.
66. Kashani, *Tafsir al-safi*, vol. 1, pp. 470–1.
67. For an example of this, consider al-Shahid al-Thani's (d. 1558) critique of *kalām*, despite him being one of the pillars of Ijtihadi thought. See Abisaab, 'Shiʿi Jurisprudence, Sunnism', p. 9.
68. Jadid al-Islam, 'Risalih dar radd-i jamaʿat-i sufiyan', p. 917.
69. Ibid. pp. 920–1.
70. Ibid. pp. 921–2.
71. Ibid. p. 922.
72. Ibid. p. 927.
73. Ibid. p. 927; The translation of the verse is from M. A. S. Abdel Haleem's version. *The Qurʾan*, p. 34.
74. SM, p. 243.
75. Ibid. pp. 109–10.
76. Ibid. p. 112.
77. Ibid. pp. 112–13.
78. SM, pp. 141; Jerome, *Vulgata* (online edition) (Since the translation here is intended to reflect the collation of the *Biblia Sacra Arabica* with the author's own rendition, I have chosen here to provide a standard biblical translation rather than to translate it from the Persian. The translation here is from the New International Version).
79. SM, pp. 144–6.
80. Ibid. p. 147.
81. It seems to me that *tiryāq-i fārūq* could have been the intended term.
82. Ibid. p. 430.
83. Ibid. p. 430.
84. Ibid. p. 430.

85. Ibid. p. 431.
86. This ellipsis is from Jadid al-Islam himself, not mine, which is why it is not between brackets.
87. Also Jadid al-Islam's ellipsis.
88. Ibid. pp. 431–2.
89. Quentin Skinner has been particularly adamant on this. See Skinner, 'Meaning and Understanding in the History of Ideas', pp. 4–7.
90. Rula J. Abisaab has noted that of the 150 works attributed to him around thirty-five are extant covering areas of law, jurisprudence, foundations of religion, exegesis, logic, philosophy, Arabic grammar and rhetoric. However, we still do not know much about his exegetical methods and his approaches to logic and philosophy. See Abisaab, 'al-Fāḍil al-Hindī'.
91. Abisaab, *Converting Persia*, p. 132; Newman, *Safavid Iran: The Rebirth of a Persian Empire*, pp. 98–9.
92. Gleave, 'Scritpural Sufism and Scriptural Anti-Sufism', p. 162.

Conclusions

Throughout this book we have reflected on different dimensions of Jadid al-Islam's polemical work and, through it, on the genre of *dalāʾil al-nubuwwa* in the post-classical period more generally. Through considering the *Sayf al-muʾminin* as representative of broader developments in the later stages of the history of the genre, we cannot fail to notice a seemingly contradictory – although perhaps complementary – characteristic of early modern polemics. While these texts continuously resort to the same tropological repertoire that was used throughout the classical period, they are also malleable enough to draw from a wide variety of intertextual references in order to address debates that are more specific to a certain time and place. This latter aspect is what makes these works historically grounded, thus compensating for the shortage of biographical information on some of their authors, as in Jadid al-Islam's case. However, the persistence of classical motifs forces us to reexamine common assumptions about concepts such as 'originality' or 'innovation', to give a fairer appraisal of what the reproduction of these tropes implies. If we think of the writing of polemics primarily as an exercise in piety intended to strengthen the author's – and by extension, the community's – religious convictions, it is clear that the pursuit of novelty is subordinated to the need to provide the soundest arguments in favour of one's own faith. This urge is even more pronounced among converts like Jadid al-Islam, partly because of their need to prove their commitment to their new coreligionists, but also as an act of self-reassurance. This being the case, polemicists have had to revisit every single argument and provide all the evidence at their disposal – whether commonplace or novel – to make their cases. This explains the inclusion of old motifs alongside less commonly used sources, arguments and tropes.

Aside from this, the recourse to classical motifs in Jadid al-Islam's work – as in the works of other authors of *dalāʾil* – has the function of anchoring the text within a well-established, and therefore intellectually authoritative, tradition. What is crucial to emphasise here, however, is that this use of tropes is not purely formulaic or stagnant. Perhaps the richest example to counteract any thesis that would point towards a stifled genre would be our author's engagement with the biblical codex in light of his discussion on the theme of *taḥrīf*. The fact that Jadid al-Islam could boast of a deep familiarity with the Bible was not in itself as outstanding in his generation as it would have in an Abbasid, an early Mongol, or even a Mamluk context, when only a small minority of convert polemicists could claim such knowledge. By the early modern period, as we have seen, the circulation of biblical translations, supported by the patronage of courts and missionary institutions, as well as by the technological revolution of the printing press in some cases, facilitated access to the biblical text among Muslim scholars of non-convert backgrounds. This levelled the ground between Muslim-born and convert polemicists to a certain extent. Partly as a direct consequence of this development, convert polemicists like Jadid al-Islam needed to resort to more elaborate displays of authoritative knowledge of the tradition they sought to refute. In this context, the discussion on the Vulgata and the re-dimensioning of the theme of *taḥrīf* as a historically traceable and multi-layered phenomenon acquires a higher significance: if the falsification of the Scriptures is understood not only as the result of the assembly of the original biblical corpus, but also of the translation of the Latin Vulgate (further corrupted through the *Biblia Sacra Arabica*); then there would be an implicit redemption of the primordial biblical scriptures and of those who, like Jadid al-Islam, had once relied on them for religious guidance. This of course explains the inclusion of ʿAli's translation of the forty Suras of the Torah.

As for Jadid al-Islam's recourse to complementary non-biblical sources throughout his text, aside from their historical value, they serve different functions. To begin with, they help enhance the author's intellectual authority in the knowledge of both the Christian and the Muslim archives and traditions. More importantly, they allow him to establish common ground with different hypothetical audiences. The hadith quotations and the anti-Sufi arguments could appeal to sectors of the ulama who were not primarily concerned with interreligious arguments for their own sake. In contrast, however, the Christian references in the text can barely be said to serve a missionary purpose, aimed at a hypothetical Christian audience. They rather represent another layer to the author's credentialisation before his Muslim readership. From a thematic point of view, bringing about intra-Christian debates on the validity of papal authority or hinting at Trentine dissidence on the canonical status of the Latin Vulgate (as in the case of the passing reference to Melchor Cano) adds a deeper dimension to the arguments against the institutional and scriptural authority of Christianity (particularly Catholicism in this case).

As for the social impact of the genre, many questions regarding the reception of Jadid al-Islam's work remain unanswered. The fact that there is evidence of its being read and cited in the Qajar period, in the context of theological debates that were *not* continuations of the cycle started by Jerome Xavier, suggests that by then it had attained the status of a nearly canonical work, at least among a select group of Iranian scholars. Perhaps the most enigmatic aspect of this kind of literature is the fact that, despite the persistence of classical motifs and the use of different kinds of intertextual references, other classical exponents of *dalāʾil* are barely ever explicitly cited. This makes it hard to provide an accurate assessment of the transmission of works of the genre, given that it is not entirely clear to what extent early modern authors like Jadid al-Islam were familiar with the works of Ibn Qutayba, Ibn Hazm, ʿAli al-Tabari, Turmeda and their likes. The reproduction of classical motifs alone does not suffice to give a full diagnosis on this matter. It could have very well been that, just as Muslim scholars in the Abbasid period repeated a fixed set of biblical quotes because of their lack of access to the full biblical codex, post-classical polemicists could have been familiar only with those motifs of *dalāʾil* literature that permeated into other genres, albeit as tangential references. As would be expected, this also seems to have changed with the passing of time, and hence the verbatim references to Jadid al-Islam in the work of Naraqi in the nineteenth century. It is however significant that the choice of the latter author would be to quote Jadid al-Islam – that is, a local Iranian example – rather than a more classical figure in the tradition of *dalāʾil al-nubuwwa*. Was this due to the decidedly Shiʿi character of Jadid al-Islam's polemics, with his fusion of themes and sources related to both *dalāʾil al-nubuwwa* and *dalāʾil al-imāma*? Was it an implicit recognition of his intellectual hierarchy either as an author of *dalāʾil* literature or at the very least as a reliable informant on Christianity? We can only speculate in this regard. What seems true, in any case, is that for the most part, the polemic tradition perpetuated itself more by active emulation – that is, by the appropriation and reconfiguration of classical motifs – than by ascribing to its precursors authoritative status and by quoting or referencing them directly. In this sense, there is a marked contrast with other – admittedly more canonical – forms of knowledge in the Islamic tradition, in which the chains of transmission and the boasting of one's solid intellectual genealogies are essential to infuse a text with credibility. This is not to say that these elements are completely absent in *dalāʾil* literature, as Jadid al-Islam himself emphasised his connection to Fazil-i Hindi. However, what is different is that the intellectual genealogy here – as in other texts of the genre – serves to enhance the author's credentials in general terms, without explicitly referring to the transmission of the *dalāʾil* genre per se. In other words, while jurists, philosophers, theologians and scholars of hadith would always make a point of mentioning who taught them or with whom they read the canonical books of the discipline in question, the equivalent does not happen with authors of *dalāʾil*.

A final point to consider is the historical and political significance of works like Jadid al-Islam's in the context of the political and social turmoil of the late Safavid period. In other words, how did his production fit into – or alternatively, how did it benefit from – the interests of politically influential circles? The royal patronage and scholarly encouragement our author enjoyed does indeed demonstrate that there was a wider interest in supporting translation projects and engaging Christian missionaries through theological exchanges. The fact that Jadid al-Islam was the last link of a cycle that had its first Iranian contributor (Ahmad al-ʿAlavi) over half a century earlier also shows that this trend was not entirely dependent on specific political conjunctures, since it survived throughout periods of both tension and rapprochement between Iran and the European powers. However, the specificities of the late Safavid period did play a role in the recruitment and patronage of our author, as well as in shaping the contents of his work. The clearest example of this is of course the inclusion of the anti-Sufi and, to a lesser extent, anti-Sunni discourse within his interreligious polemics. Moreover it is also not insignificant that works like ʿAli Akbar Armani's confession memoir or Khatunabadi's translation of the Gospels also date from the late decades of the Safavid period. It reveals that the spirit of the times – with the scapegoating of the Armenians on one hand, and the intensification of an aggressive (primarily Jesuit) missionary propaganda on the other – was indeed conducive to the production of works that reflected this landscape of social and religious upheaval.

However, when considering the institutional support for projects like Jadid al-Islam's or Khatunabadi's, we should not overlook the fact that this was also the period in which the Safavid State was at its weakest. Therefore, state coercion against both non-Muslim and non-Shiʿi minorities and support for polemics (both interreligious and anti-Sufi) should be understood in part as a symptom of a waning state's plea for legitimacy. Further, we can also see in this a sign of the cooptation of positions of power by specific factions within the ulama elites interested in promoting their own understanding of Shiʿi orthodoxy. As we have seen, this latter interpretation of proper legalistic Shiʿism was often hostile to manifestations of popular piety and to the dominant schools of philosophy that had flourished in Isfahan a few decades earlier. In light of this, we should reconsider what it could mean to speak of confessionalisation in the context of the late Safavid period. If such a process were to be understood as the result of the coercive capacity of the state to promote its religious agenda, then such a framing would be inadequate for the study of the milieu in question. However, if we were to speak rather of the sociological fact of the sectarianisation of discourse and the radicalisation of religious positions in the context of state decomposition, then we could probably find in this term – or in any other term that could be used to describe this process, for that matter – a useful analytical tool. The same can be said of the process of sectarianisation of the interreligious branch of the genre of *dalāʾil al-nubuwwa* itself, as in the case of its Shiʿitisation at the hands of Jadid al-Islam, through the inclusion of sources and arguments from the intra-Muslim *dalāʾil al-imāma* tradition. If anything, the clearest residue of the traditional understanding of confessionalisation, as used by Reinhard and Schilling (that is, as a Catholic vs Protestant phenomenon), would be in our author's appropriation of anti-Catholic arguments and critiques of the papacy to provide his refutation of Christianity with a supposedly impartial dimension.

Finally, regardless of the sincerity of Jadid al-Islam's conversion or lack thereof (neither of which would be of particular scholarly interest), the defections within the ranks of the Portuguese Augustinians at the time of the failed Portuguese–Persian alliance against Oman are of course symptomatic of the institutional vulnerability of the Augustinian Order as a political and diplomatic aid of the Portuguese Crown. As we have seen as well, this institutional conflict was not limited to the Augustinians but affected the larger missionary structure of the Church, resulting in factionalism and internal power struggles among the different orders. It is hardly surprising that in the context of the fragmentation of an already weak and outnumbered diaspora, some of its members would seek opportunities for self-advancement – and in certain cases, marriage – by changing their religious, and with them, political, ranks. At the end, however, Jadid al-Islam's work is more valuable for its contribution to the Iranisation and Shiʿitisation of the genre of *dalāʾil al-nubuwwa*, and even for the unequivocal Catholicisation of its discursive nemesis, than for its social and testimonial value. Thus, while the re-appropriation of old motifs and the incorporation of novel sources in the *Sayf al-muʾminin* may not suffice to fill in the documentary blanks that obscure the historical character of its author, they at least offer a unique window into the religious, political and intellectual life of late Safavid Iran. In doing so, the work in question attests to the malleability of a genre, which despite its decidedly non-canonical status, has nonetheless survived throughout centuries of Islamic intellectual tradition.

Bibliography

Primary Sources

Archives

The Hague: *Vereenigde Oostindische Compagnie* 2323, Extract uyt 'tSpahan dagregister sedert 11 September 1733 to 15 July 1734.

Rome: Archivio Storico di Propaganda Fide: Fondo di Persia, Messopotamia e i Caldei, 3 vols.

Jadid al-Islam, ʿAli Quli, *Hidayat al-zallin va taqviyyat al-muʾminin*, Tehran: Majlis Library, ms. 2089.

Published

Abdel Haleem, M. A. S. (tr.), *The Qur'an*, Oxford World's Classics (Oxford: Oxford University Press, 2004).

Anonymous, 'Risalih-i shinakht', in Mansur Sefatgol (ed.), *I'tirāfnāma: diary of Abgar ('Ali Akbar) Armani, one of new converts to Islam of Shah Sulaiman & Shah Sultan Husain Safavi's era, along with Risāla-i-Shinākht, in Gurji script on affirming Shiism by a Georgian new convert to Islam of Shah Abbas' time* (Tehran: Kitabkhanih-i Shura-yi Islami, 2010), pp. 143–212.

Anonymous, *Le Liber pontificalis*, intro. and ed. Louis-Marie Olivier Duchesne, 2 vols (Paris: Ernest Thorin, 1886).

Anonymous, *The Book of the Popes (Liber Pontificalis)*, tr. and intro. Louis Ropes Loomis (New York: Columbia University Press, 1916).

Aubin, Jean (ed.), *L'Ambassade de Gregório Pereira Fidalgo à la cour de Châh Soltân-Hosseyn, 1696*–1697 (Lisbon: Comité National Portugais pour la Célébration du 2.500e Anniversaire de la Fondation de la Monarchie en Iran, 1971).

Armani, Abgar ʿAli Akbar, 'Iʿtirafnamih', in Mansur Sefatgol (ed.), *I'tirāfnāma: diary of Abgar (ʿAli Akbar) Armani, one of new converts to Islam of Shah Sulaiman &*

Shah Sultan Husain Safavi's era, along with Risāla-i-Shinākht, in Gurji script on affirming Shiism by a Georgian new convert to Islam of Shah Abbas' time (Tehran: Kitabkhanih-i Shura-yi Islami, 2010), pp. 55–135.

Baronius, Cesare [and Odorico Rinaldi in post-1227 volumes], *Annales Ecclesiastici*, 37 vols (Bar-le-Duc, 1864–83).

Dieu, Ludovicus (Louis) de, *Historia Christi Persice, Conscripta, simulque multis modis contaminata Hier. Xavier Latine* (Leiden: Elzevir, 1639).

Calepino, Ambrogio, *Dictioranium Latinum* (Reggio nell'Emilia: Rhegium Lingobardum, 1502).

Calepino, Ambrogio, *Dictionarium Linguarum Septem* (Basel: Ex Officina Henric Petrina, 1579).

Cano, Melchor, *Melchioris Cani Episcopi Canarensis ex Ordine Praedicatorum*, ed. Jacques-Hyacinthe Serry (Madrid: Antonio Marin, 1760).

Chardin, Jean, *Voyages du Chevalier en Perse et autres lieux de l'Orient*, ed. L. Langlès, 10 vols (Paris: Le Normant, 1811).

Chick, Herbert (ed. and tr.), *A Chronicle of the Carmelites in Persia and the Papal Mission of the XVIIth and XVIIIth Centuries*, 2 vols (London: I. B. Tauris, 2012).

Eusebius Pamphilus, Bishop of Cesarea, *The Ecclesiastical History*, transl. and intro. Christian Frederick Crusé, D.D. and an Historical view of the Council of Nice by Isaac Boyle, D.D. (New York: Stanford and Swords, 1850).

Fayz-i Kashani, Muhsin, *Dah risalih-i muhaqqiq-i buzurg-i Fayz-i Kashani*, ed. Rasul Jaʿfariyan (Isfahan: Markaz-i Tahqiqat-i ʿIlmi va Dini-yi Imam Amir al-Muʾminin, 1993).

Fayz-i Kashani, Muhsin, *Tafsir al-safi*, 7 vols, ed. Sayyid Muhsin Husayni al-Amini (Tehran: Dar al-Kutub al-Islamiyya, 1998–9).

Foxe, John, *The Actes and Monuments of John Foxe*, intro. Rev. George Towsend, ed. Rev. Stephen Reed Cattley, 8 vols (London: R. Clay, 1837).

Guadagnoli, Filippo, *Apologia pro Christiana Religione* (Rome: Typography of the Congregation of Propaganda Fide, 1631).

Hazin-i Lahiji, Shaykh Muhammad ʿAli, *Rasaʾil-i Hazin-i Lahiji*, ed. ʿAli Awjabi, Miras-i Maktub 41; Zaban va Adabiyat-i Farsi 11 (Tehran: Aʾinih-i Miras: Daftar-i Nashr-i Miras-i Maktub, 1998).

Hazin-i Lahiji, Shaykh Muhammad 'Ali, *Tarikh va safarnamih-i Hazin*, ed. 'Ali Davani (Tehran: Markaz-i Asnad-i Inqilab-i Islami, 1996–7).

Hilli, Hasan b. Yusuf al-ʿAllama al-, *Al-Babu'l-Hadi 'Ashar: a Treatise on the Principles of Shi'ite theology*, tr. by William McElwee Miller (London: Royal Asiatic Society, 1928).

Hilli, Hasan b. Yusuf al-ʿAllama al-, *Nahj al-haqq wa kashf al-sidq*, ed. al-Hujjat al-Shaykh ʿAyn Allah al-Hasani al-Urmawi (Qom: Muʾassasat al-tabaʿa wa al-nashr Dār al-Hijrah, 1993).

Hilli, Hasan b. Yusuf al-ʿAllama al-, *Minhaj al-salah fi ikhtisar al-misbah*, ed. Sayyid ʿAbd Allah al-Mirdamadi (Qom: Maktabat al-ʿAllama al-Majlisi, 2009–10).

Ibn ʿArabi, Muhyi al-Din, *Fusus al-hikam*, ed. Abu al-ʿAla ʿAfifi (Beirut: Dar al-Kitab al-ʿArabi, 1946).

Ibn Babawayh, Abu Jaʿfar Muhammad b. ʿAli, *Amali al-Suduq*, intro. by Hussain al-Aʿlami (Beirut: Alaalami Library, 1980).

Ibn Babawayh, Abu Jaʿfar Muhammad b. ʿAli, *Kamal al-din wa tamam al-niʿma*, ed. ʿAli Akbar al-Ghaffari, 2 vols (Qom: Mu'assasat Nashr, 1984).

Ibn Babawayh, Abu Jaʿfar Muhammad b. ʿAli, *Kitab al-tawhid*, ed. ʿAli Akbar al-Ghaffari (Qom: Manshurat Jamaʿat fi-l-Hawza al-ʿIlmiyya, 1978).

Ibn Babawayh, Abu Jaʿfar Muhammad b. ʿAli, *ʿUyun akhbar al-Rida*, ed. Shayk Husayn al-Aʿlami, 2 vols (Beirut: Muʾassasat al-Aʿlam li-l-Matbuʿat, 1984).

Ibn Hisham, *al-Sira al-nabawiyya*, ed. Muhammad Muhyi al-Din ʿAbd al-Hamid, 4 vols (Cairo: Maktabat Muhammad ʿAli Sabih, 1963).

Ibn Qawlawayh, Jaʿfar b. Muhammad, *Kamil al-ziyarat*, ed. Javad Qayyumi al-Isfahani (Qom: Muʾassasat Nashar al-Faqaha, 2003–04).

Ibn Saʿd, Muhammad, *al-Tabaqat al-kubra*, ed. ʿAli Muhammad ʿUmar, 11 vols (Cairo: al-Nashir Maktabat al-Khanji, 2001).

Ibn Shahrashub, Abu Jaʿfar Muhammad b. ʿAli, *Manaqib al Abi Talib*, ed. Yusuf al-Biqaʿi, 4 vols (Beirut: Dar al-Adwaʾ, 1991)

Jadid al-Islam, ʿAli Quli, 'Favaʾid-i izdivaj', in Rasul Jaʿfariyan (ed.), *Miras-i Islami-yi Iran*, vol. 1 (Qom: Kitabkhanih-i Hazrat Ayat Allah al-ʿUzma Marʿsashi Najafi, 1994–5): pp. 291–310.

Jadid al-Islam, ʿAli Quli, 'Risalih dar radd-i jamaʿat-i sufiyan', in Rasul Jaʿfariyan (ed.), *Siyasat va farhang-i ruzgar-i Safavi*, vol. 1 (Tehran: Nashar-i ʿilm, 2009), pp. 895–929.

Jadid al-Islam, ʿAli Quli, *Sayf al-muʾminin fi qital al-mushrikin*, ed. Rasul Jaʿfariyan (Qom: Intisharat-i Ansariyan, 1996–7).

Jazaʾiri, Niʿmat Allah al-, *al-Anwar al-nuʿmaniyya*, ed. Muhammad Baqir Kitabchi, 4 vols (Tabriz: Matbaʿa Shirkat-i Chap, 1959–62).

Jerome (Saint), *Chronicle*, tr. Roger Pearse (Ipswich: online edition 2005), consulted online on 4 April 2019< http://www.tertullian.org/fathers/jerome_chronicle_06_latin_part2.htm>.

Jerome (Saint), *Letter of Jerome to Pope Damasus*, tr. Kevin P. Edgecomb (Berkeley: online edition, 1999), consulted online on 4 April 2019 <http://www.tertullian.org/fathers/jerome_preface_gospels.htm>.

Jerome (Saint), *Prologue to Genesis*, tr. Kevin P. Edgecomb (Berkeley: online edition, 2006), consulted online on 4 April 2019 <http://www.tertullian.org/fathers/jerome_preface_genesis.htm>.

Jerome (Saint), *Vulgata Latina* (online edition), consulted online on 7 April 2019< vulgate.org>.

Juan de Persia, *Relaciones de Don Juan de Persia*, ed. Narciso Alonso Cortés (Madrid: Real Academia Española, 1946).

Khatunabadi, Mir Muhammad Baqir, *Tarjumih-i anajil-i arbaʿa*, ed. Rasul Jaʿfariyan (Tehran: Miras-i Maktub, 2005).

Krusinski, Jan Tadeusz, *The History of the Late Revolutions in Persia, taken from the memoirs of Father Krusinski, Procurator of the Jesuits at Ispahan*, 2 vols (London: J. Pemberton, 1733).

Kulayni, Muhammad b. Yaʿqub b. Ishaq al-, *Kitab al-Kafi*, ed. ʿAli Akbar al-Ghaffari, 8 vols (Beirut: Dar al-Adwaʾ,1985).

Majlisi, Muhammad Baqir, *Bihar al-anwar*, ed. Muhammad al-Baqir al-Bihbudi, 110 vols (Beirut: Dar Ihyaʾ al-Turath al-ʿArabi, 1983).

Manucci, Nicolao, *Storia do Mogor or Mugul India 1653–1708*, tr. William Irvine, 4 vols (London, 1907–13).

Mashizi, Mir Muhammad Saʿid, *Tazkirih-i Safavi-yi Kirman*, ed. Muhammad Ibrahim Bastani Parizi (Tehran: Nashr-i ʿIlm, 1990).

Moreen, Vera B. (ed.), *Iranian Jewry during the Afghan Invasion: the Kitāb-i sar Guzasht-i Kāshān of Bābāī b. Farhād* (Stuttgart: F. Steiner, 1990).

Moreen, Vera B. (ed. and tr.), '*Risāla-yi Ṣawāiq al-Yahūd* [The Treatise *Lighting Bolts against the Jews*] by Muḥammad Bāqir b. Muḥammad Taqī al-Majlisī (d. 1699)', *Die Welt des Islams*, New Series 32/2, 1992, pp. 177–95.

Munshi, Iskandar Beg, *History of Shah ʿAbbās the Great*, tr. Roger Savory, 2 vols (Boulder, CO: Westview Press, 1978).

Naraqi, Mulla Ahmad b. Mahdi al-, *Sayf al-ummih va burhan al-millih*, ed. Sayyid Mahd Tabatabaʾi (Tehran: Pazhuhishgah-i ʿUlum va Farhang-i Islami, 2006–7).

Nicéron, Jean-Pierre, *Mémoires pour servir à l'histoire des hommes illustres de la république des lettres*, 42 vols (Paris: Briasson, 1728–41).

Nisaburi, Muhammad b. Hasan al-Fattal al-, *Rawdat al-waʿizin wa basirat al-mutaʿizin*, ed. Muhammad Mahdi Hassan al-Khurasan (Najaf: al-Matbaʿa al-Haydariyya, 1966).

Opava, Martin (see Troppau, Martin von).

Optatus of Milevis (Saint), *De Schismate Donatistarum adversus Parmeniarum* (Antwerp: Apud G. Gallet, Praefectum Typographiae Huguetanorum, 1702).

Platina, Bartolomeo, *The Lives of the Popes*, ed. and tr. William Benham, 2 vols (London: Griffith, Farran, Okeden & Welsh, 1888).

Pseudo-Tertullian, *Adversus Omnes Haereses*, ed. by F. Oehler, 1851, verse numbers by E. Kroymann, 1942, transcribed by Roger Pearse, 2001, consulted online on 9 April 2019 <http://www.tertullian.org/latin/adversus_omnes_haereses.htm>.

Qays al-Hilali, Saulaym b., *Kitab Sulaym b. Qays*, ed. Muhammad Baqir Ansar Zanjnai (Qom: Nashr al-Hadi, 1999).

Qummi, ʿAli b. Ibrahim al-(attrib.), *al-Tafsir*, ed. Tayyib al-Musawi al-Jazaʾiri, 2 vols (Najaf: Maktabat al-Huda, 1967).

Qummi, Muhammad Tahir, 'Risālih-i radd-i sufiyyih', in Raul Jaʿfariyan (ed.), *Miras-i Islami-yi Iran*, vol. 4 (Qom: Kitabkhanih-i Hazrat Ayat Allah al-ʿUzma Marʿashi Najafi, 1994–5): pp. 131–50.

Qummi, Shadhan b. Jibraʾil al-, *al-Fadaʾil* (Najaf: Manshurat al-Matbaʿa al-Haydariyya, 1962).

Radi, al-Sharif al-, *Nahj al-balagha*, ed. Subhi Salih (Beirut–Cairo: Dar al-Kitab al-Lubnani/ Dar al-Kitab al-Masri, 2004).

Richard, Francis (ed.), *Raphaël du Mans, missionaire en Perse au XVIIe s*, 2 vols., Moyen Orient et Océan Indien 9 (Paris: Société d'Histoire de l'Orient, 1995).

Rinaldi, Odorico (see Baronius).

Sanson, Nicolas, *Voyage, ou, Relation de l'état présent du royaume de Perse: avec une dissertation curieuse sur les mœurs, religion & gouvernement de cet etat* (Paris: Chez la veuve Mabre Cramoisi, 1695).

Tabari, ʿImad al-Din Abi Jaʿfar Muhammad b. Abi al-Qasim al-, *Bisharat al-mustafa li-shiʿat al-murtada*, ed. Jawad al-Qayyumi al-Isfahani (Qom: Muʾassasat al-Nashr al-Islami, 2001–2).

Tabari al-Saghir, Muhammad b. Jarir, *Dalaʾil al-imama* (Qom: Dar al-Dhakhaʾir, 1963).

Tabrisi, Ahmad b. ʿAli b. Abi Talib al-, *al-Ihtijaj*, ed. Muhammad Sadiq al-Kutubi, 2 vols (Najaf: Intisharat al-Sharif al-Radi, 2001–2).

Tafrishi, Zahir al-Din, 'Nusrat al-haqq', ed. Gudarz Rashtiyani, *Payam-i baharistan* 4/14, 2011, pp. 1224–379.

Tavernier, Jean Baptiste, *Les six voyages de Jean Baptiste Tavernier: Ecuyer, Baron d'Aubonne, qu'il a fait en Turquie, en Perse et aux Indes*, 2 vols (Paris: Gervais Clouzier, 1676–7).

Tertullian, *Adversus Marcionem*, ed. and transl. by Ernest Evans, 3 vols (Oxford: Clarendon Press, 1972).

Troppau, Martin von (Martin of Opava), *Chronicon Pontificum et Imperatorum*, ed. Anna-Dorothee von den Brincken, *Monumenta Germaniae Historica*, accessed online on 30 January 2019, <http://www.mgh.de/home/aktuelles/newsdetails/martin-von-troppau-chronicon-pontificum-et-imperatorum/040f7e5a43/?tx_ttnews[pointer]=14>.

Tihrani, Muhammad Shafiʿ, *Mirʾat -i varidat: tarikh-i suqut-i Safaviyan. Payamad-ha-yi an va farmanravaʾi-yi Malik Mahmud Sistani*, intro. Mansur Sifatgul (Tehran: Miras-i Maktub, 2004).

Wilson, Sir Arnold T. (ed. & tr.), 'History of the Mission of the Fathers of the Society of Jesus, Established in Persia by the Reverend Father Alexander of Rhodes [Translation of "Relation de la mission des Pères de la Compagnie de Iesus, Etablie dans le Royaume de Perse par le R. P. Alexandre de Rhodes', complied by Jacques de Machaud]', *Bulletin of the School of Oriental and African Studies* 3, 1925, pp. 675–706.

Xavier, Jerónimo, *Fuente de Vida, Tratado Apologético dirigido al Rey Mogol de la India en 1600*, ed. Hugues Didier (Donostia–San Sebastián: Universidad de Deusto, 2007).

Secondary Sources

Abisaab, Rula J., *Converting Persia*, International Library of Iranian Studies 1 (London–New York: I. B. Tauris, 2004).

Abisaab, Rula J., 'al-Fādil al-Hindī', in Kate Fleet, Gudrun Krämer, Denis Matringe, John Nawas, Everett Rowson (eds) *Encyclopaedia of Islam, THREE*, consulted online on 4 April 2019, <http://dx.doi.org/10.1163/1573–3912_ei3_COM_26893>.

Abisaab, Rula J., 'Shiʿi Jurisprudence, Sunnism and the Traditionist Thought (akhbārī) of Muhammad Amin Astarabadi (d. 1036/1626–7)', *International Journal of Middle Eastern Studies* 47, 2015, pp. 5–23.

Adang, Camilla, 'Guided to Islam by the Torah: The *Risāla al-hādiya* by 'Abd al-Salām al-Muhtadī al-Muḥammadī', in Camilla Adang and Sabine Schmidtke (eds), *Contacts and Controversies between Muslims, Jews and Christians in the Ottoman Empire and Pre-Modern Iran*, Istanbuler Texte und Studien 21 (Istanbul: Orient-Institut Istanbul; Wurzburg, 2010), pp. 57–72.

Adang, Camilla and Sabine Schmidtke, 'Ahmad b. Mustafa Tashkubrizade's

(d. 968/1561) polemical tract against Judaism', *Al-Qantara: Revista de Estudios Árabes* 29, no. 1, 2008, pp. 79–113.

Adang, Camilla, Maribel Fierro, and Sabine Schmidtke (eds), *Ibn Hazm of Cordoba: The Life and Works of a Controversial Thinker*, Handbuch der Orientalistik, Erste Abteilung, Nahe und der Mittlere Osten 103 (Leiden–Boston: Brill, 2013).

Aghajari, Sayyid Hashim, *Muqaddimih-i bar munasibat-i din va dawlih dar Iran-i ʿasr-i Safavi* (Tehran: Intisharat-i Tarh-i naw, 2010).

Ahmed, Shahab, *Before Orthodoxy: The Satanic Verses in Early Islam* (Cambridge, MA–London: Harvard University Press, 2017).

Alam, Muzaffar and Sanjay Subrahmanyam, 'Frank Disputations: Muslims and Christians in the Court of Jahangir (1608–11)', *The Indian Economic and Social History Review* 46, no. 4, 2009, pp. 457–511.

Algar, Hamid, 'Fayż-e Kāšānī, Mollā Moḥsen-Moḥammad', in Ehsan Yarshater (ed.), *Encyclopaedia Iranica*, vol. IX (New York: Foundation for Iranian Studies, Columbia University, 1999), fasc. 5, pp. 452–4.

Algar, Hamid, 'Naqshbandīs and Safavids: a Contribution to the Religious History of Iran and her Neighbors', in Michel Mazzaoui (ed.), *Safavid Iran and her Neighbors* (Salt Lake City: University of Utah Press, 2003), pp. 7–48.

Allard, Paul, *Histoire des persécutions pendant les deux premiers siècles*, 5 vols (Paris: Libraire Victor Lecoffre, 1898–1905).

Alonso, Carlos (ed.), 'El convento agustiniano de Ispahán durante el período 1621–1671', *Analecta Augustiniana* 36, 1973, pp. 247–308.

Alonso, Carlos, *Misioneros Agustinos en Georgia (Siglo XVII)*, Estudios de Historia Agustiniana 1 (Valladolid: Ed. Studio Agustiniano, 1978).

Álvarez, Lourdes María, 'Anselmo Turmeda: Visionary Humanism of a Muslim Convert and Catalan Prophet', in Albrecht Classen (ed.), *Meeting the Foreign in the Middle Ages* (London–New York: Routledge, 2002), pp. 172–91.

Amanat, Abbas, 'Mujtahids and Missionaries: Shīʿī responses to Christian polemics in the early Qajar Period', in Robert Gleave (ed.), *Religion and Society in Qajar Iran*, Routledge/BIPS Persian Studies Series 4 (London–New York: Routledge, 2005), pp. 247–69.

Amanat, Mehrdad, *Jewish Identities in Iran: Resistance and Conversion to Islam and the Baha'i Faith*, Library of Modern Religion 9 (New York; London: I. B. Tauris, 2011).

Amir-Moezzi, Mohammad Ali, *La preuve de Dieu. La mystique shi'ite à travers l'oeuvre de Kulaynî IXe–Xe*, Islam-Nouvelles approches (Paris: Cerf, 2018).

Amir-Moezzi, Mohammad Ali, *La religion discrète: croyances et pratiques spirituelles dans l'islam shi'ite* (Paris: Librairie Philosophique J. Vrin, 2006).

Amir-Moezzi, Mohammad Ali, 'Muḥammad the Paraclete and Alī the Messiah: New Remarks on the Origins of Islam and of Shiite Imamology' *Der Islam* 95/1, 2018, pp. 30–64.

Amir-Moezzi, Mohammad Ali, 'Note bibliografique sur le *Kitâb Sulaym b. Qays*, le plus ancien ouvrage shiʿite existent', in Mohammad Ali Amir-Moezzi, Meir Michael Bar-Asher and Hopkins (eds), *Le shîʿisme Imāmīte quarant ans après. Hommages à Etan Kohlberg*, Bibliothèque de l'École des Hautes Études, Section des Sciences Religieuses 137 (Turnhout: Brepols, 2009), pp. 33–48.

Amir-Moezzi, Mohammad Ali, 'Remarques sur les critères d'authenticité du hadith et l'autorité du juriste dans le shi'isme imâmite', *Studia Islamica* 85, 1997, pp. 5–39.

Anthony, Sean W., 'The Satanic Verses in Early Shiʿite Literature: a Minority Report on Shah Ahmed's Before Orthodoxy', *Shii Studies Review* 3, Issues 1–2, 2019, pp. 215–52.

Anzali, Ata, *"Mysticism" in Iran: The Safavid Roots of a Modern Concept* (Columbia, SC: University of South Carolina University Press, 2017).

Anzali, Ata and S. M. Hadi Gerami, *Opposition to Philosophy in Safavid Iran: Mulla Muḥammad-Ṭāhir Qummī's Ḥikmat al-ʿĀrifīn*, intro. and critical edition Ata Anzali and S. H. Hadi Gerami, Islamicate Intellectual History 3 (Leiden–Boston: Brill, 2018).

Arendzen, John, 'Marcionites', in *The Catholic Encyclopedia*, vol. 9 (New York: Robert Appleton Company, 1910), consulted online on 4 April 2019, <http://www.newadvent.org/cathen/09645c.htm>.

Arjomand, Said Amir, 'The Office of *Mulla-Bashi* in Shiʿite Iran', *Studia Islamica* 57, 1983, pp. 135–46.

Arjomand, Said Amir, *The Shadow of God and the Hidden Imam: Religion, Political Order, and Societal Change in Shi'ite Iran from the Beginning to 1890* (Chicago: University of Chicago Press, 1984).

Ashk Shirin, Ebrahim, 'Muḥammad Khalīl Qā'inī', in David Thomas and John Chesworth (eds), *Christian-Muslim Relations. A Bibliographical History. Volume 12: Asia, Africa and the Americas 1700–1800,* The History of Christian-Muslim Relations 36 (Leiden–Boston: Brill, 2018), pp. 274–7.

Asín Palacios, Miguel, 'El original árabe de Disputa del Asno contra Fr. Anselmo Turmeda', *Revista de Filología Española* 1, 1914, pp. 1–51.

Aslanian, Sebouh, *From the Indian Ocean to the Mediterranean: The Global Trade*

Networks of Armenian Merchants from New Julfa (Berkeley: University of California Press, 2011).

Aslanian, Sebouh, 'Social Capital, Trust, and the Role of Networks in Julfan Trade: Informal and Semi-formal Institutions at Work', *Journal of Global History* 1, no. 3, November 2006, pp. 383–402.

Aubin, Jean, 'Introduction', in *L'Ambassade de Gregório Pereira Fidalgo à la cour de Châh Soltân-Hosseyn, 1696*–1697, ed. Jean Aubin (Lisbon: Comité National Portugais pour la Célébration du 2.500e Anniversaire de la Fondation de la Monarchie en Iran, 1971), pp. 11–26.

Ayoub, Mahmoud, *Redemptive Suffering in Islām: a Study of the Devotional Aspects of 'Āshūrā' in Twelver Shī'ism* (The Hague: Mouton Publishers, 1978).

Azfar Moin, A, *The Millennial Sovereign: Sacred Kingship and Sainthood in Islam* (New York: Columbia University Press, 2012).

Babaie, Sussan, Kathryn Babayan, Ina McCabe and Massumeh Farhad (eds), *Slaves of the Shah: New Elites of Safavid Iran*, The Library of Middle East History 3 (London: I. B. Tauris, 2004).

Babayan, Kathryn, *Mystics, Monarchs, and Messiahs: Cultural Landscapes of Early Modern Iran*, Harvard Middle Eastern Monographs 35 (Cambridge, MA: Harvard University Press, 2002).

Babayan, Kathryn, 'The Waning of the Qizilbash: The Spiritual and the Temporal in Seventeenth Century Iran' (PhD diss., Princeton University, 1993).

Baer, Marc David, *Honored by the Glory of Islam: Conversion and Conquest in Ottoman Europe* (Oxford: Oxford University Press, 2008).

Baer, Marc David, 'Review of: *Contested Conversions to Islam: Narratives of Religious Change in the Early Modern Ottoman Empire,* by Tijana Krstić', *Journal of Islamic Studies* 23, no. 3, September 2012, pp. 391–4.

Baer, Marc, Ussama Makdisi and Andrew Shryock, 'Tolerance and Conversion in the Ottoman Empire: A Conversation', *Comparative Studies in Society and History* 54, no. 4, 2009, pp. 927–40.

Bammel, Ernest, 'Christian Origins in Jewish Tradition', *New Testament Studies* 13, 1967, pp. 317–35.

Bar Asher, Meir, 'Ḥorr-e 'Āmeli', in Ehsan Yarshater (ed.), *Encyclopaedia Iranica,* vol. XII (New York: Foundation for Iranian Studies, Columbia University, 1996), fasc. 5, pp. 478–9.

Bashir, Shahzad, 'Shah Isma'il and the Qizilbash: Cannibalism in the Religious History of Early Safavid Iran', *History of Religions* 45, no. 3, February 2006, pp. 234–56.

Bayhom-Daou, Tamima, '*Kitāb Sulaym ibn Qays* Revisited', *Bulletin of the School of Oriental and African Studies* 78, no. 1, 2015, pp. 105–19.

Bdaiwi, Ahab, 'The Isfahan School of Philosophy', in Salim Ayduz, Caner Dagli, Ibrahim Kalin (eds), *The Oxford Encyclopaedia Philosophy, Science, and Technology in Islam*, vol. 1 (Oxford: Oxford University Press, 2014), pp. 405–9.

Behloul, Samuel-Martin, 'The Testimony of Reason and Historical Reality: Ibn Ḥazm's Refutation of Christianity', in Camilla Adang, Maribel Fierro and Sabine Schmidtke (eds), *Ibn Hazm of Cordoba: The Life and Works of a Controversial Thinker*, Handbuch der Orientalistik, Erste Abteilung, Nahe und der Mittlere Osten 103 (Leiden–Boston: Brill, 2013), pp. 457–83.

Beier, Robert, 'Einführung', in *Anselm Turmeda, Des Esesls Streitrede: eine altkatalanische Satire*, tr. and ed. Robert Beier (Berlin: Lit-Verlag, 2009), pp. 1–13.

Beier, Robert, 'Una coincidència textual entre la Tuḥfa d'Anselm Turmeda/ 'Abdallāh al-Tarjumān I el tractat no. 21 del Germans de la Puresa-Nova aportació a la qüestió de l'autenticitat de la Tuḥfa', *Xarc Al-Andalus* 9, 1993, pp. 83–8.

Benigni, Elisabetta, 'The Many Languages of the Self in the Early Modern Mediterranean: Anselm Turmeda/'Abdallāh Al-Tarjumān (1355–1423) – Friar, Muslim Convert and Translator', in Claire Norton (ed.), *Conversion and Islam in the Early Modern Mediterranean: The Lure of the Other* (London–New York: Routledge, 2017), pp. 194–221.

Bernardini, Michele, 'Giovan Battista and Gerolamo Vecchietti in Hormuz', in Rudi Matthee and Jorge Flores (eds), *Portugal, the Persian Gulf and Safavid Persia*, Acta Iranica 52 (Leuven: Peeters, 2011), pp. 265–81.

Bevilacqua, Alexander, *The Republic of Arabic Letters: Islam and the European Enlightenment* (Cambridge, MA: The Belknap Press of Harvard University Press, 2018).

Bourgain, Pascale, 'Silvestre dans le Liber Pontificalis', in Olivier Guyotjeannin et Emmanuel Poulle (eds), *Autour de Gerbert d'Aurillac, le Pape de l'an mil* (Paris: École des Chartes, 1996), pp. 355–7.

Browne, Edward Granville, *A Literary History of Persia*, 4 vols (Cambridge: Cambridge University Press, 1930).

Bruijn, J. T. P. de, 'Dieu, Louis (Ludovicus) de', in Ehsan Yarshater (ed.), *Encyclopaedia Iranica*, vol. VII (New York: Foundation for Iranian Studies, Columbia University, 1995), fasc. 4, pp. 397–8.

Brunner, Rainer, *Die Schia und di Koranfälschung*, Abhandlungen für die Kunde des Morgenlandes 53.1 (Würzburg: Ergon, 2001).

Bulliet, Richard, 'Conversions Stories in Early Islam', in Michael Gervers and

Ramzi Jibran Bikhazi (eds), *Conversion and Continuity: Indigenous Christian Communities in Islamic Lands*, Papers in Medieval Studies 9 (Toronto: Pontifical Institue of Medieval Studies, 1990), pp. 123–33.

Butler, Pierce, *Legenda aurea = Légende dorée = Golden Legend: A Study of Caxton's Golden Legend with Special Reference to its Relations to the Earlier English Prose Translation* (Baltimore: J. Murphy, 1899).

Calasso, Giovanna, 'Récits de conversions, zèle dévotionnel et instruction religieuse dans les biographes des 'gens de Basra' du Kitab al-Tabaqat d'Ibn Sa'd', in Mercedes García-Arenal (ed.), *Conversions islamiques. Identités religieuses en Islam méditerranéen/Islamic Conversions. Religious Identities in Mediterranean Islam* (Paris: Maisonneuve et Larose), pp. 19–48.

Calmard, Jean, 'France ii. Relations with Persia to 1789', in Ehsan Yarshater (ed.), *Encyclopaedia Iranica*, vol. X (New York: Foundation for Iranian Studies, Columbia University, 1990), fasc. 2, pp. 127–31.

Calmard, Jean, 'Shi'i Rituals and Power II. The Consolidation of Safavid Shi'ism: Folklore and Popular Religion', in Charles Melville (ed.), *Safavid Persia. The History and Politics of an Islamic Society*, Pembroke Persia Papers 4 (London–New York: I. B. Tauris; Centre of Middle Eastern Studies, University of Cambridge, 1996), pp. 139–90.

Camps, Arnulf, *Jerome Xavier S.J. and the Muslims of the Mogul Empire: Controversial Works and Missionary Activity* (Schöneck-Beckenried, Switzerland: Nouvelle Revue de Science Missionaire, 1957).

Carnoy-Torabi, Dominique, 'A biblioteca esquecida dos missionários do Ispaão/ The Forgotten Library of the Isfahan Missionaries', *Oriente* [Fundação Oriente, Lisbon] 19, 2008, pp. 94–105.

Castro Romano, *Vincenzo de, Difesa della causa di S. Marcellino, I, Pont. Rom.* (Rome: Stamperia Mordacchini, 1819).

Chaudhuri, Kirti Narayan, *Trade and Civilisation in the Indian Ocean: An Economic History from the Rise of Islam to 1750* (Cambridge: Cambridge University Press, 1985).

Cole, Juan, *Sacred Space and Holy War: The Politics, Culture and History of Shi'ite Islam* (London–New York: I. B. Tauris, 2005).

Cole, Juan, 'Shi'i Clerics in Iraq and Iran, 1722–1780: the Usuli-Akhbari Conflict Reconsidered', *Iranian Studies* 18, no. 1, Winter 1985, pp. 3–34.

Corbin, Henri, 'Annuaire 1976–1977: Shî'isme et christianisme à Ispahan au XVIIe siècle: L'œuvre de Sayyed Ahmad 'Alavî Ispahânî', in *Itinéraire d'un enseignement: Résumé des conférences à l'École pratique des hautes études (Section des sciences religieuses) 1955–1979* (Tehran: Institut français de recherche en Iran, 1993), pp. 169–73.

Cutillas, José, 'Don Juan de Persia', in David Thomas and John Chesworth (eds), *Christian-Muslim Relations. A Bibliographical History (1600–1700). Volume 9: Southern and Central Europe 1600–1700*, The History of Christian-Muslim Relations 31 (Leiden–Boston: Brill, 2017), pp. 75–7.

Cutillas, José, 'Spain: Relation with Persia in the 16th and 17th Centuries', *Encyclopædia Iranica*, online edition, 2018, consulted online on 24 August 2019 <http://www.iranicaonline.org/articles/spain-relations-persia-16–17-century>.

Cutillas, José, 'Las Relaciones de Don Juan de Persia : una imagen exótica de Persia narrada por un musulmán shií convertido al cristianismo a principios del s. XVII', *Sharq al-Andalus* 16/17, 2005, pp. 213–27.

Dakake, Massi Maria, 'Love, Loyalty and Faith: Defining the oundaries of the Early Shi'ite Community', PhD dissertation (Princeton University, 2000).

Decock, Wim, 'Law and the Bible in Spanish Neo-Scholasticism', in Brent Strawn (dd.), *The Oxford Encyclopedia of the Bible and Law*, vol. 2 (Oxford–New York: Oxford University Press, 2015), pp. 325–31.

Demiri, Lejla, *Muslim Exegesis of the Bible in Medieval Cairo: Najm al-Dīn al-Ṭūfī's (d. 716/1316). A Critical Edition and Annotated Transation with an Introduction*, History of Muslim-Christian Relations 19 (Leiden–Boston: Brill, 2013).

Demiri, Lejla, '*Taḥrīf* in der vormodernen muslimischen Literatur', in Timo Güzelmansur (ed.), *Das koranische Motiv der Schriftfälschung (taḥrīf) durch Juden und Christen: Islamische Deutungen und christliche Reaktionen*, CIBEDO Schriftenreihe 3 (Regensburg: Friedrich Pustet, 2014), pp. 15–45.

Didier, Hugues, 'Jerome Xavier', in David Thomas and John Chesworth (eds), *Christian-Muslim Relations. A Bibliographical History Volume 11 South and East Asia, Africa and the Americas (1600–1700)*, The History of Christian-Muslim Relations 33 (Leiden–Boston: Brill, 2016) pp. 84–91

Didier, Hugues, 'Jerónimo Xavier, un Navarro en la India', in Vibha Maurya and Mariela Insú *Actas del I Congreso Iberasiático de Hispanistas Siglo de Oro e Hispanismo General (Delhi, 9–12 de noviembre, 2010)*(Pamplona: Publicaciones del GRISO/ Servicio de Publicaciones de la Universidad de Navarra, 2011), pp. 147–58.

Duchesne, Louis-Marie Olivier, 'Introduction', in *Le Liber pontificalis*, intro. and ed. Louis-Marie Olivier Duchesne, 2 vols (Paris: Ernest Thorin, 1886), pp. I–CCLXII.

Duchesne, Louis-Marie Olivier, *Histoire ancienne de l'Église chrétienne*, 3 vols (Paris: Fontemoing, 1906–10).

Dubray, Charles Albert, 'Ambrogio Calepino', in *The Catholic Encyclopedia*, vol. 3 (New York: Robert Appleton Company, 1908), consulted online on 9 April 2019<http://www.newadvent.org/cathen/03169a.htm>.

Ellis, Havelock and John Addington Symonds, *Sexual Inversion: A Critical Edition*, ed. Ivan Crozier (Basingstoke–New York: Palgrave Macmillan,2008).

Erginbaş, Vefa, 'Problemaizing Ottoman Sunnism: Appropriation of Islamic History and Ahl al-Baytism in Ottoman Literary and Historical Writing in the Sixteenth Century', *Journal of the Economic and Social History of the Orient* 60, 2017, pp. 614–46.

Epalza, Míkel de, *La Tuḥfah, autobiografía y polémica islámica contra el Cristianismo de Abdallāh al-Taryumān (Fray Anselmo Turmeda)* (Rome: Accademia Nazionale dei Lincei, 1971). Reprinted as *Fray Anselmo Turmeda (Abdallāh al-Taryumān) y su polémica islamo-cristiana. Edición, traducción y studio de la Tuḥfa* (Madrid: Hiperión, 1994).

Epalza, Míkel de, 'Nuevas aportaciones a la biografía de fray Anselmo Turmeda (Abdallah al-Tarchuman)', *Analecta Sacra Tarraconensia* 38, 1965, pp. 87–158.

Faroqhi, Suraiya, *The Ottoman Empire and the World Around it*, The Library of Ottoman Studies 7 (London–New York: I. B. Tauris, 2004).

Fenlon, John Francis. "Hexapla', *The Catholic Encyclopedia, vol.* 7 (New York: Robert Appleton Company, 1910), consulted online on 9 April 2019, <http://www.newadvent.org/cathen/07316a.htm>.

Ferrier, Ronald W. and John R. Perry, 'East India Company (The British)', in Ehsan Yarshater (ed.), *Encyclopaedia Iranica*, vol. VII (New York: Foundation for Iranian Studies, Columbia University, 1996), fasc. 6, pp. 644–7.

Fischel, Walter J., 'The Bible in Persian Translation: A Contribution to the History of Bible Translations in Persia and India', *The Harvard Theological Review* 45, no. 1, January 1952, pp. 3–45.

Flannery, John M, *The Mission of the Portuguese Augustinians to Persia and Beyond (1601–1747)*, Studies in Christian Mission 43 (Leiden–Boston: Brill, 2013).

Floor, Willem, 'Dutch-Persian Relations', in Ehsan Yarshater (ed.), *Encyclopaedia Iranica*, vol. VII (New York: Foundation for Iranian Studies, Columbia University, 1996), fasc. 6, pp. 603–13.

___________,'The Rise and Fall of Mirza Taqi, the Eunuch Grand Vizier', *Studia Iranica* 26, 1997, pp. 237–66.

Flores, Jorge, *Unwanted Neighbors: The Mughals, the Portuguese, and Their Frontier Zones* (New Delhi: Oxford University Press, 2018).

__________, *The Mughal Padshah: A Jesuit Treatise on Emperor Jahangir's Court and Household*, ed. and tr. Jorge Flores, Rulers and Elites 6 (Leiden–Boston: Brill, 2015).

Frazee, Carles A., *Catholics and Sultans: The Church and the Ottoman Empire, 1453–1923* (London: Cambridge University Press, 2006).

Gaudeul, Jean-Marie and Robert Caspar, 'Textes de la tradition musulmane concernant le *tahrif* (falsification) des écritures', *Islamochristiana* 6, 1980, pp. 61–104.

García-Arenal, Mercedes and Fernando Rodríguez Mediano, *Converted Muslims, the Forged Lead Books of Granada, and the Rise of Orientalism*, tr. Consuelo López-Morillas, Numen Book Series 142 (Leiden–Boston: Brill, 2013).

García-Arenal, Mercedes, 'Dreams and Reason: Autobiographies of Converts in Religious Polemics', in Mercedes García-Arenal (ed.), *Conversions islamiques. Identités religieuses en Islam méditerranéen/Islamic Conversions. Religious Identities in Mediterranean Islam* (Paris: Maisonneuve et Larose), pp. 89–118.

García Hernán, Enrique, 'The "Persian Gentelmen" at the Spanish Court', in Rudi Matthee and Jorge Flores (eds), *Portugal, the Persian Gulf and Safavid Persia, Acta Iranica* 52 (Leuven: Peeters, 2011), pp. 283–99.

Giorgi, Ignazio, 'Appunti intorno ad alcuni manoscritti del "Liber Pontificalis"', *Archivio della Società romana di storia patria* 20, 1897, pp. 247–312.

Girard, Aurélien, 'Des manuels de la langue entre mission et erudition orientaliste au XVIIme siècle: les grammaires de l'arabe des Caracciolini', *Studi Medievali e Moderni: arte, letteratura, storia* 16, no. 1, 2010, pp. 279–95.

Girard, Aurélien, 'Teaching and Learning Arabic in Early Modern Rome: Shaping a Missionary Language', in Jan Loop, Alastair Hamilton and Charles Burnett (eds), *The Teaching and Learning of Arabic in Early Modern Europe*, The History of Oriental Studies 3 (Leiden–Boston: Brill, 2017), pp. 189–212.

Gleave, Robert, 'Early Shiite Hermeneutics and the Dating of *Kitāb Sulaym ibn Qays*', *Bulletin of the School of Oriental and African Studies* 78, no. 1, 2015, pp. 83–103.

Gleave, Robert, 'Imāmī Shīʿī Refutations of *qiyās*', in Bernard Weiss (ed.), *Studies in Islamic Legal Theory*, Studies in Islamic Law and Society 13 (Leiden–Boston–Cologne: Brill, 2002), pp. 267–91.

Gleave, Robert, *Inevitable Doubt: Two Theories of Shīʿī Jurisprudence*, Studies in Islamic Law and Society 12 (Leiden–Boston–Cologne: Brill, 2000).

Gleave, Robert, 'Scriptural Sufism and Scriptural Anti-Sufism: Theology and

Mysticism amongst the Shī'ī Akhbāriyya', in Ayman Shihadeh (ed.), *Sufism and Theology* (Edinburgh: Edinburgh University Press, 2007), pp. 158–76.

Gleave, Robert, *Scripturalist Islam: the History and Doctrines of the Akhbārī Shī'ī School*, Islamic Philosophy, Theology and Science. Texts and Studies (Leiden–Boston: Brill, 2007).

Glei, Reinhold F., and Roberto Tottoli, *Ludovico Marracci at Work. The Evolution of his Latin Translation of the Qur'ān in the Light of his Newly Discovered Manuscripts with an Edition and a Comparative Analysis of Sura 18*, Series Arabica-Latina 1 (Wiesbaden: Harrassowitz Verlag, 2016).

Gooren, Henri, 'Towards a New Model of Religious Conversion Careers: the Impact of Social and Institutional Factors', in *Paradigms, Poetics, and Politics of Conversion*, ed. Jan N. Bremmer, Wout J. van Bekkum and Arie L. Molendijk (Leuven–Paris–Dudley, MA: Peeters, 2006), pp. 25–40.

Ghougassian, Vazken S., *The Emergence of the Armenian Diocese of New Julfa in the Seventeenth Century*, University of Pennsylvania Armenian Texts and Studies 14 (Atlanta: Scholars Press, 1998).

Giunashvili, Helen and Tamar Abuladze, 'Researches on Persian and Georgian-Persian Historical Documents of Nader Shah's Times from Georgian Depositories', *Analytica Iranica* 4–5, 2013, pp. 189–211.

Graf, Tobias P., *The Sultan's Renegades: Christian-European Converts to Islam and the Making of the Ottoman Elite, 1576–1610* (Oxford: Oxford University Press, 2017).

Green, Nile, *Terrains of Exchange: Religious Economies of Global Islam* (New York: Oxford University Press, 2015).

Griffith, Sidney H., *The Bible in Arabic: The Scriptures of the "People of the Book" in the Language of Islam* (Princeton: Princeton University Press, 2013).

Grypeou, Emmanouela and Helen Spurling, *The Book of Genesis in Late Antiquity: Encounters between Jewish and Christian Exegesis*, Jewish and Christian Perspective Series 24 (Leiden: Brill, 2013).

Gulbenkian, Roberto, *The Translation of the Four Gospels into Persian*, Schriftenreihe der Neuen Zeitschrift für Missionswissenschaft 29 (Immensee: Nouvelle Revue de science missionnaire, 1981).

Ja'fariyan, Rasul, *Din va siyasat dar dawrih-i Safavi* (Qom: Ansariyan, 1991/2).

Ja'fariyan, Rasul, 'Muqaddimih-i muhaqqiq', in Rasul Ja'fariyan (ed.) *Sayf al-mu'minn fi qital al-mushrikin* (Qom: Intisharat-i Ansariyan, 1996–7), pp. 13–54.

Ja'fariyan, Rasul, *Safaviyyih dar 'arsih-i din, farhang va siyasat*, 3 vols (Qom: Pizuhishkadih-i Hawzih va Danishgah, 2000–1).

Jaʿfariyan, Rasul, and Maryam Sadiqi, *Az Darband ta Qatif: Guzarishi az guftiguha-yi masihi-islami dar dawrih-i Safavi va Qajar* (Tehran: Nashr-i ʿIlm, 2016).

Jones, Linda G., *The Power of Oratory in the Medieval Muslim World* (Cambridge: Cambridge University Press, 2012).

Haʾiri, ʿAbdul-Hadi, 'Reflections on the Shi'i Responses to Missionary Thought and Activities in the Safavid Period', in Jean Calmard (ed.), *Etudes Safavides* (Paris–Tehran: Institut Français de Recherche en Iran, 1993), pp. 151–64.

Haʾiri, ʿAbdul-Hadi, *Nakhustin ruyaruyiha-yi andishihgaran-i Iran ba du ruyih-i tamaddun-i burzhuvazi-yi Gharb* (Tehran: Amir Kabir, 1988).

Hamilton, Alastair, 'The Qur'an as Chrestomathy in Early Modern Europe', in Jan Loop, Alastair Hamilton and Charles Burnett (eds), *The Teaching and Learning of Arabic in Early Modern Europe*, The History of Oriental Studies 3 (Leiden–Boston: Brill, 2017), pp. 213–29.

Hallaq, Wael B., 'Notes on the Term *qarīna* in Islamic Legal Discourse', *Journal of the American Oriental Society* 108, no. 3, July–September 1988, pp. 475–80.

Hallaq, Wael B., *Sharīʿa Between Past and Present: Theory, Practice and Modern Transformations* (Cambridge: Cambridge University Press, 2009).

Halft, Dennis, 'Hebrew Bible Quotations in Arabic Transcription in Safavid Iran of the 11th/17th Century: Sayyed Aḥmad ʿAlavī's Persian Refutations of Christianity', *Intellectual History of the Islamicate World* 1, nos. 1–2, 2013, pp. 235–52.

Halft, Dennis, 'Hovhannēs Mrkʿuz Jułayecʿi', in David Thomas and John Chesworth (eds), *Christian-Muslim Relations. A Bibliographical History. Volume 12 Asia, Africa and the Americas 1700–1800*, The History of Christian-Muslim Relations 36 (Leiden–Boston: Brill, 2018), pp. 260–5.

Halft, Dennis, 'Pietro Della Valle', in David Thomas and John Chesworth (eds), *Christian-Muslim Relations. A Bibliographical History. Volume 10: Ottoman and Safavid Empires 1600–1700*, The History of Christian-Muslim Relations 32 (Leiden–Boston: Brill, 2017), pp. 515–21.

Halft, Dennis,'Schiitische Polemik gegen das Chrsitentum im safawidischen Iran des 11/17 Jarhunderts: Sayyid Aḥmad ʿAlawī's *Lawāmiʿ-i rabbānī dar radd-i šubha-yi naṣrānī*', in Camilla Adang and Sabine Schmidtke (eds), *Contacts and Controversies between Muslims, Jews and Christians in the Ottoman Empire and Pre-Modern Iran*, Istanbuler Texte und Studien 21 (Istanbul: Orient-Institut Istanbul; Wurzburg, 2010), pp. 273–334.

Halft, Dennis, 'The Arabic Vulgate in Safavid Persia: Arabic Printing of the Gospels, Catholic Missionaries, and the Rise of Shīī Anti-Christian Polemics' (PhD dissertation, Freie-Universität Berlin, 2016).

Hartmann, Ulrich, 'Staat und Religion in Transoxanien im frühen 16. Jahrhundet', *Zeitschrift der Deutschen Morgenländischen Gesellschaft* 124, no. 2, 1974, pp. 332–69.

Herzig, Edmund, 'The Deportation of the Armenians in 1604–1605 and Europe's Myth of Shah 'Abbas I', in Charles Melville (ed.), *Pembroke Papers 1* (Cambridge: Cambridge University Press, 1990), pp. 59–71.

Herzig, Edmund, 'The Family Firm in the Commercial Organisation of Julfa Armenians', in Jean Calmard (ed.), *Etudes Safavides* (Paris–Tehran: Institut Français de Recherche en Iran, 1993), pp. 287–304.

Heyberger, Bernard, 'Polemic Dialogues between Christians and Muslims in the Seventeenth Century', *Journal of Economic and Social History of the Orient* 55, 2012, pp. 495–516.

Hodgson, Marshall G. S., *The Venture of Islam, Volume 3: the Gunpower Empires and Modern Times* (Chicago: University of Chicago Press, 2009).

Horst, Ulrich, *Päpstlich Unfehlbarkeit wider konziliare Superiorität? Studien zur Geschichte eines (ekklesiologischen) Antagonismus vom 15. bis zum 19. Jahrhundert*, Pabedorn: Ferdinand Schöning, 2016.

Hourani, George F., 'Ibn Sina on Necessary and Possible Existence', *Philosophical Forum* 4, no. 1, 1972, pp. 74–86.

Ikas, Wolfgang-Valentin, 'Martinus Polonus' Chronicle of the Popes and Emperors: A Medieval Best-Seller and Its Neglected Influence on Medieval English Chroniclers', *The English Historical Review* 116, No. 466, April 2001, pp. 327–41.

Kara, Seyfeddin, *In Search of 'Alī Ibn Abī Ṭālib's Codex: History and Traditions on the Earliest Copy of the Qur'ān*, with a foreword by James Piscatori (Berlin: Gerlach Press, 2018).

Khan, Gulfishan, 'Late 16th- and Early 17th-Century Contestations of Catholic Christianity at the Mughal Court', in Chad M. Bauman and Richard Fox Young (eds), *Constructing Indian Christianities: Culture, Conversion and Caste* (London–New York; Delhi: Routledge, 2014), pp. 61–85.

Kiefer, René, 'John', in John Barton and John Muddiman (eds), *The Oxford Bible Commentary. The Gospels* (New York: Oxford University Press, 2001), pp. 186–242.

Kirsch, Johann Peter, 'Pope John XXI', in *The Catholic Encyclopedia*, vol. 8 (New York: Robert Appleton Company, 1910), consulted online on 9 April 2019 <http://www.newadvent.org/cathen/08429c.htm>.

Kister, Meir Jacob, 'A Bag of Meat: A Study of an Early *Ḥadīth*', *Bulletin of the School of Oriental and African Studies* 33, no. 2, 1970, pp. 267–75.

Koertner, Mareike, 'We Have Made Clear the Signs – Dalā'il al-Nubūwa: Proofs of Prophecy in Early Ḥadīth Literature' (PhD dissertation: Yale University, 2014).

Kohlberg, Etan, 'Beḥār al-Alnwār', in Ehsan Yarshater (ed.), *Encyclopaedia Iranica*, vol. IV (New York: Foundation for Iranian Studies, Columbia University, 2002), fasc. 1, pp. 90–93.

Kohlberg, Etan and Mohammad Ali Amir-Moezzi (eds), *Revelation and Falsification: the Kitāb al-qirā'āt of Aḥmad b. Muḥammad al-Sayyārī*, Studies on the Qur'ān 4 (Leiden–Boston: Brill, 2009).

Kroell, Anne, 'East India Company (French)', in Ehsan Yarshater (ed.), *Encyclopaedia Iranica*, vol. VII (New York: Foundation for Iranian Studies, Columbia University, 1996), fasc. 6, pp. 647–49.

Kroell, Anne, *Louis XIV, la Perse et Mascate* (Paris: Société d'Histoire de l'Orient, 1977).

Kristić, Tijana, *Contested Conversions to Islam: Narratives of Religious Change in the Early Modern Ottoman Empire* (Stanford: Stanford University Press, 2011).

Kueny, Kathryn, 'Abraham's Test: Islamic Male Circumcision as Anti/Ante-Covenantal Practice', in John C. Reeves (ed.), *Bible and Qur'ān: Essays in Scriptural Intertextuality*, Symposium Series 24 (Leiden–Boston: Brill, 2004), pp. 161–82.

Langen, Joseph, *Geschichte der römischen Kirche*, 4 vols (Bonn: M. Cohen, 1885).

Laoust, Henri, 'Les fondements de l'imamat dans le Minhâǧ d'al-Ḥillī', *Revue des études islamiques* 46, 1978, pp. 3–55.

Laoust, Henri, *Les schismes dans l'Islam: introduction à une étude de la religion musulmane* (Paris: Payot, 1983).

Lazarus-Yafeh, Hava, *Intertwined Worlds: Medieval Islam and Bible Criticism* (Princeton: Princeton University Press, 1992).

Lazarus-Yafeh, Hava, 'Some Neglected Aspects of Medieval Muslim Polemics against Christianity', *The Harvard Theological Review* 89, no. 1, January 1996, pp. 61–84.

Lewisohn, Leonard, 'Sufism and the School of Iṣfahān: *Taṣawwuf* and *'Irfān* in Late Safavid Iran ('Abd al-Razzāq Lāhījī and Fayḍ-i Kāshānī on the Relation of *Taṣawwuf*, *Ḥikmat* and *'Irfān*', in Leonard Lewisohn and David Morgan (ed.), *The Heritage of Sufism, Vol. III: Late Classical Persianate Sufism: the Safavid and Mughal Period (1501–1750)* (Oxford: Oneworld, 1999), pp. 63–134.

Lockhart, Laurence, 'European Contacts with Persia, 1350–1736', in Peter Jackson and Laurence Lockhart (eds), *Cambridge History of Iran, vol. 6: The Timurid and Safavid Periods* (Cambridge: Cambridge University Press, 1986), pp. 373–411.

Lockhart, Laurence, *The Fall of the Safavid Dynasty and the Afghan Occupation of Persia* (Cambridge: Cambridge University Press, 1958).

Loomis, Louis Ropes, 'Introduction', *The Book of the Popes (Liber Pontificalis),* tr. and intro. Louis Ropes Loomis (New York: Columbia University Press, 1916), pp. ix–xxii.

Loop, Jan, *Johann Heinrich Hottinger: Arabic and Islamic Studies in the Seventeenth Century* (Oxford: Oxford University Press, 2013).

Loureiro, Rui Manuel, 'The Persian Ventures of Fr. António de Gouveia', in Rudi Matthee and Jorge Flores (eds), *Portugal, the Persian Gulf and Safavid Persia,* Acta Iranica 52 (Leuven: Peeters, 2011), pp. 249–64.

Love, Rosalind C. (ed. and tr.), *Three Eleventh-century Anglo-Latin Saints' Lives: Vita S. Birini, Vita et Miracula S. Kenelmi and Vita S. Rumwoldi* (Oxford: Clarendon Press, 1996).

Maeda, Hirotake, 'Slave Elites Who Returned Home: Georgian Vālī-king Rostom and the Safavid Household Empire', in *Memoirs of the Department of the Tokyo Bunko,* 69. (Tokyo Bunko, 2011), pp. 97–127.

Mahdavi, Muslih al-Din, *Zindiginamih-i ʿAllamih-i Majlisi,* 2 vols (Tehran: Sazman-i Chap va Intisharat-i Vizarat-i Farhang va Irshad-i Islami, 1999–2000).

Malcolm, Noel, 'Comenius, Boyle, Oldenburg, and the Translation of the Bible into Turkish', *Church History & Religious Culture* 87, no. 3, July 2007, pp. 327–62.

Malcolm, Noel, 'Comenius, the Conversion of the Turks, and the Muslim-Christian Debate on the Corruption of Scripture', *Church History and Religious Culture* 87, no. 4, 2007, pp. 477–508.

Malcolm, Noel, *Useful Enemies: Islam and The Ottoman Empire in Western Political Thought, 1450–1750* (Oxford: Oxford University Press, 2019).

Matthee, Rudi, 'Christians in Safavid Iran: Hospitality and Harassment', *Studies on Persianate Societies* 3, 2005, pp. 44–72.

Matthee, Rudi, 'Confessions of an Armenian Convert: the *I'tirafnama* of Abkar ('Ali Akbar) Armani', in Hani Khafipour (ed.), *The Empires of the Near East and India: Source Studies of the Safavid, Ottoman and Mughal Literate Communities* (New York: Columbia University Press, 2019), pp. 11–31.

Matthee, Rudi, 'Diplomatic Contacts between Portugal and Iran in the Reign of Sah Tahmasp, 1524–1576', in Rudi Matthee and Jorge Flores (eds), *Portugal, the Persian Gulf and Safavid Persia,* Acta Iranica 52 (Leuven: Peeters, 2011), pp. 219–47.

Matthee, Rudi, 'Georgia vii. Georgians in the Safavid Administration', in Ehsan Yarshater (ed.), *Encyclopaedia Iranica*, vol. X (New York: Foundation for Iranian Studies, Columbia University, 2001), fasc. 5, pp. 493–6.

Matthee, Rudi, 'Gorgin Khan', in Ehsan Yarshater (ed.), *Encyclopaedia Iranica*, vol. XI (New York: Foundation for Iranian Studies, Columbia University, 2002), fasc. 2, pp. 163–5.

Matthee, Rudi, 'Jesuits in Safavid Persia', in Ehsan Yarshater (ed.), *Encyclopaedia Iranica*, vol. XIV (New York: Foundation for Iranian Studies, Columbia University, 2008), fasc. 6, pp. 634–8.

Matthee, Rudi, 'Introduction', in Rudi Matthee and Jorge Flores (eds), *Portugal, the Persian Gulf and Safavid Persia*, Acta Iranica 52 (Leuven: Peeters, 2011), pp. 1–7.

Matthee, Rudi, 'Merchants in Safavid Iran: Participants and Perceptions', *Journal of Early Modern History* 3–4, 1999–2000, pp. 233–68.

Matthee, Rudi, 'Poverty and Perseverance: the Jesuit Mission of Isfahan and Shamakhi', *Al-Qantara* 36/2, July–December 2015, pp. 463–501.

Matthee, Rudi, *Persia in Crisis: Safavid Decline and the Fall of Isfahan*, International Library of Iranian Studies 17 (London–New York: I. B. Tauris, 2012).

Matthee, Rudi, 'The Career of Mohammad Beg, Grand Vizier of Shah 'Abbas II (r. 1642–1666)', *Iranian Studies* 24, No. 1/4, 1991, pp. 17–36.

Matthee, Rudi, 'The Politics of Protection: Iberian Missionaries in Safavid Iran ender Shāh ʿAbbās I (1587–1629)', in Camilla Adang and Sabine Schmidtke (eds), *Contacts and Controversies between Muslims, Jews and Christians in the Ottoman Empire and Pre-Modern Iran*, Istanbuler Texte und Studien 21 (Istanbul: Orient-Institut Istanbul; Wurzburg, 2010), pp. 245–71.

Matthee, Rudi, *The Politics of Trade in Safavid Iran: Silk for Silver, 1600–1730* (Cambridge–New York: Cambridge University Press, 1999).

Matthee, Rudi, *The Pursuit of Pleasure: Drugs and Stimulants in Iranian History, 1500–1900.* (Princeton: Princeton University Press, 2005).

Matthee, Rudi, 'The Safavids under Western Eyes: Seventeenth-Century European Travellers to Iran', *Journal of Early Modern History* 13, 2009, pp. 137–71.

Mazzaoui, Michel, *The Origins of the Safawids: Shi'ism, Sufism, and the Ghulat*, Freiburger Islamstudien 3 (Mainz: Rheingold-Druckerei; Wiesbaden: Franz Steiner, 1972).

McChesney, Robert, *Waqf in Central Asia: Four Hundred Years in the History of a Muslim Shrine, 1480–1889* (Princeton: Princeton University Press, 1991).

Melchert, Christopher, 'Khargūshī, *Tahdhīb al-asrār*', *Bulletin of the School of Oriental and African Studies* 73, no. 1, 2010, pp. 29–44.

Michel, Thomas F., *A Muslim Theologian's Response to Christianity: Ibn Taymiyya's Al-Jawab al-Sahih* (Demar, NY: Caravan Books, 1984).

Moazzen, Maryam, *Formation of a Religious Landscape: Shiʿi Higher Learning in Safavid Iran*, Islamic History and Civilization, Studies and Texts 151 (Leiden–Boston: Brill, 2017).

Moazzen, Maryam, 'Institutional Transformation or Clerical Status Quo? New Insights into the Career and Work of Sayyid Mīr Muḥammad Bāqir Khvātūnabādī', *Studia Iranica* 45/1, 2016, pp. 65–88.

Modarressi, Hossein, 'Early Debates on the Integrity of the Qur'ān: A Brief Survey', *Studia Islamica* 77, 1993, pp. 5–39.

Modarressi, Hossein, 'Rationalism and Traditionalism in Shīʿī Jurisprudence: a Preliminary Survey', *Studia Islamica* 59, 1984, pp. 141–58.

Modarressi, Hossein, *Tradition and Survival: A Biographical Survey of Early Shīʿite Literature, Volume 1*, Oneworld Reference Library (Oxford: Oneworld, 2003).

Monferrer Sala, Juan Pedro, 'Fray Anselmo Turmeda', in David Thomas and Alex Mallett (eds), *Christian-Muslim Relations. A Bibliographical History. Volume 5 (1350–1500)*, The History of Christian-Muslim Relations 20 (Leiden–Boston, Brill, 2013), pp. 326–9.

Moreen, Vera B., 'A Seventeenth-Century Iranian Rabbi's Polemical Remarks', in Michel Mazzaoui (ed.), *Safavid Iran and her Neighbors* (Salt Lake City: University of Utah Press, 2003), pp. 157–68.

Moreen, Vera B., *Iran's Jewry's Hour of Peril and Heroism: A Study of Babai ibn Lutf's Chronicle, 1617–1662* (New York: American Academy of Jewish Research, 1987).

Moreen, Vera B., 'The Problems of Conversion among Iranian Jews in the Seventeenth and Eighteenth Centuries', *Iranian Studies* 19, nos. 3–4, Summer-Autumn 1986, pp. 215–28.

Moreen, Vera B., 'The Status of Religious Minorities in Safavid Iran 1617–61', *Journal of Near Eastern Studies* 40, no. 2, April 1981, pp. 119–34.

Morimoto, Kazuo, 'How to Behave Toward *Sayyids* and *Sharīfs*: A Trans-sectarian Tradition of Dream Accounts', in Kazuo Morimoto (ed.), *Sayyids and Sharifs in Muslim Societies: The living links to the Prophet* (London–New York: Routledge, 2012), pp. 15–35.

Morimoto, Kazuo, 'The Earliest ʿAlid Genealogy for the Safavids: New Evidence for the Pre-dynastic Claim to the *Sayyid* Status', *Iranian Studies* 43, no. 4, 2010, pp. 447–69.

Moura Carvalho, Pedro, *Mir'at al-quds (Mirror of Holiness): A Life of Christ for Emperor Akbar: a commentary on Father Jerome Xavier's text and the miniatures of Cleveland Museum of Art, Acc. no. 2005.145*, with a translation by Wheeler Thackston, Sources and Studies in Islamic Art and Architecture 12 (Leiden: Brill, 2012).

Muhajir, Ja'far al-, *al-Hijra al-'amiliyya ila Iran fi al-'asr al-Safawi: asbabuha al-tarikhiyya wa nata'ijuha al-thaqafiyya wa al-siyasiyya* (Beirut: Dar al-Rawda, 1989).

Nasr, Seyyed Hossein, 'Religion in Safavid Persia', *Iranian Studies* 7, nos. 1–2, Studies on Isfahan: Proceedings of the Isfahan Colloquium, Part I, Winter-Spring, 1974, pp. 271–86.

Nasr, Seyyed Hossein, 'The School of Isfahan', in Mian Mohammad Sharif (ed.), *A History of Muslim Philosophy*, vol. 2 (Wiesbaden: Harrassowitz, 1963–6.), pp. 932–61.

Newman, Andrew J., 'Clerical Perceptions of Sufi Practices in Late Seventeenth-Century Persia: Arguments over the Permissibility of Singing (*Ghinā*)', in Leonard Lewisohn and David Morgan (ed.), *The Heritage of Sufism, Vol. III: Late Classical Persianate Sufism: the Safavid and Mughal Period (1501–1750)* (Oxford: Oneworld, 1999), pp.135–64.

Newman, Andrew J., 'Fayd al-Kashani and the rejection of the clergy/state alliance: Friday prayer a politics in the Safavid period', in Linda S. Walbridge (ed.), *The Most Learned of the Shi'a: the Institution of the Marja' Taqlid* (New York: Oxford University Press, 2001), pp. 34–52.

Newman, Andrew J., 'The Myth of the Clerical Migration to Safawid Iran: Arab Shii Opposition to 'Alī al-Karakī and Safawid Shiism', *Die Welt des Islams* 33, no. 1, 1993, pp. 66–112.

Newman, Andrew J., 'The Nature of the Uṣūlī/Akhbārī Dispute in Late Ṣafawid Iran. Part 1: 'Abdallāh al-Samāhijī's *Munyat al-Mumārisīn*', *Bulletin of the School of Oriental and African Studies* 55, no. 1, January 1992, pp. 22–51.

Newman, Andrew J., *Safavid Iran: The Rebirth of a Persian Empire*, Library of Middle East History 5 (New York–London: I. B. Tauris, 2006).

Newman, Andrew J., 'Sufism and Anti-Sufism in Safavid Iran: The Authorship of the Ḥadīqat al-Shī'a Revisited', *Iran* 37, 1999, pp. 95–108.

Newman, Andrew J., 'Towards a Reconsideration of the "Isfahān School of Philosophy": Shaykh Bahā'ī and the Role of the Safawid 'Ulamā', *Studia Iranica* 15, no. 2, 1986, pp. 165–99.

Nizami, Khaliq Ahmad, *Akbar and Religion* (Delhi: Idarah-i-Adabiyat-i-Delli, 1989).

Oestereich, Thomas, 'Pope St. Gregory VII', in *The Catholic Encyclopedia*, vol. 6 (New York: Robert Appleton Company, 1909), consulted online on 9 April 2019 <http://www.newadvent.org/cathen/06791c.htm>.

Oldoni, Massimo, 'Gerberto e la sua storia, I', *Studi medievali*, 3rd series, vol. 18, 1997, pp. 629–704.

Ometto, Franco, 'Khatun Abadi, the Ayatollah who Translated the Gospels', *Islamochristiana* 28, 2002, pp. 55–72.

Ortega García, Pedro, 'Juan Tadeo de San Eliseo, 1574–1634', *Kalakorikos*, no. 17, 2012, pp. 161–83.

Pelletier, André, *Lettre d'Aristée à Philocrate* (Paris: Cerf, 1962).

Peters, Edward, *The Magician, the Witch, and the Law* (Philadelphia: University of Pennsylvania Press, 1978).

Pfeiffer, Judith, 'Confessional Ambiguity vs. Confessional Polarization: Politics and the Negotiation of Religious Boundaries in the Ilkhanate', in Judith Pfeiffer (ed.), *Politics, Patronage, and the Transmission of Knowledge in 13th–15th Century Tabriz*, Iran Studies 8 (Leiden–Boston: Brill, 2014), pp. 129–68.

Pfeiffer, Judith, 'Conversion Versions: Sultan Öljeytü's Conversion to Shiʿism (709/1309) in Muslim Narrative Sources', *Mongolian Studies* 22, 1999, pp. 35–67.

Piemontese, Angelo Michele, 'Leggere e scrivere "Orientalia" in Italia', *Annali della Scuola Normale Superiore di Pisa. Classe di Lettere e Filosofia* Series III, vol. 23, no. 2, 1993, pp. 427–53.

Pizzorusso, Giovanni, 'La preparazione linguistica e controversistica dei misionari per l'Oriente islamico: scuole, testi, insegnanti a Roma e in Italia', in Bernard Heyberger, Mercedes García-Arenal, Emanuela Colombo, Paola Vismara (eds), *L'Islam visto da Occidente. Cultura e religione del Seicento europeo di fronte all'Islam, Atti del Convegno (Milano, 17–18 ottobre 2007)* (Milan: Marietti 1820, 2009): pp. 253–88.

Pizzorusso, Giovanni, 'Filippo Guadagnoli, i Caracciolini e lo studio delle lingue orientali e della controversia con l'Islam a Roma nel XVII secolo', *Studi Medievali e Moderni: arte, letteratura, storia* 16, no. 1, 2010, pp. 245–78.

Pourjavady, Reza and Sabine Schmidtke, "Alī Qulī Jadīd al-Islām', in Kate Fleet, Gudrun Krämer, Denis Matringe, John Nawas and Everett Rowson (eds), *Encyclopaedia of Islam, THREE*, Consulted online on 8 April 2019, <http://dx.doi.org/10.1163/1573-3912_ei3_COM_23210>.

Pourjavady, Reza, 'Muslim Polemics against Judaism and Christianity in 18th Century Iran. The literary sources of Āqā Muḥammad `Alī Bihbahānī's (1144/1732–1216/1801) *Radd-i shubahāt-i al-kuffār*', *Studia Iranica* 1, 2006, pp. 69–94.

Powell, Avril A., *Muslims and Missionaries in Pre-Mutiny India*, London Studies on South Asia 7 (London–New York: Routledge, 2008).

Rashtiyani, Gudarz, 'Muqaddimih-i Musahhih', in Zahir al-Din Tafrishi, *Nusrat al-haqq*, ed. Gudarz Rashtiyani, *Payam-i baharistan* 4, no. 14, 2011, pp. 1224–44.

Reinhard, Wolfgang, '"Gegenreformation als Modernisierung?" Prolegomena zu einer Theorie des konfessionellen Zeitalters', *Archiv für Reformationsgeschichte* 68, 1977, pp. 226–52.

Reinhard, Wolfgang, 'Zwang zur Konfessionalisierung? Prolegomena zu einer Theorie des konfessionellen Zeitalters', *Zeitschrift für Historische Forschung* 10, no. 3, 1983, pp. 257–77.

Rezvani, Babak, 'The Islamization and Ethnogenesis of the Fereydani Georgians', *Nationalities Papers* 36, no.4, 2008, pp. 593–623.

Richard, Francis, 'Capuchins in Persia', in Ehsan Yarshater (ed.), *Encyclopaedia Iranica*, vol. IV (New York: Foundation for Iranian Studies, Columbia University, 1990), fasc. 7, pp. 786–8.

Richard, Francis, 'Carmelites in Persia', in Ehsan Yarshater (ed.), *Encyclopaedia Iranica*, vol. IV (New York: Foundation for Iranian Studies, Columbia University, 1990), fasc. 7, pp. 832–4.

Richard, Francis, 'L'apport des missionnaires européens à la connaissance de l'Iran en Europe et de l'Europe en Iran', in Jean Calmard (ed.), *Etudes Safavides* (Paris–Tehran: Institut Français de Recherche en Iran, 1993), pp. 251–66.

Richard, Francis, 'Le Franciscain Dominus Germanus de Silésie, grammairien et auteur d'apologie en persan', *Islamochristiana* 10, 1984, pp. 92–5.

Richard, Francis, 'Les frères Vecchietti, diplomates, érudits et aventuriers', in Alastair Hamilton, Mauritz H. van den Boogert and Bart Westerweel (eds), *The Republic of Letters and the Levant*, Intersections 5 (Leiden–Boston: Brill, 2015), pp. 11–26.

Richard, Francis, 'Les manuscripts persans rapportés par les frères Vecchietti et conservés aujourd'hui à la Bibliothèque Nationale', *Studia Iranica* 9, no. 2, 1989, pp. 291–300.

Richard, Francis, 'Le Père Aimé Chézaud, controversiste et ses manuscrits persans', *Nāmeh-ye Bahārestān: International Iranian Journal for Research into Islamic Manuscripts* 6–7/11–12, Spring–Winter 2005–2006, pp. 7–18.

Richard, Francis, 'Trois conférences de controverse islamo-chrétienne en Géorgie vers 1665–1666', *Bedi Kartlisa* 40, 1982, pp. 253–9.

Richard, Francis, 'Un augustin portugais renégat apologiste e de l'Islam chiite au début du XVIIIe siècle', *Moyen Orient et Océan Indien* 1, 1984, pp. 73–85.

Rizvi, Saiyid Athar Abbas, *Religious and Intellectual History of the Muslims in Akbar's Reign, with special reference to Abu'l Fazl, 1556–1605* (Delhi: Munshiram Manoharlal Publishers, 1975).

Rizvi, Sajjad H., 'A Sufi Theology Fit for a Shī'ī King: The *Gawhar-i Murād* of 'Abd al-Razzāq Lāhījī (d. 1072/1661–2)', in Ayman Shihadeh (ed.), *Sufism and Theology* (Edinburgh: Edinburgh University Press, 2007), pp. 83–98.

Rizvi, Sajjad H., 'Isfahan School of Philosophy', in Ehsan Yarshater (ed.), *Encyclopaedia Iranica*, vol. XIV (New York: Foundation for Iranian Studies, Columbia University, 2007), fasc. 2, pp. 119–25.

Rizvi, Sajjad H., 'Mollā Ṣadrā Širāzi', *Encyclopædia Iranica*, online edition, 2005, consulted online on 20 September 2016, <http://www.iranicaonline.org/articles/molla-sadra-sirazi>.

Rizvi, Sajjad H., 'Mullā 'Alī Nūrī', in Reza Pourjavady (ed.), *Philosophy in Qajar Iran*, Handbook of Oriental Studies/ Handbuch der Orientalistik: Section One, The Near and Middle East 127 (Leiden–Boston: Brill, 2019), pp. 125–78.

Rizvi, Sajjad H., 'Sayyid Niʿmat Allāh al-Jazāʾirī and his Anthologies: Anti-Sufism, Shi'ism and Jokes in the Safavid World', *Die Welt des Islams* 50, 2010, pp. 224–42.

Rizvi, Sajjad H., 'Shī'ī Polemics at the Mughal Court: the Case of Qaẓī Nūrullāh Shūshtarī', *Studies in People's History* 4, no.1, 2017, pp. 53–67.

Rizvi, Sajjad H., 'The *takfīr* of the Philosophers (and Sufis) in Safavid Iran', in Camilla Adang, Hassan Ansari, Maribel Fierro and Sabine Schmidtke (eds), *Accusations of Unbelief in Islam: A Diachronic Perspective on Takfīr*, Islamic History and Civilization 123 (Leiden–Boston: Brill, 2016), pp. 244–70.

Roemer, Hans, 'The Safavid Period', in Peter Jackson and Laurence Lockhart (eds), *Cambridge History of Iran, vol. 6: The Timurid and Safavid Periods* (Cambridge: Cambridge University Press, 1986), pp. 189–350.

Rota, Giorgio, 'The Death of Tahmāspqoli Xān Qājār According to a Contemporary Ragusan Source (How to become a Renegade, 2)', in Markus Ritter, Ralph Kauz and Birgitt Hoffmann (eds), *Iran und iranisch geprägte Kulturen. Studien zum 65 Geburtstag von Bert G. Fragner*, Beiträge zum Iranistik 27 (Wiesbaden: Dr Ludwig Reichert Verlag, 2008), pp. 54–63.

Roychoudhury, Makhanlal, *The Din-i-Ilahi or the Religion of Akbar* (Calcutta: Calcutta University Press, 1941).

Rubin, Uri, 'Nūr Muḥammadī' in P. Bearman, Th. Bianquis, C. E. Bosworth, E. van Donzel, W. P. Heinrichs (eds), *Encyclopaedia of Islam, Second Edition*, consulted online on 6 April 2019, <http://dx.doi.org/10.1163/1573-3912_islam_SIM_5985>.

Rubin, Uri, 'Pre-existence and light; aspects of the concept of Nūr Muḥammad', *Israel Oriental Studies* 5, 1975, pp. 62–119.

Said Reynolds, Gabriel, *A Muslim Theologian in a Sectarian Milieu: Abd al-Jabār and the Critique of Christian Origin*, Islamic History and Civilization 56 (Leiden–Boston: Brill, 2004).

Said Reynolds, Gabriel, 'On the Qur'anic Accusation of Scriptural Falsification (*taḥrīf*) and Christian Anti-Jewish Polemic', *Journal of the American Oriental Society* 130, no. 2, April–June 2010, pp. 189–202.

Sarrió Cucarella, Diego R., *Muslim-Christian Polemics across the Mediterranean: The Splendid Replies of Shihāb al-Dīn al-Qarāfī (d. 684/1285)*, History of Christian-Muslim Relations 23 (Leiden–Boston: Brill, 2014).

Saleh, Walid, 'A Fifteenth-Century Muslim Hebraist: al-Biqā'ī and his Defense of Using the Bible to Interpret the Qur'ān', *Speculum* 83, no. 3, July 2008, pp. 629–54.

Savory, Roger, *Iran under the Safavids* (New York: Cambridge University Press, 1980).

Savory, Roger, 'Relations between the Safavid State and its Non-Muslim Minorities 1', *Islam and Christian-Muslim Relations* 14, no. 4, 2003, pp. 435–58.

Scarcia, Gianroberto, 'al-Ḥurr al-'Āmili', in P. Bearman, Th. Bianquis, C. E. Bosworth, E. van Donzel, W. P. Heinrichs (eds), Encyclopaedia of Islam, Second Edition, Consulted online on 28 August 2019, <http://dx.doi.org/10.1163/1573-3912_islam_SIM_2969>

Scheffner, Ryan, 'The Bible through a Qur'ānic Filter: Scripture Falsification (*Taḥrīf*) in 8th- and 9th-Century Muslim Disputational Literature' (PhD dissertation: Ohio State University, 2016).

Schilling, Heinz, 'Die Konfessionalisierung im Reich. Religiöser und gesellschaftlicher Wandel in Deutschland zwischen 1555 und 1620', *Historische Zeitschrift* 246, 1988, pp. 1–45.

Schmidtke, Sabine, 'The Muslim Reception of Biblical Materials: Ibn Qutayba and his *A'lām al-nubuwwa*', *Islam and Christian-Muslim Relations* 22, no. 3, July 2011, pp. 249–74.

Schmidtke, Sabine, *The Theology of al-'Allāma al-Ḥillī (d. 726/ 1325)*, Islamkundliche Untersuchungen 152 (Berlin: Klaus Schwarz Verlag, 1991).

Schmitt, Jean-Claude, *La conversion d'Hermann le Juif: autobiographie, histoire et fiction* (Paris: Éditions du Seuil, 2003).

Sells, Michael A. (ed.), *Early Islamic Mysticism: Sufi, Qur'an, Miraj, Poetics and Theological Writings*, The Classics of Western Spirituality 86 (Mahwa, NJ: Paulist Press, 1996).

Skinner, Quentin, 'Meaning and Understanding in the History of Ideas' *History and Theory* 8, no. 1, 1969, pp. 3–53.

Sifatgul, Mansur, 'Muqaddimih-i musahhih', in Mansur Sefatgol (ed.), *I'tirāfnāma: diary of Abgar ('Ali Akbar) Armani, one of new converts to Islam of Shah Sulaiman & Shah Sultan Husain Safavi's era, along with Risāla-i-Shinākht, in Gurji script on affirming Shiism by a Georgian new convert to Islam of Shah Abbas' time* (Tehran: Kitabkhanih-i Shura-yi Islami, 2010), pp. 15–54.

Sifatgul, Mansur, *Sakhtar-i nihad va andishih-i dini dar Iran-i 'asr-i Safavi: tarikh-i tahavvulat-i dini-yi Iran dar sadih-ha-yi dahum ta davazdahum-i Hijri-i qamari* (Tehran: Mu'assasih-i Khadamat-i Farhangi-yi Rasa, 2002–3).

Sindawi, Khalid, '"Fāṭima's Book" A Shī'ite Qur'ān?', *Rivista degli studi orientali.* 78, Fasc. 1/2, 2004, pp. 57–70.

Sindawi, Khalid, 'Jesus and Ḥusayn Ibn 'Alī Ibn 'Abū Ṭālib: a Comparative Study', *Ancient Near Eastern Studies* 44, 2007, pp. 50–65.

Sindawi, Khalid, 'The Image of Ḥusayn Ibn 'Alī in "Maqātil" Literature', *Quaderni di Studi Arabi* 20/21, 2002, pp. 79–104.

Snow, David A. and Richard Machalek, 'The Convert as a Social Type', *Social Theory* 1, 1983, pp. 259–89.

Snow, David A.,'The Sociology of Conversion', *Annual Review of Sociology* 10, 1984, pp. 167–90.

Spicehandler, Ezra, 'The Persecution of the Jews of Isfahan under Shah 'Abbās II (162–1666)', *Hebrew Union College Annual* 46, 1975, pp. 331–56.

Stern, Samuel M., ''Abd al-Jabbār's Account of how Christ's Religion was Falsified by the Adoption of Roman Customs', *The Journal of Theological Studies* 19, no. 1, April 1968, pp. 128–85.

Stewart, Devin J. (tr.), 'The Autobiography of Yūsuf al-Baḥrānī', in Dwight Fletcher Reynolds (ed.) *Interpreting the Self: Autobiography in the Arabic Literary Tradition* (Berkeley: University of California Press, 2001), pp. 217–23.

Stroumsa, Sarah, 'The Signs of Prophecy: The Emergence and Early Development of a Theme in Arabic Theological Literature', *The Harvard Theological Review* 78, no. 1–2, January–April 1985, pp. 101–14.

Subrahmanyam, Sanjay, *The Career and Legend of Vasco da Gama* (Cambridge: Cambridge University Press, 1997).

Szpiech, Ryan, *Conversion and Narrative: Reading and Religious Authority in Medieval Polemic* (Philadelphia: University of Pennsylvania Press, 2013).

Teles e Cunha, João, 'The Eye of the Beholder: The Creation of a Portuguese Discourse on Safavid Iran', in Rudi Matthee and Jorge Flores (eds), *Portugal, the Persian Gulf and Safavid Persia*, Acta Iranica 52 (Leuven: Peeters, 2011), pp. 11–50.

Thomas, David, 'Ali l-Ṭabarī', in David Thomas and Barabra Roggema (eds) *Christian-Muslim Relations: A Bibliographical History. Volume 1 (600–900)*, The History of Christian-Muslim Relations 11 (Leiden–Boston: Brill, 2009), pp. 669–74.

Thomas, David, *Christian Doctrines in Islamic Theology*, The History of Muslim-Christian Relations 10 (Leiden–Boston: Brill, 2008).

Thomas, David, 'Ibn Qutayba', in David Thomas and Barabra Roggema (eds) *Christian-Muslim Relations: A Bibliographical History. Volume 1 (600–900)*, The History of Christian-Muslim Relations 11 (Leiden–Boston: Brill, 2009), pp. 816–18.

Thomas, David (ed.), *Routledge Handbook of Christian-Muslim Relations* (London: Routledge, 2017).

Thomas, David, 'The Bible in Early Muslim Anti-Christian Polemic', *Islam and Christian-Muslim Relations* 7, 1996, pp. 29–38.

Thomson, Rodney M., 'William of Malmesbury's Edition of the "Liber Pontificalis"', *Archivum historiae Pontificiae* 16, 1978, pp. 93–112.

Tiburcio, Alberto, 'Abgar 'Alī Akbar Armanī', in David Thomas and John Chesworth (eds), *Christian-Muslim Relations. A Bibliographical History. Volume 12 Asia, Africa and the Americas 1700–1800*, The History of Christian-Muslim Relations 36 (Leiden–Boston: Brill, 2018), pp. 256–59.

Tiburcio, Alberto, "Alī Qulī Jadīd al-Islām, António de Jesus', in David Thomas and John Chesworth (eds), *Christian-Muslim Relations. A Bibliographical History. Volume 12: Asia, Africa and the Americas 1700–1800*, The History of Christian-Muslim Relations 36 (Leiden–Boston: Brill, 2018), pp. 266–73.

Tiburcio, Alberto, 'Aimé Chézaud', in David Thomas and John Chesworth (eds), *Christian-Muslim Relations. A Bibliographical History. Volume 10: Ottoman and Safavid Empires 1600–1700*, The History of Christian-Muslim Relations 32 (Leiden–Boston: Brill, 2017), pp. 592–7.

Tiburcio, Alberto, 'Convert Literature, Interreligious Polemics, and the 'Signs of Prophethood' Genre in Late Safavid Iran (1694–1722): the Work of 'Alī Qulī Jadīd al-Islām (d. *circa* 1722)' (PhD dissertation, McGill University, 2014).

Tiburcio, Alberto, 'Filippo Guadagnoli', in David Thomas and John Chesworth (eds), *Christian-Muslim Relations. A Bibliographical History (1600–1700). Volume 9: Southern and Central Europe 1600–1700*, The History of Christian-Muslim Relations 31 (Leiden–Boston: Brill, 2017), pp 749–55.

Tiburcio, Alberto, 'Muslim-Christian Polemics and Scriptural Translation in Safavid Iran: ʿAli Qoli Jadid al-Eslām and his Interlocutors', *Iranian Studies* 50, no. 2, 2017, pp. 247–69.

Tiburcio, Alberto, 'Some Aspects of Conversion Narratives in Late Safavid Iran and their Circulation: The Case of ʿAlī Akbar Armanī', *Eurasian Studies*, special vol.: Sandra Aube and Maria Szuppe (eds), with the collaboration of Anthony T. Quickel: *Channels of Transmission : Family and Professional Lineages in the Early Modern Middle East*, 15, no. 2 2017, pp. 350–72.

Tihrani, Agha Buzurg, *al-Dhariʿa ila tasanif al-shiʿa*, 25 vols (Beirut: Dar al-Awdaʾ, 1983).

Tolan, John V., *Faces of Muhammad: Western Perceptions of the Prophet of Islam from the Middle Ages to Today* (Princeton–Oxford: Princeton University Press, 2019).

Tolan, John V., *Saracens: Islam in the European Medieval Imagination* (New York: Columbia University Press, 2002).

Tolan, John V., *Sons of Ishmael: Muslims through European Eyes in the Middle Ages* (Gainsville: University of Florida Press, 2013).

Tottoli, Roberto, *Biblical Prophets in the Qur'ān and Muslim Literature*, Routledge Studies in the Qur'ān (London–New York: Routledge, 2002).

Trentini, Andrea, 'Guadagnoli controversista e islamologo, un'analisi dell'edizioni dell'Apologia (1631, 1637)', *Studi Medievali e Moderni: arte, letteratura, storia* 16, no. 1, 2010, pp. 297–314.

Truschke, Audrey, *Culture of Encounters: Sanskrit at the Mughal Court*, South Asia Across the Disciplines (New York: Columbia University Press, 2016).

Turner, Colin, *Islam without Allah?: The Rise of Religious Externalism in Safavid Iran* (Richmond; Surrey, Curzon: 2000).

Urvoy, Dominique, 'Le sense de la polémique anti-biblique chez Ibn Ḥazm', in Camilla Adang, Maribel Fierro and Sabine Schmidtke (eds), *Ibn Hazm of Cordoba: The Life and Works of a Controversial Thinker*, Handbuch der Orientalistik, Erste Abteilung, Nahe und der Mittlere Osten 103 (Leiden–Boston: Brill, 2013), pp. 485–96.

Vollandt, Ronny, *Arabic Versions of the Pentateuch: A Comparative Study of Jewish, Christian, and Muslim Sources*, Biblia Arabica 2 (Leiden–Boston: Brill, 2015).

Vollandt, Ronny, 'Che portono al ritorno quì una Bibbia Arabica integra: A history of the Biblia Sacra Arabica (1671–73)', in Samir Khalil and Juan Pablo Monferrer-Sala (eds), *Graeco-Latina et Orientalia: Studia in honorem Angeli Urbani heptuagenarii* (Cordoba: Cordoba Near Eastern Research Unit; Beirut: Centre de Documentation et de Recherches Arabes Chrétiennes/Oriens Academic, 2013), pp. 401–18.

Volz, John, 'Melchior Cano', in *The Catholic Encyclopedia*, vol. 3 (New York: Robert Appleton Company, 1908), consulted online on 9 April 2019, <http://www.newadvent.org/cathen/03251a.htm>.

Walter, Peter, 'Melchor Cano. *De Logis Theologicis* (1563)', in Oda Wischmeyer (ed.), *Handbuch der Bibel-Hermeneutiken von Origenes bis zur gegenwart* (Berlin–Boston: De Gruyter, 2016), pp. 507–18.

Walter, Peter, 'Quelle oder Steinbruch? Über den Umgang der Dogmatik mit der Bibel', in Karl Lehmann and Ralf Rothenbusch (eds), *Gotteswort in Menschenwort: die eine Bible as Fundamet der Theologie* (Freiburg: Herder, 2014), pp. 79–103.

Windler, Christian, 'Katholische Mission und Diasporareligiosität: Christen europäischer Herkunft im Safavidenreich', in Henning P. Jürgens and Thomas Weller (eds), *Religion und Mobilität zum Verhältnis von raumbezogener Mobilität und religiöser Identitätsbildung im frühneuzeitlichen Europa*, Veröffentlichungen des Instituts für Europäische Geschichte, Beiheft 81 (Göttingen–Oakville, CT: Vadenhoeck &Ruprecht, 2010), pp.183–212.

Windler, Christian, 'La curie romaine et la cour safavide au XVIIe siècle: projets missionaires et diplomatie', in Maria Antonietta Visceglia (ed.), *Papato e politica internazionale nella prima età moderna* (Rome: Viella, 2013), pp. 505–23.

Windler, Christian, *Missionare in Persien: Kulturelle Diversität und Normenkonkurrenz im globalen Katholizismus (17–18. Jahrhundert)*, Externa 12 (Cologne: Böhlau, 2018).

Zarrinkub, ʿAbd al-Husayn, *Dunbalih-i justuju dar tasavvuf-i Iran* (Tehran: Muʾassasih-i Intisharat-i Amir Kabir, 1987).

Index

ʿAbbas I
decline of the Qizilbash, 156
ghulām corps, 13
relations with Armenian Christians, 11–12
relations with Catholic missionaries, 19, 20–1, 22, 40–1
relations with Georgian Christians, 12–13
theological debate at the court of, 42
translations of Christian writings, 40–1
ʿAbbas II
relations with French missionaries, 21
repression of religious minorities, 13–14
Acquaviva, Rodolfo, 38
Akbar the Great
Christian missionaries at the court of, 38–9
dīn-i ilāhī (the divine religion), 38
Persian translation of the Gospels, 39–40
Akhbaris, 172–3
Al-Andalus, 5, 44
al-ʿAmili, Ahmad b. Zayn al-ʿAbidin al-ʿAlavi, 42–3, 44–6, 68, 182
al-ʿAmili, al-Hurr, 99, 158, 164, 173
António de Gouvea, 11, 18
António de Jesus, Padre
ambassadorial mission to Iran, 18, 24–5
conversion of the Shahrimanian family, 26
early life of, 24
relations with Pereira Fidalgo, 25
see also Jadid al-Islam, ʿAli Quli
Anzali, Ata, 157
Apologia pro Christiana Religione (Guadagnoli)
ad hominem attacks on Muhammad, 45, 124, 126
adultery of Muhammad, 127–8
Aimé Chézaud's knowledge of, 46, 47
Arabic versions of as missionary tools, 44–5, 126
idol worship as encouraged by Muhammad, 126, 128–31
interpretation of the Qur'an as proscribed, 127
Jadid al-Islam's knowledge of the *Apologia*, 48, 123–4
on Muslim ritual practices as idolatry, 126–7
as refutation of the *Misqal-i safa*, 44
on the sanctity of the Qur'anic Scripture, 124
the *Sayf al-mu'minin* as refutation of, 30, 48, 50, 124, 131
taḥrīf of the Bible, 125–6
Arjomand, Said Amir, 156, 157
Armani, Abgar ʿAli Akbar, 16, 68, 183
Armenians
Armenian Catholics, 22, 26
forced conversions to Islam, 12, 41–2
Gregorian church, 22, 23
hostility towards the Catholic missionaries, 23, 25, 27
importance of trade to, 16
Muhammad ʿAli Jadid al-Islam (renegade priest), 58

Armenians (*cont.*)
religious repression of, 13–16, 183
responses to Chézaud's refutation of *Misqal-i safa*, 48
in Safavid Iran, 11–12, 41–2
voluntary conversions to Islam, 15, 16
Astarabadi, Muhammad Baqir (Mir Damad), 42, 157
Augustinian Order, 19–20, 21, 22, 23, 24, 184

Baer, Marc D., 3
Baha' al-Din al-ʿAmili (Shaykh-i Baha'i)
on dietary regulations, 139–40
hatred of the Armenian Christians, 12
protection of Vardapet Yovhan, 15
al-Bahrani, Yusuf, 99
al-Bakri, Abu Hassan, 99–100
Baluchis, 2
Bayat, Uruch Beg, 29
al-Bayhaqi, Abu Bakr, 95
Beg, Grand Vizier Muhammad, 14, 17, 47
Beg, Hasan Quli, 9, 26–7, 29
Belchior dos Anjos, 11
Bible
Arabic Bible manuscripts, 52
Biblia Sacra Arabica, 52, 57, 72–4, 145–6
biblical knowledge of Jadid al-Islam, 68–9
converts to Islam's knowledge of, 66–7, 69, 180
intentional misrepresentation of by converts, 67, 69
Melchizedek, 22, 77–8, 167
Muslim scholars' references to, 66, 69
Pauline letters, 71
questions of *taḥrīf* in, 125–6
Roman Arabic Vulgate, 41, 43, 50, 51–2, 57
Sunni readings of biblical passages, 78–9
as a tool of *tafsīr* (Qur'anic exegesis), 67
translation of the Gospels into Persian, 39–40, 50–1
see also Latin Vulgate
Bihar al-anwar, 55, 99, 102, 106

Calepino, Ambrogio, 76, 102, 160, 162
Camp, Arnulf, 6
Cano, Melchor, 113
Caracciolini order, 43
Carnoy-Torabi, Dominque, 52, 108, 114
Catholic missionaries
apostasy of Catholic missionaries, 9, 10, 184
Armenian hostility towards, 23, 25, 27
Augustinian Order, 19–20, 21, 22, 23, 24, 184
Carmelite Order, 20, 23
conversion of Shahrimanian family, 22–3, 26
debates with the ulama, 48–9
as diplomatic attachés, 18, 24
French missionaries, 21
Gregorian Armenian hostility towards, 23
internal rivalries, 20, 24
linguistic instruction of, 43–4
mixed successes of, 21–3
at the Mughal court, 38–9
Nicolau de Melo, 19–20
in pre-Safavid Iran, 19–20
relations with ʿAbbas I, 19, 20–1, 22, 40–1
in Safavid Iran, 11, 18, 41–2
Chardin, Jean, 48, 49, 139
Chézaud, Aimé, 21, 46–8, 123
Christian missionaries, 56; *see also* Catholic missionaries; Jesuits
Comenius, Jan Amos, 125–6
confessionalisation paradigm
critiques of, 3
and Safavid Iran, 3–4, 10, 183
in *Sayf al-mu'minin*, 116
Sunni Islam in the Ottoman Empire, 2–3, 10
term, 2
conversion narratives, 28–9
converts

apostasy of Catholic missionaries, 9, 10, 184
Armenian forced conversions to Islam, 12, 41–2
Armenian voluntary conversions to Islam, 15, 16
as authors of religious polemics, 6, 94
convert scholars in Isfahan, 96, 99, 154
Georgian converts in the *ghulām* corps, 13, 16–17, 156
Jewish converts to Islam, 17, 81
knowledge of the Bible, 66–7, 69, 180
the Shahrimanian family, 22–3, 26
Council of Trent, 41, 72, 108, 113
Cristobal de Vega, 39

dalā'il al-nubuwwa (signs of the prophecy) literature
fārqālīṭ, 74–6
figure of the Prophet in, 95
genre of, 67–8, 179–81, 184
hadith in, 95–7
intra-Muslim theological discussions, 95
Jadid al-Islam's status as an author of, 181–2
proofs for the legitimacy of the tenets of Shi'ism, 78
refutations of Christian tenets, 77
Sunni readings of biblical passages, 78–9
taḥrīf (scriptural falsification) in, 70
David IV, 22
Della Valle, Pietro, 44, 46
Dieu, Ludovicus de, 109
Don Juan de Persia (Uruch Beg Bayat), 29

Eanes Pereira, Gil, 38
Ecchelensis, Abraham, 45
El'azar, Yehudah b., 58
Erginbaş, Vefa, 3
Eusebius of Caesarea, 110

al-Farisi, Salman, 115–16
Fava'id-i izdivaj (*The Benefits of Marriage*), 27, 132, 133–6
Fayz-i Kashani, Mulla Muhsin, 156, 165–6
Flores, Jorge, 2, 6
France, 18, 21

Georgian Christians
conversions to Islam, 13
in the *ghulām* corps, 13, 16–17, 156
in Safavid Iran, 12–13
Germanus of Silesia, 45–6
Gesu Maria, Paolo Simone di, 41
ghulām corps, 13, 16–17, 156
Goa, 19, 20, 25, 38–9
Góis, Bento de, 39
Gregorian Church, 22, 23
Gregory XIII, 41, 52
Grimon, Leon, 39
Guadagnoli, Filippo, 52; see also *Apologia pro Christiana Religione* (Guadagnoli)

Hadiqat al-Shī'a, 157–8
hadith
the birth of Husayn, 106–7
the creation myth, 99–101
in *dalā'il* literature, 95–7
Jadid al-Islam's knowledge of Shi'i hadith collections, 55, 78, 96–7, 99, 103–5, 107
linking Husayn to Jesus, 102–3
the month of Muharram, 104
Muhammad's idol worship, 129
Muhammad's offer of sacrificed meat to idols, 129, 139
predestination of Muhammad's mission, 98–101
premonition of Husayn's martyrdom, 104–6
in *Risalih dar radd-i jama'at-i sufiyan*, 163–4
sacrifice of Husayn in Karbala, 101–2
sacrifice of Ismael, 101–2
in *Sayf al-mu'minin*, 96–107
Shi'i hadith collections, 96
as a source of legal and theological truth, 97
Halft, Dennis, 6, 41, 43, 50, 68

Hazin-i Lahiji, Shaykh Muhammad ʿAli, 57
Henriques, Francisco, 38
Herzig, Edmund, 1, 11
al-Hilli, al-ʿAllama, 103–4, 159, 164, 173
Hindi, Fazil-i, 30, 96, 103–4, 172–3
Holy Trinity, 40, 73, 114, 124, 129, 162
Husayn (Sultan)
  decline of the Safavid era, 14
  Jadid al-Islam as interpreter for, 26
  patronage of the Armenians, 16
  Persian-Portuguese alliance, 25
  protection of the Carmelites, 23
  Sayf al-muʾminin's dedication to, 30
  translations of Christian writings into Persian, 50–1

Ibn ʿArabi, Muhyi al-Din, 158, 159, 162
Ibn Babawayh, 96, 98, 102, 105
Ibn Hazm of Cordoba, 5, 67, 70, 81, 139, 181
Ibn Ishaq, 74, 95
Ibn Qawlawayh, 106
Ibn Qutayba, Abu Muhammad ʿAbd Allah b. Muslim, 67, 74, 181
Ibn Taymiyya, 70, 160
ijtihād, 97, 103, 141–2
Imam Riza, 98, 159
Iran *see* Safavid Iran
Isfahan
  Augustinian Order in, 24
  Catholic missions in, 9, 14, 20, 21, 22, 24
  convert scholars in, 96, 99, 154
  missionary library in, 52, 108, 114
  monasteries of, 20, 22
  New Julfa, 11, 15, 16, 22, 24, 46–7, 48
  Sufis in, 156, 164
al-Isfahani, Abu Nuʿaym, 95
Iskandar Beg Munshi, 12
Islam
  dietary customs and restrictions, 139
  medieval European knowledge of, 124–5
Islamic jurisprudence
  contextual indication (*qarīna*), 148–9
  hadith as sources of legal truth, 97
  ijtihād, 97, 103, 141–2, 148
  legal principles within social norms, 141–2, 144
  Usuli–Akhbari dispute, 97, 103, 104
Ismael, 80, 82–3, 84–5, 101–2
Ismaʿil, 155

al-Jabbar, ʿAbd, 5, 70, 71, 95, 115, 133
Jadid al-Islam, ʿAli Quli
  anti-Sufi position, 154, 172
  biblical knowledge of, 68–9
  condition as a convert, 6
  conversion of, 6, 9, 10, 26–9
  early life of, 24
  Hidayat al-zallin, 49–50
  historical and political milieu of, 182–3
  as interpreter for Shah Sultan Husayn, 26
  knowledge of Shiʿi hadith collections, 55, 78, 96–7, 99, 103–5, 107
  the Pauline theme, 71–2
  polemical writings of, 9, 29–30
  Shiʿi knowledge of, 97
  status as a *dalāʾil* author, 181–2
  teachers, 96
  use of extra-scriptural sources, 94, 180
  see also António de Jesus, Padre; *Risalih dar radd-i jamaʿat-i sufiyan*; *Sayf al-muʾminin*
Jadid al-Islam, Muhammad ʿAli, 58
Jahangir, 39, 40
al-Jahiz, 70, 95
al-Jazaʾiri, Niʿmat Allah, 159, 163–4
Jerome, Saint
  Chronicon, 110
  letter to Pope Damasus I, 114
  on ritual prostration, 129
  see also Latin Vulgate
Jesuits
  Aimé Chézaud, 21, 46–8, 123
  French missionaries, 21, 46–8
  French–Iberian rivalry and, 24
  missionaries in Hormuz, 19
  Polish Jesuit missionaries, 16, 23
  Portuguese missionaries, 38, 39
  see also Xavier, Jerome (Jerónimo)
Jesus, 133–6

Jews
  converts to Islam, 17, 81
  Jewish polemical debates, 58
  Jewish scripture as proof of the prophecy of Islam, 47–8
  religious repression of, 13, 16
  see also Torah
Julayeci, Dawit, 46, 47
Julayeci, Yovhannes Mrkuz, 57

Khalifih Sultan and Grand Vizier, 13–14
Khan, Levan, 16
Khatunabadi, Mir Muhammad Baqir, 50–1, 183
Kircher, Athanasius, 45
Krstić, Tijana, 2, 3, 28, 68, 78–9
Krusinski, Jan Tadeusz, 16

Lahuri, ʿAbd al-Sattar, 39
language/linguistics
  language instruction for Catholic missionaries, 43–4
  problems of the Arabic Bible translation (*Sayf al-muʾminin)*, 52–3
  qarīna, term, 148–9
  translations of Christian writings into Persian, 40–1, 50–1
languages/linguistics
  the Paraclete and links to ḥ-m-d trilateral root, 74
Latin Vulgate
  canonical status of, 72, 73, 112, 113, 116, 181
  collation with the *Roman Arabic Vulgate*, 41
  critique of the validity of in *Sayf al-muʾminin*, 56–7, 58, 72–4, 75–6, 84, 154, 167, 168, 169, 170–1
  epithet given to Noah, 145–6
  Jadid al-Islam's reinterpretation of, 50, 55
  in the missionary library, Isfahan, 52, 108
  taḥrīf and the translation of, 149, 180
  unigenitus, term, 102
Lazarus-Yafeh, Hava, 66, 67
Leitão, Duarte, 39

al-Maghribi, Samawʾal, 81, 139
Majlisi, Muhammad Baqir, 15, 55, 99–100, 102, 106, 158, 173
Majlisi, Muhammad Taqi, 156, 157
Malvasia, Bonaventura, 44, 45, 46
Manucci, Niccolao, 42
Marcellinus, 110–11
Marracci, Ludovico, 45, 46
marriage
  apology for celibacy in the Qurʾan, 136
  defense of marriage, 132–3
Martellotto di Martinafranca, Francesco, 43–4
Martyn, Henry, 56–7
Matthee, Rudi, 2, 11, 13, 14, 15, 21
Misqal-i safa (*Burnisher of Purity*) (al-ʿAmili), 43, 44–6, 47
Monserrate, António de, 38, 39
Mosaic Law, 77, 78, 80
Mughal India
  Akbar the Great's syncretic religion strategy, 38
  Christian missionaries in, 38–9
  Portuguese exploration in Asia, 18–19
  religious minority populations, 2
  theological debate in, 42
Muhammad
  accusations of adultery in the *Apologia*, 127–8
  ad hominem attacks on in the *Apologia*, 45, 124, 126
  and the birth of Husayn, 106–7
  the creation myth, 99–101
  dalāʾil literature, 95
  dalāʾil-themed hadith, 95–6
  incident of the Satanic Verses, 130
  the offer of sacrificed meat to idols, 129, 139
  as the Paraclete, 75, 98–9
  as proponent of idol worship, 126, 128–31
  in *al-Sira al-nabawiyya*, 74, 95
Murad b. ʿAbd Allah, 68, 70, 71, 114

al-Naraqi, Mulla Ahmad b. Mahdi, 56–7, 58, 181
Nicolau de Melo, 19–20

al-Nisaburi, Muhammad b. Hasan
al-Fattal, 55, 106

Oman, 25, 184
Ottoman Empire
alliance with the French, 18, 21
confessionalisation of, 2–3
Muslim–Christian interactions, 1
Sunnitisation of, 2–3, 10

the Paraclete
in the Christian tradition, 74
in contemporary theological debates, 49
fārqālīṭ (the Greek Paraclete), 74–6
Islamic interpretation of, 48, 74
link to ḥ-m-d trilateral root, 74
as the Prophet Muhammad, 75, 98–9
Paul, Saint
accusations of pantheism, 170
consumption of meat sacrificed for
idols, 166–7
forgeries of, 71
marital relations, 138
persecution of Christians, 133–4
priestly celibacy, 133
transgression of Mosaic Law, 168
Paul of Antioch, 125
Pereira Fidalgo, Gregório, 25, 27
Peter, Saint, 109
Peter the Venerable, 125
Pfander, Karl Gottlieb, 56
Philip II, 19, 39
philosophy, 164–6, 172–3
Pinheiro, Manuel, 39, 40
polemical writings
of al-ʿAmili, 42–3
anti-Islamic polemics, 124–5
of Baqir Majlisi, 15
biblical passages as signs that foretell
the coming of Islam, 66
classical motifs in, 179–80, 181
within *dalāʾil* literature, 67–8
dietary customs and restrictions,
138–40
of Henry Martyn, 56–7
images and idols for worship, 146
Jewish polemical debates, 58
of Karl Pfander, 56
mid-seventeenth century, 55–8
Misqal-i safa (*Burnisher of Purity*)
(al-ʿAmili), 43, 44–6, 47
reception in the Qajar period, 55–6
reception of the works of, 181–2
and the repression of non-Muslim
populations, 15
role of converts, 6, 94
Roman Arabic Vulgate (Raimondi), 41,
43
scholarship on, 4–6
state support for, 183
theological debate in Persia, 42
see also *Apologia pro Christiana
Religione* (Guadagnoli); *Risalih
dar radd-i jamaʿat-i sufiyan* (Jadid
al-Islam); *Sayf al-muʾminin* (Jadid
al-Islam); Xavier, Jerome (Jerónimo)
Portugal, 18–19, 20, 25
prophecy
biblical prophets, 66
dalāʾil genre, 67–8
from within Islamic sources, 95
popular tales of the prophets, 66
scriptural proofs of, 67
see also the Paraclete
prophets
moral authority of, 145
in Shiʿa Islam, 145
Protestant missionaries, 56

Qaʾini, Muhammad Khalil, 57–8
al-Qarafi, Shihab al-Din, 5, 67, 71, 77,
139
al-Qasim b. Ibrahim, 70
Qizilbash, 3, 13, 155–6
Qummi, Muhammad Tahir-i, 157–8,
162, 163–4
Qurʾan
apology for celibacy, 136
and the *Book of Fatima*, 87
Christian treatments of in polemical
writings, 124–5
interpretation of the Qurʾan as
proscribed, 127
Latin translations of, 124–5

tafsīr (Qur'anic exegesis), 67, 130–1
taḥrīf (scriptural falsification), 69, 115
Qutayba, Abu Muhammad 'Abd Allah b. Muslim Ibn, 67

Raimondi, Giovanni Battista, 41, 43
Rashid, Ma'mar b., 95
Ribeiro, Estevão, 39
Richard, Francis, 46–7, 58
Rigordi, François, 21, 46
Risalih dar radd-i jama'at-i sufiyan (Jadid al-Islam)
comparison between Christian priesthood and Sufi *pīrhood*, 159–60, 163
composition of, 154
genealogy of the term 'Sufi', 160
hadith-based arguments, 163–4
links between Sufism and paganism, 160–2, 169
paganism and the worship of images, 162–3
on Sufi philosophy, 164–5
Sufism's ties to Christian scripturalism, 166–7
Rizzo, Sergio (Sarkis al-Rizzi), 44, 52
Rota, Gorgio, 1, 13

Sadra, Mulla, 156
Safavid Iran
anti-Sufi refutations, 157
Armenian Christians, 11–12, 41–2
Catholic missionaries in, 11, 18, 41–2
Catholic missionaries in pre-Safavid Iran, 19–20
Christian minorities in, 10–11
clerical hierocracy, 156
confessionalisation paradigm, 3–4, 10
decline of, 14–15, 182–3
dietary customs and restrictions, 139
French–Iranian relations, 21
Georgian Christians in, 12–13
Persian–Portuguese relations, 19–20, 25
religious minority populations, 2, 4
repression of non-Muslim populations, 4, 13–18
Safavid Shi'itisation, 3, 184
scholarship on, 1, 4–5
Sufism in, 155–6
Safavid–Ottoman war, 11, 12
San Alberto, Elia di, 23, 24, 25
Sánchez, Tomás, 132–3
Sanson, Nicolas, 49, 139
Satanic Verses, 130
Savory, Roger, 11, 12
Sayf al-mu'minin (Jadid al-Islam)
adultery of Muhammad, 127–8
'Ali's rendition of the forty Suras, 50, 54–5, 180
anti-Sufi passages, 154, 167–71, 172
the 'awaited one' as the Prophet Muhammad, 80–2
biblical passages as signs that foretell the coming of Islam, 66
blending of Sunni and Christian scriptures, 127
on blood consumption, 142–3
on Christian morality, 132
Christian sources in, 98, 107–14
circumcision of Abraham, 84–6
condemnation of Sunnism, 83–4, 85–6
confessionalisation paradigm in, 116
contention between Christian factions, 109–10
critique of celibacy and monastic life, 136–7
critique of the validity of Saint Jerome, 56–7, 58, 72–4, 75–6, 84, 154, 167, 168, 169, 170–1
defense of marriage, 132–3
discussions of dietary regulations, 140–2
distinction between the old and the new covenants, 80–5
divisions within the hierocracy of the Catholic Church, 110–12
etymological arguments for the term *angelus* (angel), 76
fārqālīṭ (the Greek Paraclete), 74–6
figure of Saint Paul, 71–2
hadith in, 96–107
idol worship as encouraged by Muhammad, 128–31

Sayf al-mu'minin (Jadid al-Islam) (*cont.*)
idolatry in Muslim ritual practices, 126–7, 146–9
lack of modesty in Christian women, 137–8
moral authority of prophets, 145
motif of the blood-libel, 131–2
Muslim and Christian references combined, 114–16
paganism and the worship of images, 170–1
pantheism of Saint Paul, 170
problems of the Arabic Bible translation, 52–3
prohibition of wine, 143–5
question of Scriptural falsification, 53
reference to Melchor Cano, 111–13
as refutation of Guadagnoli's *Apologia*, 30, 48, 50, 124, 131
relations between Muslims and the People of the Book, 131
Shi'i readings of biblical proofs, 78–86, 89
sources for, 51–2, 53–4, 180–1
substitution of the Mahdi for Michael, 86–7
Sufi/Christian connection, 167–8
Sufi/Christian/ Pagan connection, 168–9
taḥrīf analysis in, 71–4, 86, 101–2, 113–15, 124, 141–2, 145–6, 148
on the Twelfth Imam, 79, 80, 85, 86–8
use of legal principles to explain social norms, 141–2, 144, 148–9
Shabistari, Shaykh Mahmud, 170
Shahrimanian family, 22–3, 26
Shi'ism
infallibility of prophets, 145
links with Sufism, 155, 158
Safavid Shi'itisation, 3, 184
Twelver Shi'ism, 10, 155, 157, 161
al-Sira al-nabawiyya (Ibn Ishaq), 74, 95
Spain, 19, 20, 29, 113
storytellers (*quṣṣāṣ*), 66–7
Sufism
Abu Muslimnamih tradition, 157, 158
anti-Sufi passages in *Sayf al-mu'minin*, 154, 167–71, 172
anti-Sufi refutations, 157–9
Hadiqat al-Shi'a text, 158
'irfān (high Sufism), 156, 157
links with Shi'ism, 155, 158
paganism and the worship of images, 170–1
in Safavid Iran, 155–6
Sufi/Christian connection, 166–8
Sufi/Christian/ Pagan connection, 168–9
waḥdat al-wujūd (unity of existence), 73, 158, 160, 163, 164, 167–8
see also *Risalih dar radd-i jama'at-i sufiyan* (Jadid al-Islam)
Sulayman, 14, 15, 23
Sunni Afghans, 2
Sunni Islam
condemnation of Sunnism in *Sayf al-mu'minin*, 86, 127, 128, 130, 131
the *dalā'il* genre and, 78, 96
the infallibility of prophets, 145
in the Ottoman Empire, 2–3, 10
Sunni readings of biblical passages, 78–9
Sunni Sufi orders, 155
Sylvester II, 111

al-Tabari, 'Ali b. Rabban, 67, 68, 70, 94, 181
Tadeo de San Eliseo, Juan, 40–1
Tafrishi, Zahir al-Din, 57
tafsīr, 67, 130–1
Tahmasp, 12
taḥrīf (scriptural falsification)
in the Bible, 125–6
within the *dalā'il* genre, 180
in debates between the ulama and missionaries, 49
historical genesis of, 70, 71
in the Qur'an, 69, 115
in *Sayf al-mu'minin*, 71–4, 86, 101–2, 113–15, 124, 141–2, 145–6, 148

substitution of the Mahdi for Michael, 86–7
taḥrīf al-maʿnā, 70, 75
taḥrīf al-naṣṣ, 69–70, 71, 75–6
understandings of, 69–70
al-Tamimi, Sayf b. ʿUmar, 71
Tashkubrizade, Ahmad Mustafa, 68
Tavernier, Jean-Baptiste, 13, 26
Teimuraz I of Kakhet'i, 12
Tertullian, 110
Theodotion, 72
Torah
ʿAli's rendition of the forty Suras, 50, 54–5, 180
Arabic translation of, 52–4
Jewish scripture as proof of the prophecy of Islam, 47–8
Turmeda, Anselm, 68, 94, 181
Twelver Shiʿism, 10, 155, 157, 161

Usuli–Akhbari dispute, 97, 103, 104
Usulis, 166, 172–3

Valle, Pietro della, 43
Vasco da Gama, 18
Vecchietti, Giovanni Battista, 39–40

Xavier, Jerome (Jerónimo)
al-ʿAlavi, Ahmad's response to, 42–3, 68
critique by Ludovicus de Dieu, 109
discussions of dietary regulations, 140–2
Fuente de Vida, 40, 146
Aʾinih-i haqq-numa (*The Truth-Reflecting Mirror*), 40, 42, 43, 47, 146
polemical writings, 40, 42, 43, 55
scholarship on, 5
translation of the Gospels into Persian, 39–40

Yovhan, Vardapet, 15, 24

Zahidiyya order, 155

EU representative:
Easy Access System Europe
Mustamäe tee 50, 10621 Tallinn, Estonia
Gpsr.requests@easproject.com

www.ingramcontent.com/pod-product-compliance
Lightning Source LLC
Chambersburg PA
CBHW070350240426
43671CB00013BA/2460
* 9 7 8 1 4 7 4 4 4 0 4 7 9 *